Chilton's
Complete Guide to Motorcycles and Motorcycling

Chilton's Complete Guide to Motorcycles and Motorcycling

Don Koch

Chilton Book Company
Radnor, Pennsylvania

Copyright © 1974 by Donald W. Koch
First Edition   All Rights Reserved
Published in Radnor, Pa., by Chilton Book Company
and simultaneously in Ontario, Canada
by Thomas Nelson & Sons, Ltd.

Designed by Carole L. DeCrescenzo
Manufactured in the United States of America

Library of Congress Cataloging in Publication Data
Koch, Donald.
   Chilton's complete guide to motorcycles and motor-cycling.

   1. Motorcycles. 2. Motorcycling. I. Title.
II. Title: Complete guide to motorcycles and motor-cycling.
TL440.K58   1974   629.22′75   74-17365
ISBN 0-8019-6069-X .
ISBN 0-8019-6089-4 (pbk.)

Thanks Are Due the Following Organizations
for their Cooperation and Assistance
in the Preparation of this Book:

American Honda Motors Corporation; *AMA NEWS*;
American Motorcycle Association; Bates Industries, Inc.;
Bultaco International, Ltd.; Cosmopolitan Motors, Inc.;
CYCLE WORLD; Harley-Davidson Motor Company;
Kawasaki Motors Corporation; Montessa Motors, Inc.;
National Highway Traffic Safety Administration;
National Safety Council; PABATCO (Hodaka motorcycles);
Vetter Fairing Company; and Yankee Motor Company.

    DWK

For **Norman** and **Suzanne**
and the memory of **JY** and
my old Super Hawk

Contents

Introduction	What This Book Is About	1
Chapter 1	Buying a Road Motorcycle	5
Chapter 2	Buying an Off-Road Motorcycle	28
Chapter 3	Motorcycle Ownership	50
Chapter 4	Knowing Your Motorcycle	63
Chapter 5	Motorcycling Safety	77
Chapter 6	Preventive Maintenance	98
Chapter 7	Bike Tripping	113
Chapter 8	Competition Cycling	132
Chapter 9	The Accessory Market	151
Chapter 10	Motorcycling and the Environment	170
	Glossary	191
	Index	195

Chilton's Complete Guide to Motorcycles and Motorcycling

Introduction: What This Book Is About

I

Two decades ago, less than half a million motorcycles were registered in the United States. The cycles of that day and age were heavy, cumbersome and prone to all manner of mechanical ills. Today, however, the situation is very different.

Nearly 4 million motorcycles are in operation throughout the United States. Students, businessmen, construction workers, scientists, housewives, teachers and just plain people are using motorcycles to get to work, to do their chores, to go visiting and to get away from it all. For motorcycles can do all these things more economically and more ecologically (not to mention more enjoyably) than can four-wheeled vehicles.

Every year, more and more persons are turning toward motorcycles as a new way to get from one point to another. Motorcycle manufacturers, in turn, are tailoring their products to this new clientele, who demand levels of performance, smoothness and reliability that were unheard of even a decade ago. Gone forever are the days of hard starting, rough running motorcycles that too often required constant attention if they were to work at all.

The new breed of motorcycles seem, in comparison, nearly as comfortable to drive as an automobile and almost as easy to operate as a bicycle. Many experienced riders would argue that motorcycles do indeed combine the best features of an automobile and a bicycle. Be this as it may, motorcycles nevertheless offer the prospective rider a unique experience available from no other wheeled vehicle. They also require of their operators a special blend of skill and knowledge. Knowing how to operate an automobile—or a bicycle—is no guarantee whatsoever that a prospective rider can safely and

Motorcycling is a sport for women too. An increasing number of women are learning to operate their own motorcycles.

effectively operate a motorcycle. Nor can a recent convert assume that he or she knows instinctively the best kind of motorcycle to purchase or how to maintain that motorcycle properly. No book can teach a reader all that he needs to know of these matters. A single experience is often worth more than a thousand words about that experience. The following pages, however, offer a comprehensive introduction to the subject of buying, operating and maintaining a motorcycle.

II

Despite the vast differences between a modern motorcycle and the machines of yesterday, every motorcycle is part of a tradition stretching back to the first time a rider threw his leg over the first primitive motorcycle. Few riders today can recall the Henderson Four, the Brough Superior, the Vincent twin or the Norton Manx. Yet most every motorcycle produced today owes a part of its ancestry to these and other less legendary motorcycles.

The contemporary motorcycle also owes much to the world of motorcycle competition. In motorcycling, more so than in the automotive field, a direct link exists between the racetrack and the production line. Race bred improvements quickly find their way onto the production line. Many of the design features we commonly associate with modern motorcycles existed a few years back only on exotic racing cycles. The racing innovations of today will in turn most likely become the production features of tomorrow's motorcycles.

In recognition of these facts, the following pages examine the sport of motorcycling as merely the most recent stage in an evolutionary process already several generations old. Since motorcycle competition in its many forms is so integral a part of the sport, this book also provides a brief introduction to the various forms of motorcycle competition practiced throughout the country.

III

Never before have there existed so many motorcyclists nor so many different kinds of motorcycles from which to pick and choose. Along with this growth in participants and products has come, however, a growth in problems. The motorcycling community is no longer a small band of adventurers whom the public will allow to do as they please. Motorcyclists are becoming increasingly accountable for their actions both on the road and off.

In the wake of a growing environmental awareness there has emerged the demand for new constraints on motorcycle manufacturers and users. If the sport of motorcycling is to survive, each of us must demonstrate an awareness of and concern for both our own selfprotection and the protection of the environment. Rider safety and environmental protection are the two principal issues presently confronting motorcyclists. In order to preserve present freedoms we must develop a new ethic of individual and collective responsibility for our actions. Motorcycling has become for better or worse an issue of public concern and we must all act accordingly.

Protection of the land, conservation of air quality standards, the avoidance of noise pollution and user safety measures are issues that an earlier generation of motorcyclists could conveniently ignore. Yet times have changed. This book provides no easy solutions to the twin problems of rider safety and environmental protection. It does, however, offer a short course in these matters and it points the way toward some possible answers. Each reader must decide how he or she intends to deal with the issues of safety and the environment. The following pages simply state the facts and point out the consequences that may result from various courses of action or inaction.

IV

In addition to all his other roles, a motorcyclist is also a consumer of goods and services. Like every other consumer, he needs to know what the marketplace can offer him and what cautions to exercise while shopping for goods and services. In recent years, various statutes have been enacted to protect the consumer from himself and from those who would do him harm. Nevertheless, the rule of *caveat emptor* still holds true. The buyer must beware.

More specifically, a consumer must take pains to do the right thing and to do things right. In other words, he needs to decide both what he should do and how to go about doing it. Not only must he decide, for example, what kind of insurance to buy but from whom to buy it and at what limits of coverage. Similarly, he must decide whether to finance the purchase of his motorcycle and if he is going to finance it, with what lending institution and on what terms.

It is not the purpose of this book to tell consumers what they should do or how they should go about doing it. Nor will the reader find any particular brand or kind of motorcycle or accessory marked as a best buy or the best in its class. The book you are about to read is not simply a how-to book nor a shopping guide. Instead, more than anything else, it is a consumer manual intended to provide you, the consumer, with an introduction to every phase of motorcycling from the art of buying a used motorcycle to the physics of cornering to how to prepare for a long distance cycling trip. In matters that may adversely affect a rider's health, welfare or pocketbook, some stern warnings are offered. For the most part, however, the following pages focus less on what you should do than on what you need to know in order to reach your own decisions. The facts—along with some statements of opinion—are contained herein. It is up to the reader to do with them as he or she sees fit.

Chapter 1

Buying A Road Motorcycle

So you want to buy a motorcycle? Or you already own a motorcycle and want to get a bigger or newer one. Or you would not want one for yourself, but your son wants to buy one. Or perhaps you plan to haul your goggles and old silk scarf out of storage since word has spread that nowadays one meets the nicest people on a motorcycle.

Whatever your reasons for wanting a motorcycle—and the why does not much matter—you will soon discover that the motorcycle market is filled to capacity with various makes and models of two-wheeled vehicles. Manufacturers from a dozen or more lands are clamoring for their share of the American motorcycle market. The products they offer for sale range from minibikes with a 3 cubic inch powerplant to earth shaking superbikes that produce upward of 70 horsepower. And the price of buying a motorcycle varies proportionately, from as little as a few hundred dollars for a minibike or a well-used small displacement motorcycle to nearly three thousand dollars for an exotic, limited production racing machine or a fully equipped heavyweight touring motorcycle.

Many prospective motorcycle owners and the majority of current motorcyclists intending to trade know approximately how large and how costly a motorcycle they plan to purchase. Yet even within a particular category of motorcycles, for example medium capacity touring bikes produced in Japan, there is a bewildering variety of choices. Should a rider place his bet on the sensational Guzzlefire V-3 with its new isoplastic suspension system? Or ought he bet his money on the three-stroke Yamadakta with its slick paint job and fine sounding exhaust system? The Yamadakta, of course, comes with a 6 month/36,000 mile guarantee, but then again the Guzzlefire just last week won three important races in California.

Dilemmas such as these need not drive a prospective motorcyclist back to the world of four-wheeled transportation. The confusion and uncertainty surrounding the purchase of a motorcycle, and especially the uncertainty that surrounds the purchase of a first two-wheeler, can readily be reduced to manageable proportions. The secret, though it is an entirely obvious one, lies in deciding as clearly as possible just what your objectives and priorities are. What is most important to you in a motorcycle? What is less important? And what does not much matter? Once these decisions have been made, it is a relatively simple task to match them up with the various motorcycles available in any given price range. Corporate managers and organizational planners call this technique management by objectives or MBO. It hardly deserves so mysterious and imposing a title. Actually, this method of decision making involves little more than the application of common sense and a bit of forethought to the solution of everyday problems.

The following pages of this chapter are devoted to an examination of the considerations involved in selecting a road bike. We will first survey the variety of road-going motorcycles on the market and then examine some of the purchasing considerations that might sway a buyer in one direction or another.

Road-going motorcycles comprise the single largest category of two-wheeled vehicles. They therefore deserve first consideration. The issue of selecting a motorcycle for off-road use will be dealt with in the following chapter. Many of the shopping techniques and purchasing principles outlined in this chapter apply, however, with equal weight to the purchase of a dirt-going motorcycle. Consequently, those readers interested solely in buying an off-road motorcycle will find it worth their while to consider the contents of this chapter before proceeding to Chapter 2.

What Is a Road-Going Motorcycle?

Road-going motorcycles come in every size and shape from 50 cc midgets to 1200 cc touring goliaths. For it is not size or weight or cost that distinguishes a road going motorcycle, but a particular set of design features.

Road bikes, as the name implies, are intended for use on hard surfaced roadways. By hard surfaced, we are referring primarily to asphalt or concrete roads and, secondarily, to packed or oiled dirt roads of the sort that exist everywhere in rural America. A considerable number of road-going motorcycles, which were once called street scramblers in the advertising literature, claim to be dual purpose motorcycles. To a limited extent they are, since a rider can operate them with some safety and comfort on the highway and along trails. But these motorcycles are engineered largely for roadway use with the addition of some outward and a few inward concessions to dirt riding. Consequently, the dirt environment in which street scrambler style motorcycles perform best are the kind that give tires and suspension systems a relatively smooth, level surface. The road going heritage of a street scrambler motorcycle becomes immediately apparent when a rider attempts to negotiate deep sand, gravel, mud or a slippery uphill climb.

Among motorcycles, more than in the automotive world, form tends to follow function. Road going motorcycles, whether they are intended exclusively or largely for use on hard surfaces, exhibit a number of similar design features. What are these features? Chapter 4 includes a more detailed description, but here is a partial listing:

BUYING A ROAD MOTORCYCLE

A typical road-going motorcycle: the Honda CB-350. Note the ample gas tank, medium rise handlebars, long wide seat, passenger hand rail, low slung exhaust pipes and close mounted front fender.

The Frame Road going motorcycles typically employ a heavy steel frame designed to support from a quarter ton to nearly one half a ton of weight, yet resist the flexing that produces dangerous handling. The frame and swing arm assembly generally offer a compromise geometry that permits high speed stability and a fair degree of low speed maneuverability.

The frame design and overall construction of a road-going motorcycle distributes slightly more vehicle weight on the rear wheel than up front. A typical road bike will have an unladen weight distribution on the order of 45 percent front/55 percent rear. This somewhat rearward balance (which is increased with a rider in place) allows a motorcycle to achieve excellent rear wheel traction and light, positive steering control.

The Suspension Road-going suspension systems are characterized by stiff springing, a moderate length of travel, and only limited opportunity for on the spot adjustment. The stiff springing contributes to a firm ride and a high resistance to steering wander. The hydraulic front suspension of a road-going motorcycle generally provides five to six inches of fork leg travel, which becomes progressively stiffer as the fork legs near their point of maximum compression. The rear suspension assembly employs a coiled spring surrounding an automotive style shock absorber unit. The shock absorber unit generally has a three-way adjustment to compensate for varying passenger loads.

Engine Characteristics Road-going motorcycles generally operate at moderate to high engine speeds; therefore, low-speed engine flexibility and tractor-like pulling power are not crucial. Most engine designs therefore employ large carburetors, a high bore-to-stroke ratio, moderately "hot" valve or port timing, and two, three or more cylinders. High-performance, high-speed engines are the rule among road-going motorcycles.

Gas Tank and Seat A road going motorcycle must be capable of traveling considerable distances in a single day. Consequently, long, wide and (usually) well-padded seats are common. As a rule of thumb, the top of the seat is 30 to 32 inches above the ground. This relatively low seat height allows a rider sufficient leverage to control a motorcycle at rest or low speeds and it helps maintain a low center of gravity.

Fenders In order to protect a rider and passenger from water on the roadway, the fenders of a road-going motorcycle are mounted close to the tread surface. Usually, they extend at their rearmost point approximately to the centerline of the axle. Steel construction is the rule, though a few manufacturers employ aluminum fenders.

Exhaust System Sharp bends in an exhaust system restrict the free flow of exhaust gases. So the exhaust system sweeps gently forward and downward from the engine, passing beneath the foot pegs and exiting to the rear of the motorcycle at a point about two feet or less above the ground. A low mounting point offers the additional advantage of placing the dangerously hot exhaust piping as far away as possible from a rider's legs and hands. Double wall constructed exhaust pipes are used by at least a few manufacturers. This pipe within a pipe design serves to deaden the exhaust racket, present a cooler outer surface than is the case with single wall pipes and prevent discoloration of the chrome plating from exhaust heat, which some riders find unattractive.

Tires and Wheel Rims Wide tires and wheels are of little value on a road-going motorcycle. The wheel rims of a road bike are therefore moderately narrow with a slightly larger tire used in back than in front. On pure road-going motorcycles, the front tire employs a circumferential rib pattern that resembles the tread design of a tractor or an aircraft tire while the rear tire has a universal style pattern similar to the tread design on passenger car tires. Motorcycles intended for dual purpose riding use either a universal pattern tire on the front and rear wheels or, less commonly, an open lug pattern trail tire, which gives improved traction and steering control on dirt surfaces.

In summary, road-going motorcycles are designed from the ground up for highway use. As a result of much trial and error, cycle manufacturers have come to accept a relatively uniform set of design solutions to the problem of building a stable road-going motorcycle. Most highway bikes have a distinctive look that differs from other kinds of motorcycles. It is important to remember that these distinctive features are more than skin deep. Simply adding the appropriate tires, tank, seat and exhaust pipes will not convert a dirt bike into a pure road-going motorcycle. Nor can a motorcycle designed for use on the highway be readily converted into a true off-road cycle.

The Varieties of Road-Going Motorcycles

Although road-going motorcycles are a separate breed unto themselves, there exists within the breed obvious and important differences. A visit to any large motorcycle dealership will confirm the fact that road-going motorcycles come in a variety of shapes and sizes. Little, insect-like minibikes, modest looking motorcycles and sleek-lined machines rest there on the showroom floor waiting for a customer to breath life into their cylinders. Which one should a customer select?

A motorcycle salesman may not say so in as many words, but motorcycles are traditionally grouped into three broad categories on the basis of their weight and engine size. The smaller motorcycles, generally under 250 cc in engine size, are classified as lightweights. Motorcycles with an engine displacement in the range of 250 cc to 500 cc fall into the category of middleweight vehicles. Motorcycles with an engine larger than 500 cc (or 30 cubic inches) deserve to be placed in the heavyweight category.

Like any division of reality into presumably distinct groupings, these three categories overlap to a certain extent. For example, a 450 cc twin cylinder Honda and the 250 cc Bultaco are both technically middleweight motorcycles. Yet, on the basis of its weight, bulk and lively performance, the Honda might reasonably be classified as a heavyweight while the light, agile Bultaco has much in common with lightweight motorcycles. The point is that these three motorcycle categories are not absolute types, but merely approximate classifications. Thus a motorcyclist who owns a machine near the top of the lightweight category might decide he wants a larger, more powerful motorcycle near the bottom of the heavyweight category. In that case he could consider purchasing a used 650 cc motorcycle or one of the 500 cc motorcycles produced in Japan, England, Germany or Italy. He might also consider buying a 450 cc motorcycle that, although not technically a heavyweight, will offer a level of performance and handling virtually identical to that of a 500 cc motorcycle.

How should a prospective buyer decide what kind of motorcycle is best suited to his needs? The answer is that he must first decide how and where he expects to use that motorcycle. Does he plan only to ride back and forth to school or work over city streets? Will he take occasional trips on a crosstown expressway, or every now and then go up to the hills for an afternoon of trail riding? Would he want to ride his motorcycle out to the hills, or trailer it behind an automobile? Is there a strong possibility he might take occasional trips requiring a full day's ride and the use of interstate roads? Does the heft and bulk of a heavyweight motorcycle worry him? Or does he need a long wheelbased touring machine that can comfortably eat up half a thousand miles of pavement in a single day?

The answer to these and related questions will determine the motorcycle size best suited to a rider's needs. Each size of motorcycle is designed to accomplish a given set of objectives that can be fulfilled only at the cost of sacrificing other objectives. In other words, it is invariably necessary to trade off one or more objectives in order to satisfy those objectives or needs that are foremost in a rider's mind. A motorcycle can be especially fast or light, or economical or comfortable, or reliable or maneuverable. In fact, it may exhibit a number of these characteristics. But it simply cannot achieve all of them.

Lightweight Motorcycles The smallest class of motorcycles, the lightweights, are light in weight (usually under 300 pounds), economical to operate (from 50 to 100 or more miles per gallon) and relatively inexpensive to purchase, insure and repair. Moreover, lightweight motorcycles make excellent dual purpose trail vehicles that can be ridden back and forth to school or work during the weekday, then used on the weekend for trail riding. Since small bore bikes weigh so little (often under 200 pounds) they can readily be loaded into the back of a pickup truck or rolled onto a motorcycle trailer.

On the other hand, lightweight motorcycles present a number of draw-

The Kawasaki 90 is a lightweight utility vehicle that yields excellent fuel economy and dependable around town transportation.

backs. The very smallest models barely produce sufficient power to keep up with city traffic much less get away from it. Even the bigger motorcycles in the lightweight category are rarely powerful enough to cruise for extended periods of time at turnpike speeds and they have only limited passenger carrying capacity. Trying to carry a passenger along at 60 MPH or more on a lightweight motorcycle is neither comfortable nor conducive to rider safety or mechanical longevity. Almost by definition, lightweight motorcycles are not (except for a few of the most powerful 250 cc machines) equipped with the tires, brakes, suspension systems or engine output necessary to haul a 300 pound burden any significant distance. Every once in a while we hear of a motorcyclist who rode his 175 cc Hummingbird Flash all the way from Alaska to the tip of Tierra del Fuego or some equally improbable point. Perhaps he did complete the trip as claimed. Rest assured that his journey was an endless series of trials and tribulations that only the brave or foolish would endure.

As a final consideration, lightweight motorcycles must be ridden with special care. Though easy to operate, lightweights have small, narrow section tires that can navigate roadway obstructions less readily. The shorter wheelbase and smaller inertia of a lightweight makes it all the more susceptible to veering from its intended path. Many riders think of a lightweight motorcycle as a motor powered bicycle. Instead, it is a full fledged motorcycle and should be treated with appropriate caution. A lightweight motorcycle can not accelerate as suddenly as more powerful bikes, but it can just as abruptly bring its operator into contact with a wide variety of stationary objects.

Middleweight Motorcycles The middleweight category encompasses the popular 250 cc, 350 cc and 500 cc displacement sizes. Middleweight motorcycles vary substantially in weight, from 250 pounds to 425 pounds; in horsepower, from 20 HP to 60 HP; and in cost, from $800 to $1,600. Since competition for the middleweight market is so fierce, motorcycle manufacturers offer a diversity of models. Not so long ago a prospective customer had his choice of two middleweight engine sizes, 250 cc or 500 cc, and only two different engine designs, single cylinder or twin cylinder (the latter usually being a four-stroke engine). Today, that same customer has his choice of two-stroke or four-stroke engine designs in nearly every middleweight engine size and he must select from among one, two, three and even four cylinder layouts.

A few years back, knowledgeable motorcyclists would have considered a four cylinder 350 cc motorcycle too expensive and too complex for any purpose other than factory supported road racing. Those same motorcyclists would have condemned the notion of a two-stroke, three cylinder motorcycle of 500 cc capacity to the junkpile of unworkable ideas. Today, however, both these designs have yielded commercially successful road bikes.

The popularity of middleweight motorcycles is a natural consequence of the fact that they do so many things so well. Middleweights are light and agile enough to thread their way through city traffic with ease. They are sufficiently light that most riders, including many women, have no difficulty

The Honda 450 twin is a reliable yet sophisticated middleweight that offers a time tested mechanical layout.

managing their weight. Yet middleweights offer spirited performance and they can smartly negotiate sharp curves and blast down straightaways at a speed of 100 MPH or more. The larger middleweights are adequate for extended highway cruising and they can safely handle the additional burden of a passenger. These big middleweight motorcycles are none too agile on trails though they will negotiate dirt roads with little difficulty. The smaller middleweights, however, in the range of 250 cc to 350 cc, make excellent dual purpose motorcycles. They are large enough to be ridden comfortably on the highway, yet they will negotiate all but the roughest of back country trails. Indeed, the very best of the dual purpose middleweights are equally at home on and off the highway.

Despite the fact that middleweight road bikes do many things very well, they are not the perfect choice for every rider. Middleweights lack the agility and economy of a lightweight and the larger middleweight motorcycles are often too heavy for operation on any kind of soft surface. Moreover, many of the larger middleweights are expensive to purchase and to maintain. The three and four cylinder designs common among the big middleweights yield spirited performance at the cost of considerable mechanical complexity, which usually means greater initial cost and additional upkeep.

The smaller middleweights can generally cruise for moderate distances at highway speed so long as they are not burdened with excessive weight or adverse road conditions. They do not, however, provide an especially comfortable ride. Larger middleweight motorcycles do better in this respect. Their wheelbase, power output and overall size are sufficient to transport a rider down the highway comfortably and safely. Most of the larger, more powerful middleweights lack the torque and bulk necessary for luxurious touring comfort or scorching boulevard acceleration. Yet they can double as excellent around town transportation and occasional medium distance touring mounts.

Heavyweight Motorcycles Heavyweight motorcycles often tip the scales at little more than the larger middleweights. But the typical heavyweight motorcycle offers an engine displacement of 750 cc and a horsepower rating in the neighborhood of 60 HP. The very largest and most powerful motorcycles in this category weigh upward of 500 pounds and produce about 70 horsepower. But even an older British 650 cc twin or a 600 cc BMW legitimately fall into the heavyweight class.

Heavyweight motorcycles, then, are big and fast. Indeed, for the traditional rider they are what the sport of motorcycling is all about: stable handling, attractive design, searing acceleration and long distance cruising comfort. In keeping with this tradition, most heavyweight motorcycles are a pleasure to behold and to ride. More than any other kind of motorcycle, a heavyweight bike captures the essence of motorcycling along an open road. A heavyweight performs like a purebred hunting dog. It will survive in the city, but only out in the countryside is it content and in its natural element.

The ownership of a big bore motorcycle does not come cheaply, however. First there is the price tag, which is usually well in excess of $1,500 and often in the neighborhood of $2,000. Next come the operating expenses, which include gas mileage that is often only a step above the mileage an economy car will deliver. Then too, the maintenance and repair expenses can prove substantial. Tires, oil, tune-ups and the other routine expenses of

This 1,000 cc Harley-Davidson Sportster offers a classic blend of big bike handling and awesome horsepower.

motorcycle ownership are roughly equal to the cost of maintaining a small economy car. Major rebuilding work on a three or four cylinder heavyweight can also prove costly. In the realm of motorcycles as in the automotive world, more cylinders, means more power, more complexity, more sophistication and more expense.

Because of their size and power, heavyweight motorcycles are hardly ideal traffic bikes. They lack the low speed agility and light balance needed for stop and go traffic riding. A heavyweight can, of course, be ridden in heavy traffic. It is no pleasure to do so, however. This is especially true of the larger heavyweights, those in the over 500 pound category, when they are operated by a rider weighing in at 150 pounds or less. Once a heavyweight is rolling down the highway, a rider's weight and strength matter little. At very low speeds, however, heavyweight motorcycles handle sluggishly; therefore, careful balance and considerable physical effort are needed to keep them upright and traveling in the right direction.

Like a high performance sports car, heavyweight motorcycles are intended for use on the open road. To operate them exclusively in a city makes no more sense than maintaining a Ferrari automobile for use in a large metropolitan area. If you do not anticipate using the performance and long distance riding capacity of a heavyweight, then it makes little sense to own one.

As a final consideration, large capacity motorcycles are not suitable for off-road use. Their steering geometry, ground clearance, tire tread pattern and weight all conspire to make off-road operation a tiresome and dangerous task. Indeed, any kind of loose or soft surface, as a gravel road or patch of sand, is difficult to negotiate on a large capacity road-going motorcycle. The massive power output of a heavyweight road bike should be applied only to hard surfaced roads, and preferably roads uncongested with low speed traffic.

These three motorcycle categories encompass most every kind of road-going cycle presently available in the United States. The only motorcycles not directly included in the preceding discussion are minibikes and motorcycle/sidecar combinations. So at this point we will briefly examine these two extremes of the motor driven cycle market.

Minibikes are scaled down lightweight motorcycles (see the accompanying photographs). The typical minibike employs a small capacity engine of 100 cc or less in a low, short frame coupled with small wheels that are always less than 18 inches in diameter and sometimes as small as 12 inches. Everything that has been said in regard to lightweight motorcycles applies with special force to minibikes. The small wheels, short wheelbase and miniature design scale of the minibike preclude riding double or operating it in traffic. The minibike is primarily a learning vehicle for youngsters and a fun bike for adults wishing to cruise around a parking lot, a fairground or a campsite. Portability, simplicity and economy are the principal virtues of a minibike. When they are used within the range of their limitations, minibikes make an excellent source of recreational entertainment. They were never intended, however, to serve as basic urban transportation vehicles nor should they be so used.

The motorcycle/sidecar combination and the tricycle (a motorcycle with parallel rear wheels connected by a common axle) are technically multi-track vehicles. At the same time these hybrid designs employ a single front wheel with a motorcycle style suspension and riding position. European tax laws look favorably on three-wheeled vehicles; therefore, motorcycle sidecars have been popular in England and on the Continent for many years. Although three-wheeled vehicles have never captured a significant share of the American motorcycle market, they are occasionally used in this country ei-

One style of minibike. Honda's SL 70 is a scaled down replica of that manufacturer's larger dual purpose motorcycles.

This Harley-Davidson minibike features wide, small diameter wheels and a 90 cc two-stroke engine.

ther as utility vehicles, generally among police departments, or as exotic alternatives to the single track motorcycle.

Sidecar equipped motorcycles are slower and less maneuverable than the basic solo vehicle to which the sidecar is attached. Moreover, the cost of a sidecar is high, their availability is limited on this side of the Atlantic and once a sidecar has been attached it is no simple matter to detach it for an afternoon of solo riding. A sidecar also requires the heft and power of a heavyweight motorcycle so an owner must be willing to commit a major financial investment. A factory fresh sidecar outfit will usually cost more than the price of a compact automobile.

There are, obviously, sound reasons for the lack of privately owned sidecar

16 CHILTON'S COMPLETE GUIDE TO MOTORCYCLES

Although popular in Europe, the motorcycle/sidecar combination remains an exotic breed on this side of the Atlantic.

outfits in this country. But sidecar owners, though few in number, are vocal advocates of their sport. Sidecars, they admit, are not for everyone. Nevertheless, the sidecar and motorcycle combination offers a high level of stability and comfort. In traffic, a sidecar equipped motorcycle is less maneuverable than a single track vehicle, yet it is much more agile than an automobile. Moreover, a motorcycle with sidecar can be operated safely in the wintertime; it will readily negotiate snowpacked and even icy roads. Learning to drive a sidecar well requires practice in mastering the intricacies of a vehicle that almost never tends to track in a straight line. Because a sidecar wheel is asymmetrically located, braking, cornering and accelerating generate unequal forces, for which an operator must learn to compensate. The pleasure of sidecar ownership comes partly from mastering these skills and partly from knowing that nobody else in town is likely to show up with so exotic a motor vehicle.

Road-going motorcycles differ with respect to their size and also their state of tune. State of tune, as it is used here, refers not to whether a motorcycle is properly tuned up (with the ignition, valves and carburetor adjusted) but to the amount of power its engine is designed to produce. The same basic engine assembly—consisting of the engine cases, crankshaft, connecting rods and pistons—can be a mild mannered, ho-hum powerplant or a screaming competition engine. The difference depends largely on such factors as carburetion, valve timing, compression ratio, flywheel weight, valve and port size and exhaust system design.

Not so many years ago motorcycle manufacturers commonly produced two or even three versions of the same basic motorcycle design so that a rider could select the state of tune appropriate to his needs. The bygone Vincent Series B twin, for example, could be purchased in the mildly tuned Rapide version, in a high performance Black Shadow model or in the form of a radically tuned version that was appropriately called the Black Lightning. A number of manufacturers continue to follow the practice of issuing the same motorcycle in two or more states of tune. Thus, Triumph riders have the opportunity to choose between a comfortably equipped single-carburetor model or the faster, dual-carburetor version known as the Bonneville. Japanese manufacturers are less prone to market the same engine in two or more different states of tune than to offer the same basic engine in two or more different sizes or to offer more than one engine in the same size category. As an example, consider the Honda four cylinder and the Kawasaki three cylinder motorcycles. A rider can buy the same basic engine in a 350 cc, 500 cc or 750 cc capacity, with the entire motorcycle scaled to the power output of the engine. Alternately, Kawasaki manufactures a 750 cc two-stroke, three cylinder motorcycle and a 900 cc four-stroke, four cylinder motorcycle. These two motorcycle engines produce approximately the same peak horsepower, yet they are engineered for significantly different uses.

The advertising literature or a salesman's pitch may suggest that a particular motorcycle is all things to all people. Do not believe it. In this age of specialization, no engineering staff or marketing division expects to produce a two-wheeled vehicle with universal appeal. Instead, manufacturers design their products to meet best the needs of a particular audience. Therefore two motorcycles with similar price tags and equally glowing paint jobs may be intended to serve very different functions.

For the purposes of consumer convenience we can divide these different uses, and the accompanying states of tune, into a few broad categories. The three we will examine are utility motorcycles, designed with an eye to practicality; performance motorcycles, which are engineered for speed; and cruising motorcycles, for the long distance rider. For the sake of simplicity these three kinds of motorcycles will be referred to as plain janes, hot rods and easy riders. Let's look at each of these motorcycle types in turn.

Plain Janes Sporting ingredients so heavily flavor American motorcycling that few pure utility motorcycles are available in the United States. The true plain jane motorcycle is invariably painted black and tuned for extreme mechanical longevity above all else. A plain jane might not set any speed records, but with proper care it will still be slogging about the countryside or cityscape long after its competitors have traveled their final mile.

The best examples of a plain jane motorcycle, such as the British Panther or the Czechoslovakian Jawa, are largely unknown outside Europe. But many nicely painted motorcycles loaded with gleaming chrome and polished alloy are little more than plain janes decked out in some fancy trim. The trim, of course, is there simply to sell the bike; underneath rests a durable engine and no nonsense suspension system that are gluttons for punishment. Few motorcycle dealers will admit that any model on their showroom floor is a plain jane. Wait, however, until the salesman allows that the little Guzzlefink twin sitting over there in the corner may not be the fastest bike around, but it sure is dependable and starts like a charm. With that kind of introduction you can reasonably suppose that the Guzzlefink twin is a plain jane in disguise. To confirm your suspicion, check the weight and horsepower rating of the Guzzlefink against its competition. If it weighs more and produces less horsepower than its competitors, there is even more reason to believe that the Guzzlefink twin is a plain jane.

Perhaps the best method of identifying plain janes is to talk with a variety of motorcycle owners and especially owners who have accumulated a substantial number of miles on the odometer of their motorcycles. For it is a characteristic of plain janes that they continue to run for years with tractor-like reliability. Especially good candidates for the plain jane category are motorcycles that have been developed from larger capacity models. When a manufacturer scales down a motorcycle, he often does little more than reduce the bore or stroke of the engine and substitute a smaller frame. For reasons of economy, many of the engine and running gear components designed for the larger motorcycle are carried over to the smaller model. The result is a motorcycle with a variety of overdesigned and understressed parts.

Hot Rods The hot rod goes by a number of different names. It may be called a boulevard cruiser or a cafe racer. Regardless of what it is called, the hot rod motorcycle offers maximum horsepower and rapid acceleration, even at the cost of smooth idling, low speed torque or extended engine life. A hot rod may be difficult to ride in traffic and ill-suited to interstate touring, but it is the quickest and most dazzling method on two wheels of getting from point A to a not-so-distant point B.

The design features that characterize most hot rod motorcycles include light overall weight, high compression ratios, extended valve timing, wide valves or ports, large carburetors and a non-restrictive exhaust system. Due

BUYING A ROAD MOTORCYCLE 19

The Kawasaki 500 triple retains the well deserved reputation as a middleweight hot rod. If offers performance levels equal to those of most heavyweight motorcycles.

to these features, the hot rod is neither simple to drive, economical to operate nor easy to service. It does, however, provide the flashing performance and sleek good looks that many riders demand from a motorcycle.

The fastest and best known motorcycle hot rods fall into the heavyweight category. But not all high performance motorcycles are heavyweights. Some of the most sophisticated and elegant hot rods have an engine capacity and a price tag well below that of a heavyweight. Yet their acceleration, handling and stopping power place them nearly on a par with full-fledged road racers of only a few years ago. These small scale street racers are masterful works of technology that can provide an experienced rider with most all the sensations of a full bore competition motorcycle at a fraction of the cost and bother of the real thing.

Easy Riders The easy rider is a smooth, powerful, and durable long distance touring motorcycle that will roll along comfortably for days on end. Many of the more luxurious middleweights make excellent cruising motorcycles. But a true easy rider is invariably a heavyweight motorcycle with an engine of 750 cc or more (the smaller BMWs are an exception to this rule), a power rating in the vicinity of 60 horsepower or better and a price tag around the $2,000 mark.

The sheer size of an easy rider precludes trail riding and removes any pleasure from maneuvering in heavy traffic. Once an easy rider is out on the highway, however, its engine will settle down to a contented hum as rider, passenger and baggage are whisked along the roadway in comfort and style. Crosswinds, pavement joints, cattleguards and other obstacles to bother-free motorcycling diminish in significance on an easy rider: it just keeps on rolling along.

For the motorcyclist with a well upholstered bank account and a passion for long distance touring, the easy rider is the only way to go. Prospective buyers with less wherewithal (commonly known as cash) or only a mild in-

The power, dependability and smoothness of this Honda CB-750 qualifies it as an excellent choice for the rider seeking a heavyweight touring machine.

The Harley-Davidson FXE 1200: a fast, comfortable heavyweight for the man who wants the virtues of a hot rod and an easy rider. Note the use of front and rear hydraulic disc brakes.

terest in long distance riding can generally find an adequate middleweight compromise to the easy rider. Some of the same manufacturers that produce easy riders (such as Honda and BMW) also market scaled down middleweight versions that approach the luxury of a full size touring motorcycle, but at a lower cost and with less loss of low speed agility. Then, too, various manufacturers produce a heavyweight motorcycle, such as the 750 cc Triumph or the Moto Guzzi 750 Sport, that can best be described as performance oriented touring bikes. These dual purpose heavyweights may not offer the full comfort of a pure easy rider or the sheer acceleration of a true hot rod. But they present an appealing compromise for the rider who would try to have his cake and eat it too.

Some Purchasing Considerations

In summary, there are three basic categories of road-going motorcycles: the lightweights, the middleweights, and the heavyweights. Additionally, we have identified three types of motorcycles: plain janes, hot rods and easy riders. The relationship between these three categories or sizes and the different types of motorcycles is shown in diagram form in the accompanying chart. The shaded boxes indicate motorcycle combinations that either do not exist, as a lightweight easy rider, or that are uncommon, as plain jane style heavyweight.

A TOPOLOGY OF ROAD-GOING MOTORCYCLES

	Lightweights	Middleweights	Heavyweights
Plain Janes	Lightweight Plain Jane	Middleweight Plain Jane	
Hot Rods	Lightweight Hot Rod	Middleweight Hot Rod	Heavyweight Hot Rod
Easy Riders		Middleweight Easy Rider	Heavyweight Easy Rider

Which one (or more) of these boxes a consumer should focus his attention on will depend upon his needs, his experience, his desires and his budget.

The kind of motorcycle a consumer needs will depend in turn on how he intends to use a motorcycle. The preceding explanation of motorcycle sizes and types has outlined the various uses to which each kind of motorcycle is best suited. Thus the rider intent on long distance touring would concentrate his attention on heavyweight crusing bikes while a motorcyclist searching for a high performance motorcycle to use around town with occasional trips to the countryside would confine his shopping to middleweight hot rods.

The majority of riders, however, purchase a motorcycle not to indulge a passion for long distance touring nor to enjoy blazing acceleration above all else. Instead, they seek a machine that offers a reasonable balance of performance, dependability and economy. The plain jane motorcycles available on the American market nicely fulfill these requirements. Compared to a high-performance superbike in the 750 cc category, the plain jane is no speed

This Suzuki 250 offers the middleweight rider a blend of strong performance, smooth handling and excellent stopping power. Note the hydraulically assisted front disc brake.

demon. Nor is it a slouch. Most middleweight plain janes have enough power to outrun nearly any passenger car on the road today.

Moreover, the plain jane, when outfitted with street scrambler or on-road/off-road accessories, makes an excellent dual purpose motorcycle. Easy rider touring bikes are simply too heavy for use in the dirt while hot rods have inappropriate tires and engines that are too highly tuned for enjoyable dirt riding. Yet a plain jane, though also a bit overweight for off-road use, produces the smooth, controllable flow of power to the rear wheel that is so necessary for riding in the dirt.

Previous motorcycling experience is an equally important consideration in selecting a motorcycle. No sensible hunter would recommend that an inexperienced shooter begin his career with the purchase of a Holland and Holland .600 express rifle. Nor should a beginning motorcyclist start his riding career with a 750 cc superbike. A high performance heavyweight motorcycle in the hands of an inexperienced rider can be as dangerous as the Holland and Holland .600 elephant gun in the hands of an inexperienced hunter. Just as a shooter graduates to progressively larger firearms, so should a motorcyclist graduate to progressively larger and faster motorcycles.

On the other hand, a beginning motorcyclist should not necessarily restrict his shopping to lightweight motorcycles. Like any other sportsman, he needs to have in his possession equipment appropriate to the task at hand. No elephant hunter should venture into the woods equipped only with a .22 caliber rifle. By the same token, a motorcyclist planning to ride along a freeway back and forth to work requires the bulk and performance of a middleweight motorcycle. Perhaps he could get by with a lightweight if the distance involved were short and the road uncongested. A middleweight motorcycle, perhaps in the range of 350 cc, would prove a more sensible and safer choice.

A prospective customer should also bear in mind that whatever his present level of experience may be, frequent riding will soon make him a more experienced motorcyclist. Consequently, a machine that is ideally fitted to his current experience and capabilities might soon seem inadequate. The solution is for a rider, especially if he is buying a first motorcycle, to buy a model one step larger than he feels is appropriate to his present experience level. Or in the event that a prospective customer is torn between buying a 250 cc motorcycle or a 350 cc cycle, it would be prudent (all other considerations being equal) for him to purchase the larger bike. It may require an entire season of riding, but he will "grow into" the larger machine. Buying the bigger of two motorcycles may actually prove economical in the long run. A motorcyclist who feels he has outgrown a cycle will usually trade it in for a larger model, despite the financial loss he suffers. By buying a slightly oversize (relative to his experience) motorcycle, a rider can postpone or even eliminate altogether the loss that usually accompanies the trade up to a larger and more expensive motorcycle.

For better or worse, motorcycle ownership owes as much to the kingdom of the spirit as it does to the realm of reason. In other words, motorcyclists as a group are often motivated by illogical wants as much as by rational needs. Few motorcyclists have any earthly need for a 750 cc superbike that can ac-

The Benelli 750 cc six is a study in crisp Italian styling and enormous mechanical sophistication.

celerate from a dead stop to 60 MPH in five seconds or less. Nevertheless, a number of motorcyclists presently ride such machines and many more riders wish they could afford to own them.

Motorcyclists longing to own a vehicle with a price tag and a power rating far out of proportion to their needs would do well to first reconsider their decision in light of the cautionary advice offered earlier in this chapter. There exist no statutes to prevent a rider from engaging in the two-wheeled equivalent of hunting rabbits with an elephant gun. Motorcyclists are therefore free to so indulge themselves. Yet any rider whose imagination exceeds the limits of prudence should act with full knowledge of what he is doing. He is advised to bear in mind the words of Euripedes: "I know indeed the evil of that which I propose, but my inclination gets the better of my judgment."

The final and often limiting consideration when shopping for a motorcycle is the question of how much it costs. The issue at hand is not simply the price tag itself but the total cost of getting a motorcycle on the road. To the cost of obtaining ownership you must add, as appropriate, local and state taxes, loan fees and interest, license plates and insurance. The sum of these items and not merely the price tag is the cost of the motorcycle.

The financial and legal aspects of motorcycle ownership are dealt with more thoroughly in Chapter 3, but it is appropriate to observe here that a prospective buyer has three sources from which to buy a motorcycle. He can purchase it new from a dealership; he can buy a used motorcycle from a dealer; or he can buy a used machine from a private party. If the buyer is lucky or if he is an experienced mechanic, the last choice is often the best one. But beginning motorcyclists should beware of the private party route to saving a few dollars. Motorcycles advertised in the classified section of a newspaper, on bulletin boards or for sale on consignment by a dealer include some outstanding bargains and some hopeless lemons. The problem is knowing the one from the other. An experienced mechanic can often separate the wheat from the chaff. But even the best make a mistake every now and then. If you trust your judgment or that of a friend, then try shopping the private party market. Remember, however, that although the possible gains may be great, so too are the risks high.

The next best bet is a used motorcycle from a reputable dealer. Whether or not any particular dealer is reputable can usually be determined by a few phone calls and some time spent talking with motorcyclists who have done business with him. Whether or not the particular motorcycle you have your eye on is reliable may be an altogether different matter. If your creampuff turns out to be a lemon, a reputable dealer will invariably make things right in accordance with the warranty terms he and you agreed upon beforehand. The dealer has at stake his reputation and also the possibility of selling you a new motorcycle at some time in the future. Nevertheless, remember to have him specify in advance just what his obligations will be. And do not expect miracles from the dealer. Warranty work on a used motorcycle usually represents an out of pocket expense for him and may require his mechanics to repair a brand of motorcycle they do not normally service.

Far and away the best way to purchase a motorcycle is new, from a reputable dealer. The most reputable dealer in town may not offer the lowest price in town nor be the dealer nearest to where you live. In the long run, how-

Is it a lemon or a creampuff? This Norton Commando looked clean as a whistle. But it had worn steering head bearings and a throttle that stuck wide open on its second owner.

ever, chances are he will be the best bargain around. Quality service performed courteously and in a timely fashion is so difficult to find at any price that a customer should not hesitate to travel a few extra miles or pay a few more dollars for it. Remember that aggravation, like everything else in life, has a price. Even though it may cost a few dollars more to avoid the aggravation of shoddy service, you will still be dollars ahead for doing so.

In the realm of motorcycles as most everywhere else, a consumer usually gets what he pays for. Nevertheless, bargains do exist and it behooves the wise shopper to search them out. Once a motorcycle buyer has selected the kind of motorcycle he intends to buy, such as a lightweight in street scrambler trim, he should investigate every available make and model that meets the requirements he has set down. After crossing off his list those brands that for one reason or another are out of the question, he should check the price of each remaining motorcycle. Perhaps he intended to buy a 200 cc Hondosaki. However the 175 cc Peerless Special may offer approximately the same features and performance for $90 less than the Hondosaki. Unless a shopper has his heart set on owning a Hondosaki, the Peerless Special would be the route to go—all other circumstances being equal.

Simply waiting for the appropriate moment is another way to shop smartly. Motorcycle dealers, like automobile dealers, often find themselves with an embarrassing surplus of certain models as the next year's motorcycles are hitting the showroom floor. Since the older models are already one year old and since the new models arrive in the fall, when the motorcycle market takes a seasonal dip in most parts of the country, an astute shopper stands to save a considerable amount of money by bargaining with a dealer for one of his surplus machines. If the dealer is not willing to cut his prices deep enough in September, remain patient. By January he may be ready to sell last year's model at your price. When the time comes to sell a motorcycle purchased after the end of a model year, that vehicle will bring a somewhat lower price simply because it is one year older than a motorcycle bought at the start of a model year. But until the time to sell arrives, a motorcyclist has saved himself money by purchasing a motorcycle after the new models have arrived on the showroom floor.

An observant reader might wonder why this chapter has placed the issue of cost last and not first among purchasing considerations. Surely few motorcyclists have the financial resources to take the position that price is no object.

Actually, thinking first about what you need and then asking how much it will cost can prove a money saving way to shop. A motorcyclist who decides to buy a $1,500 motorcycle will usually end up with a $1,500 (or more) motorcycle, whether he needs it or not. The shopper who specifies as precisely as possible the uses to which he will put a motorcycle may also select a $1,500 motorcycle. Yet it is equally possible that our rider will discover that a $1,000 motorcycle satisfies his objectives equally well. In that case he would have saved himself $500 by looking at price tags only after deciding what he needed.

The technique of deciding first upon your objectives then founding all subsequent decisions on the achievement of those needs may eliminate the pleasure of impulse buying. It is, however, the best possible way known to get what you want. Consider the case of Robert Woods. Back in the 1930s, Woods was an aeronautical engineer assigned the task of building a new fighter plane. He reasoned that the basic objective or need of a fighter plane was to deliver the maximum firepower. So he sketched a 39 mm cannon and then proceeded to build an airplane around it. To avoid the problem of synchronizing the cannon fire with the propeller, he arranged the gun to fire through the propeller hub. Consequently the propeller had to be gear driven. Since the cannon rested directly behind the nose of the aircraft, Woods located the engine in a midship position and connected it to the propeller via an extended driveshaft. The result of this approach to decision making by objectives was the unconventional, but highly successful P-39 fighter.

A motorcycle buyer cannot, of course, design his own vehicle. Nevertheless, by setting his objectives carefully and searching diligently for the machine that most closely fulfills them, he can enhance his chances of selecting the optimum motorcycle for his needs.

Closing the Deal

Whatever motorcycle a buyer decides to purchase and from whomever he decides to buy it, money must be exchanged and papers signed. Before closing the deal, a prospective buyer should first stop, look and listen. Is it the right motorcycle for him? Does he know everything he should about the machine? Does he feel comfortable with his decision? Will he be happy with his purchase six months, a year or two years from now?

If the answer to all these questions is an emphatic yes, then it makes sense for him to go ahead with the deal. But if he has any nagging doubts, they should not be ignored. Even the most ardent love affair between a motorcyclist and his motorcycle will soon go sour if the motorcycle turns out to be a lemon. Perhaps the best insurance against this sorry turn of events is the advice of an experienced mechanic. Such advice may cost a few dollars, but it will be money well spent.

In matters of love, as in the consumer realm, there exists a strong temptation in most of us to take the first streetcar that comes along. Try to resist the temptation. Once in a lifetime bargains are just that. They do not come along every day or every year. Opportunity, you should recall, knocks a thousand times. If you do not respond the first time, chances are you will have another opportunity shortly. In other words, he who hesitates before buying rarely loses.

Chapter 2

Buying An Off-Road Motorcycle

Not so many years ago when a motorcyclist decided to venture into the dirt, he simply turned his road-going vehicle off the pavement and proceeded to bounce about the countryside. The stiff springing and substantial weight of his motorcycle produced a rough ride while the lack of adequate ground clearance limited his mobility. Dirt riding required a high tolerance for discomfort; therefore, few motorcyclists left the road. Those riders who did frequent trails and the back country landscape generally found it necessary to build their own vehicles. Factory prepared off-road motorcycles were scarce indeed, and those few that existed were rarely more than stripped down versions of a road-going bike.

Not until the 1960s did this situation begin to change. Then, in response to a growing motorcycle market and an expanded interest in off-road competition, manufacturers began to rethink their traditional motorcycle designs. The result of this effort was a new breed of motorcycle that could go anywhere and do anything. Dirt riding became fun, so much fun in fact that fully a quarter of industry sales now go toward satisfying the off-road market. Where once a rider had to improvise his own equipment, now he must select from among many dozens of dirt-going models.

This growth in the off-road market has created an embarrassment of riches. Off-road motorcycles range in size from less than 100 cc up to 500 cc or more and in price from the cost of a lightweight street bike up to nearly $2,000. Then too, dirt-going motorcycles differ substantially, depending on the mission they are expected to accomplish. Some off-road motorcycles can maneuver precisely and comfortably at low speed, yet they lack the power and suspension design needed for high speed dirt riding. Other bikes can bound rapidly across the countryside, yet they lack the proper steering geometry

BUYING AN OFF-ROAD MOTORCYCLE

Dirt going cycles come in nearly every size imaginable. Shown here is a 90 cc Kawasaki mini-enduro.

and flow of power necessary for precision trail riding. The lightest and most maneuverable dirt bikes can be ridden comfortably on the pavement only for short distances. And the type of tires that work best on soft dirt surfaces wear quickly and grip poorly on pavement.

Since off-road environments are so radically different from the world of asphalt and concrete, no single motorcycle will perform well in both situations. Consequently, a two-wheel rider intending to venture off the road must decide precisely where his interests lie. Does he require a motorcycle that is more at home on the pavement than off? Does he want a motorcycle that is equally at home on dirt or pavement—but not ideally suited to either environment? Or is he shopping for a pure off-road motorcycle?

Off-road terrain is so diversified—from a hard packed trail to open desert, a mud hole or a rocky creekbed knee deep in water—that no motorcycle will perform at its best in all off-road environments. Therefore, even riders who have forsaken the pavement entirely must decide how much versatility they will sacrifice in order to obtain a motorcycle ideally suited for one particular terrain. A hardened desert racer or the dedicated trail rider may know precisely what kind of motorcycle he requires. But riders intending to explore a variety of off-road environments must often make some difficult and painful decisions.

It is the purpose of this chapter to provide the kind of information an off-roader requires to select a motorcycle that will fulfill his needs. The off-road motorcyclist, even more than a pavement rider, will find that he can rarely have his cake and eat it, too. Yet his task is far from hopeless. The off-road market is sufficiently large to encompass the needs of nearly every cyclist. A rider need only decide upon his requirements and shop the marketplace with those requirements in mind to locate the motorcycle most nearly suited to his purposes.

What Is an Off-Road Motorcycle?

Road-going motorcycles, as they were defined in the previous chapter, are designed for use on hard surfaced roadways. Pavement is the principal environment of road bikes, though when properly outfitted they can also negotiate dirt roads and well traveled trails. Off-road motorcycles usually carry sufficient road-going equipment to legally qualify for use on the pavement. But lights, horn, battery, turn signals and like accessories are included so that a rider may use his motorcycle for short pavement jaunts and conveniently get to or from his point of departure into the off-road environment. Many off-road riders have never had occasion to use the lights, horn or other street equipment attached to their motorcycles. Since the equipment is there, however, they can legally license their cycles for operation on any public roadway.

Beneath its lighting and related equipment, an off-road motorcycle is an all terrain vehicle designed to transport a rider down fire roads, through tall grass, up sand hills, across streams and into the desert. The more specialized off-road motorcycles will not perform equally well in all these different environments. Yet nearly every off-road cycle can negotiate a wide variety of back country terrain. In fact, an off-road cycle in the hands of an expert rider can travel up, down and over obstacles that seem wholly insurmountable by any motor vehicle.

Versatility, reliability, economy, ruggedness and agility are the principal features a rider should seek out in an off-road motorcycle. The perfect off-road motorcycle would combine tractor-like durability and pulling power with the maneuverability and lightweight strength of a hummingbird. This ideal motorcycle could gently float over fallen tree trunks and large rocks yet grip securely around fast off-camber dirt switchbacks. It would have sufficient speed to race across the high desert terrain of Southern California, yet it could crawl along the rough countryside of New England and negotiate the swampy forests of the Carolinas.

Because the perfect motorcycle does not exist and perhaps never will, no two-wheeled vehicle can excel in all these departments. Yet off-road motorcycle design has become sufficiently sophisticated that ordinary production machines (as opposed to one of a kind factory built competition motorcycles) can go, and go comfortably, most everywhere a rider might care to venture.

Any detailed look at the engineering principles upon which this sophisticated design work is based would carry us far beyond the scope of an introductory book. A reader needs no training in physics, engineering or metallurgy, however, to understand how and why an off-road motorcycle differs from the road-going variety of two-wheelers. Many of the differences are hidden from view, yet they are simple enough that most anyone can comprehend them.

BUYING AN OFF-ROAD MOTORCYCLE

The design of this Montessa 250 VR perfectly parallels its functionalism. Note the deep rimmed alloy wheels and moulded gas tank for reduced weight. Black painted engine parts are for increased heat dissipation. The tube protruding from the gas tank vents gasoline overflow.

Not all manufacturers have hit upon the same solution to the design problems surrounding the construction of a dirt going motorcycle. Although form closely follows function in the design of off-road motorcycles, not all serve precisely the same function so each manufacturer must decide for himself just what form will best accomplish a given function.

Nevertheless, the design of off-road motorcycles has become sufficiently standardized through trial and error that it is possible to describe a typical off-road motorcycle. Perhaps no one model will exactly conform to this description. But nearly every current model includes most of the typical features that define an off-road motorcycle. Here is a partial list of these features:

The Frame Off-road competition motorcycles often use chrome molybdenum steel frames to achieve maximum strength and weight. Chrome moly, as it is called, costs dearly, however, and is difficult to weld on a production basis. So most non-competition dirt bikes, and some competition models too, use mild steel frame assemblies. To keep the weight to a minimum, frame tubes are usually fastened together not with cast iron lugs (a practice once used to assemble nearly all motorcycle frames) but by direct welding to reinforced steel plates known as gussets.

Off-road motorcycles receive considerable pounding as they travel across the countryside so a sturdy frame design is mandatory. The frame tubes must rigidly retain their geometric relationship to each other whenever possible. When the frame components are called upon to receive massive shock loadings, as happens on descending from a jump, they must flex and spring back to their original shape rather than bend or crack.

Off-road riders frequently loft the front wheel of a motorcycle over various obstructions. Therefore, the frame design and overall construction must favor a rearward bias. The typical off-road motorcycle carries a slightly lower portion of its total weight on the front wheel than does a road-going motor-

Light overall weight and an effective suspension system (seen here on a Bultaco Pursang 250) is the key to controlled riding in the dirt.

cycle (weight distributions on the order of 40 percent/60 percent are common).

The Suspension Proper suspension design is the key to enjoyable off-road motorcycling. The front and rear suspension units must protect a rider from the severe jolting of rough terrain, yet permit the wheels (and hence the rider also) to travel along their intended path. Since the motion of a motorcycle wheel can be controlled only so long as it remains in touch with the ground, the suspension system is responsible for keeping the tires where they belong—in direct contact with the earth.

The front suspension of a dirt going motorcycle should be as light as possible to keep excess weight off the front wheel and it must offer plenty of shock absorbing capacity. Consequently, front suspension units make extensive use of aluminum alloy construction and permit six or even seven inches of fork travel. Spring rates are soft enough to cushion the rider and his vehicle from abrupt changes of direction, yet they provide sufficient rebound control to quickly return a front wheel to the ground. Even a brief jaunt on a true dirt going motorcycle will demonstrate that the front suspension is radically unlike the units on a road bike. The ride, which is soft and forgiving, clearly invites the operator to try his hand at jumping over a low curb or a fallen tree trunk.

BUYING AN OFF-ROAD MOTORCYCLE

Adaptability to varying terrains is so important to controllable handling that an increasing number of off-road motorcycles also make provision for quick adjustment of the front suspension. By raising or lowering the front fork tubes and by repositioning the front wheel on the lower suspension legs, a rider can tune his steering geometry to suit the varying needs of off-road travel.

Engine Characteristics Off-road motorcycles frequently operate at low speeds and rarely run at top engine speed for any significant distance. Maximum horsepower, which is developed near the top speed range of an engine, consequently counts for very little. Instead, most dirt going motorcycles require an engine that sacrifices top end horsepower for low speed torque. A broad power band will prove more useful to most dirt riders than the "peaky", highly tuned engine that produces its power only at elevated speeds.

In addition, off-road motorcycling demands a highly reliable powerplant. The pavement rider whose engine fails him will invariably find help near at hand, but the dirt going motorcyclist who experiences engine trouble is often in a lurch. If help is not nearby, he must either diagnose and repair the problem himself or hike back to civilization. And it can be a long walk.

By happy coincidence, a mildly tuned engine that produces considerable low speed power is also an inherently reliable engine. Since the various components of a mildly tuned engine are not subject to excessive stress, they are less likely to fail than the moving parts of a high performance engine.

Most road-going motorcycles (except lightweights) use a multi-cylinder engine design featuring two, three or even four cylinders. Off-road motorcycles, however, almost always employ a single cylinder design. The reasons in favor of a single, large cylinder rather than multiple cylinders are three-fold. First, the single cylinder layout, though it is not conducive to a high maximum power output, tends to produce gobs of low speed power. Low gear ratios, which are important anyway to good off-road performance, can help overcome a lack of low speed power. In the final analysis, however, there is no substitute for an engine with tractor-like, low speed pulling power. Second, a single cylinder engine is light in weight, economical to manufacture and narrow in width—so there are no overhanging engine cases to snag on a fence post, a rock or a protruding tree limb. Third, the single cylinder layout, because it contains fewer moving parts than a multi-cylinder engine, is less prone to mechanical failure.

A few manufacturers who have specialized in multi-cylinder engine design for many years, continue to produce twin cylinder off-road motorcycles. Yet this layout is favored only by dirt riders who participate in specialized off-road events such as desert racing and hill climbs.

In the domain of engine design—two-cycle *vs* four-cycle—nearly all manufacturers of pure off-road motorcycles employ the two-cycle design. Just as some of the manufacturers who specialize in two-cycle engines have switched to four-cycle engines for their top of the line road-going motorcycles, so have those manufacturers who rely on four-cycle engines for most of their line switched to two-cycle for dirt going motorcycles. Four-cycle engines (those that employ a camshaft and valves in the fashion of an automotive engine) work well enough in the dirt. But the two-cycle layout offers certain advantages. First, a two-cycle engine tends to produce the quick, low speed power favored by dirt riders. Second, the two-stroke, because it has fewer moving parts, is lighter and less complex. Third, the two-stroke carries less weight on top of the engine (where the valves, rocker arms and overhead camshaft of a four stroke powerplant are located), thereby yielding a lower center of gravity.

The two-stroke is not without its drawbacks, which include higher fuel consumption, greater susceptibility to piston failure and a less pleasant exhaust note. The advantages of the two-stroke design are sufficiently compelling, however, that it presently dominates the field of off-road motorcycling.

Gas Tank and Seat Off-road motorcycles rarely cruise at high speed for significant distances and usually employ an engine of less than 500 cc displacement. They therefore require limited gas carrying capacity, usually on the order of two or three gallons at most. The small gas tanks common to dirt going motorcycles also permit a narrow tank design and less overall weight. Since the gas tank is mounted high in a motorcycle's frame, any reduction in the weight of a tank (which is usually constructed of aluminum or fiberglass) and its contents will further reduce the center of gravity. The result is quicker and more responsive handling.

The seat on an off-road motorcycle is shorter and narrower than a road bike seat. Dirt going riders rarely carry a passenger, so only a short seat is required. A narrow width seat allows the rider to apply a firm grip with his legs. An off-road motorcyclist spends much of his time standing on the footpegs; therefore, a wide seat would hinder his riding style.

Fenders The fenders of a dirt going motorcycle are light in weight, generally constructed from fiberglass, plastic or aluminum, and mounted high off the wheel so that mud will not pack between the tire and the fender well. In order to reduce unsprung weight (see the section on *brakes* for an explanation of this concept) and to allow for sufficient clearance, the front fender is usually mounted not to the front fork legs but directly onto the motorcycle frame.

A flexible rubber mud flap is sometimes bolted to the trailing edge of the front fender in order to protect the engine fins from accumulating dirt and mud. Mud packed into the engine fins is not only unsightly, but it also deprives an engine of much needed air circulation around the hot exhaust port and forward cylinder wall.

Exhaust System The muffler and exhaust pipe assembly of an off-road motorcycle sweeps upward from the engine and exits at a point just below and behind the seat. A high pipe placement increases the likelihood that a rider will receive burns on his leg or hand from accidently touching the hot exhaust system. A high pipe tucked in close to a motorcycle's frame protects the exhaust system from damage caused by a spill or passing contact with a low obstacle. In addition, the high outlet point allows a rider to ford deep streams without fear of drawing water into his engine through a submerged exhaust pipe.

Off-road motorcycles frequently operate in areas where a fire danger exists. Hot particles of carbon from a motorcycle exhaust pipe can ignite a bed of pine needles or a pile of dry leaves. To prevent this terrible possibility, most off-road motorcycles are equipped with a spark arrester, which as the name implies will capture any burning hot particles of solid matter that would otherwise exit unextinguished through the tailpipe.

BUYING AN OFF-ROAD MOTORCYCLE

A knobby type tire. Note the rounded contour of the tire and the buttressed walls of the outer lugs to enhance traction while cornering on soft surfaces.

A trials pattern tire. Its relatively flat contour allows occasional street usage yet it provides excellent traction in the dirt.

Tires Off-road motorcycle tires can be grouped into two categories: those that are also suitable for occasional use on the pavement and those that are solely for off-road riding.

The universal type tire, described in the previous chapter, provides satisfactory traction on level, hard packed dirt surfaces. Yet its tread pattern and contour are useless on a soft or loose surface. Off-road motorcycles require tires with a wide footprint and an open block or cleated tread design. The block pattern tread provides more than a series of deep, sharply defined gripping surfaces to allow traction in sand, wet grass and soft clays. It also creates a self-cleaning action to prevent the accumulation of solid matter between the cleats. Without this self-cleaning action, any tire used on soft surfaces would soon begin to lose traction as a result of the accumulated foreign matter wedged into its tread pattern.

The trials tire, with its pattern of square blocked cleats, allows sufficient grip for all but the hardest cornering and the most treacherous surfaces a rider is likely to encounter off the road. The soft rubber compound and open tread pattern of a trials tire will cause rapid wear and less than perfect handling on the pavement. So long as a rider exercises some discretion, however, his trials tires will prove adequate for occasional pavement riding. And they will be near ideal for most off-road use.

Pure off-road tires, or "knobbies" as they are called, offer larger and more widely spaced cleats than a trials tire. Since knobbie tires provide a rounded tread contour and cleats extending far up the sidewall, they grip well even under the most adverse off-road conditions. Unfortunately, they wear too rapidly, ride too roughly and grip the pavement too poorly for highway cruising or riding on city streets.

Wheel Rims Most road-going motorcycles use steel wheel rims simply because steel rims are inexpensive to manufacture and require little maintenance. Steel rims place an additional burden of weight and inertial resistance on the suspension system of a motorcycle. Exotic dirt bikes therefore provide aluminum alloy wheels, which are not only lighter but often stronger than steel rims.

The rear wheel assembly of a dirt going motorcycle is wider than the rear wheel of a correspondingly large road-going motorcycle in order to provide better traction, while the front wheel on an off road motorcycle is frequently two or three inches larger in diameter than the rear wheel. This larger front wheel yields improved handling on rough surfaces.

Brakes Pavement riding requires strong brakes able to bring a fast moving motorcycle to a quick halt. But off-road riding usually takes place at more moderate speeds and does not provide the high traction surfaces necessary for sudden stops. Consequently, a road-going brake system can prove a liability in the soft stuff, where the danger of wheel lock-up is ever present. What the brakes on an off-road motorcycle lack in sheer stopping power they make up for in the way of light, controllable response. A good off-road braking system will rarely lock either wheel; instead, it allows a rider to measure out precise amounts of braking pressure to the front and rear tires.

In addition, motorcycle brakes designed for off-road use should be—though not all are—resistant to moisture and light in weight. The total weight of a motorcycle will influence its handling and performance. But its unsprung weight, in other words, the weight of all components attached below the suspension system, is far more important than total weight. Any decrease in the weight of these unsprung components (as tires, rims, lower fork legs and brakes) will lessen their inertial resistance to motion and correspondingly increase the vehicle's ability to respond promptly to the demands placed on it. This improved response rate readily translates into quicker and more precise handling. Since the brakes on a motorcycle constitute a large portion of the total unsprung weight, any pounds saved in their construction will translate into enhanced handling.

Footpegs Off-road riders spend much of their time operating a motorcycle from a standing position in order to obtain better balance and control. Footpeg location is therefore an especially important consideration on a back country motorcycle. The footpegs must be mounted high, for maximum ground clearance, and well to the rear, to concentrate weight toward the aft portion of an off-road motorcycle. This rearward weight distribution allows a rider to raise the front wheel of his motorcycle when clearing obstructions in his path and to concentrate maximum weight over the rear wheel for increased traction.

The rubber covered footpegs used on a road-going motorcycle provide a comfortable and vibration resistant resting point for a rider's feet. Off-road riders, who rarely operate their vehicles for extended periods of time at high speed, need not worry about vibration. Instead, they must concern themselves with a secure gripping surface that will support their full body weight even when that surface is covered with mud or wet leaves. Most off-road motorcycles are therefore equipped with metal footpegs that present a sawtooth like pattern on their top edge. These metal teeth, though they are not sharp enough to cut a rider's leg, will dig into his leather or hard rubber boot sole, thereby creating the secure platform he needs for vigorous off-road riding.

Handlebars The handlebars of a dirt going motorcycle must be wide enough to give a rider all the leverage he needs when maneuvering his machine over rough surfaces and they must be mounted far enough to the rear and high enough that he can grip them easily from a full standing position. Given these requirements, the shape and positioning of handlebars on a back country motorcycle becomes not a matter of esthetics or rider whim, but what works best. Some touring riders prefer low, narrow handlebars while other riders have a preference for high bars that sweep to the rear. Off-road riders, however, invariably rely on the flat, wide handlbar shape that experience has proven to be comfortable in both a standing and a sitting position.

A true off-road motorcycle is a specialized and sophisticated vehicle designed from the tires up to accomplish a particular mission. By adding the appropriate tires, handlebars, fenders and other accessories a rider can transform the appearance of a road going motorcycle. But that vehicle simply will not handle or perform as well in the dirt as a motorcycle specifically designed for that purpose.

The answer, of course, is not to try converting a highway motorcycle into a dual purpose vehicle, but to identify which dirt going motorcycles are designed to fulfill a particular set of rider needs. Perhaps a shopper will not find the perfect motorcycle for his requirements. Yet the chances are high that he can achieve a close fit between what he is looking for and what the marketplace offers.

The Varieties of Dirt Going Motorcycles

The previous chapter divided road-going motorcycles into lightweight, middleweight and heavyweight categories. Except for very specialized uses, such as open class hill climbs, flat track competition or desert racing, heavyweight dirt bikes are nearly a contradiction in terms. The fifty or more horsepower and four hundred pound weight of a large bore motorcycle are rarely conducive to safe, enjoyable off-road riding. Even a 250 cc motorcycle, which is barely a middleweight vehicle by road-going standards, can prove a handful to manage in the dirt. For these reasons, experienced off-road riders size up a dirt going motorcycle by somewhat different standards than a touring enthusiast would apply to the selection of a motorcycle. What are these standards? For the purpose of examining the off-road motorcycle market, we can conveniently divide the available choices into lightweight models and full size models.

Lightweights The lightweight off-road motorcycle market includes dirt going vehicles in the under 250 cc class and weighing less than 275 pounds.

Dirt going lightweights equipped with the necessary lights and other street legal equipment are suitable for limited pavement riding. Even more than road-going lightweights, small off-road motorcycles are not, however, intended for highway cruising or travel in rapid traffic. Nor do small bore lightweights offer especially comfortable or secure two-up (rider and passenger) mounts. Two full size riders will overtax the brakes, suspension and seating capacity of nearly every lightweight dirt bike on the market.

Instead, dirt going lightweights are at home beyond the world of pavement. Twisting narrow trails and rough back country travel are the proper environment for an off-road lightweight. Because of its short wheelbase, low overall weight and narrow width, the lightweight dirt bike can be maneuvered over terrain impassable by any other motor vehicle. A lightweight is more agile, less tiring and more respectful of the environment than a larger

This Hodaka 125 cc competition cycle is typical of many lightweight off-road racers. It is fast, agile and built to high standards of quality.

motorcycle. When worst comes to worst, a lightweight is also easier to push out of a mud hole or a sand wash than a heavier motorcycle.

Simply because a lightweight motorcycle is smaller and less expensive that its bigger brothers should not, however, suggest that it is any less rugged or any less serious a vehicle. The better lightweights are not simply cheapened versions of larger dirt going motorcycles for riders unable to afford the additional cost of a full size off-road motorcycle. A quality lightweight dirt bike has all the durability and integrity of a larger machine. The difference is principally a matter of size. The smaller breed of off-road motorcycles are designed for the rider who needs or wants a lighter, more maneuverable vehicle and is willing to sacrifice the power available from a larger displacement motorcycle.

Full Size Dirt Bikes In the realm of dirt going motorcycles, 250 cc marks the beginning of the full size class. The basis for this decision is simple enough. A 250 cc dirt going motorcycle equipped for street use will ordinarily weigh in the vicinity of 275 pounds (specially lightened competition models, however, weigh little more than 200 pounds) and produce between 20 and 30 horsepower. These power-to-weight ratios yield better low speed acceleration than many V8 powered passenger cars and a top speed in the neighborhood of 70 to 80 MPH. By turnpike cruising standards, a 250 cc dirt bike is no fireball. Yet its off-road capability is an altogether different matter. Few back country riders would wish to accelerate across a rough pasture from a standstill to 60 MPH in less than ten seconds or race through a sand wash at 70 MPH.

BUYING AN OFF-ROAD MOTORCYCLE 39

A full size trail bike—in this case the Harley-Davidson SX-350—provides enough off-road power for any situation in which a rider is likely to find himself.

In other words, a modern 250 cc off-road motorcycle offers as much power and speed as most riders will ever need for back country riding. Off-road motorcycles larger than 250 cc usually produce more horsepower than anybody but an experienced rider can safely handle in the dirt. To be sure, large capacity dirt motorcycles have their place. That place, however, belongs in the hands of an accomplished rider intent on such activities as desert cruising, motocross riding and other forms of competition or blasting down well kept fire roads.

Probably the principal virtue of full size, dirt going motorcycles lies not in their off-road capabilities, but in their road-going ability. Most riders who live within a short distance of dirt riding country and riders who haul their vehicles by truck or trailer rarely require a motorcycle larger than 250 cc. Motorcyclists who must ride down the highway to get off the road usually prefer a full size motorcycle simply because it is a more suitable highway cruising vehicle. Even a 360 cc dirt going motorcycle will not prove as comfortable or enjoyable for highway travel as a 250 cc road-going motorcycle. Yet the 360 cc cycle is more comfortable and perhaps safer and more reliable on the highway than a 250 cc dirt going motorcycle.

Undoubtedly, the ideal solution to the problem at hand is for a motorcyclist to purchase an off-road motorcycle suitable to his dirt riding needs and to transport it over the highway by truck or trailer. Riders who cannot accept this solution must often decide whether to purchase a motorcycle that is appropriate for moderate speed highway travel but unnecessarily heavy and powerful for dirt riding, or whether to sacrifice adequate highway riding capacity for a motorcycle that is ideally suited to their dirt riding needs. Given this choice, most motorcyclists would opt for the highway comfort of a larger capacity dirt going motorcycle. Since a rider need not use the full power of his motorcycle off the road, this decision probably represents the wisest

This factory prepared Montessa is a specialized and sophisticated vehicle designed from the ground up to accomplish a particular mission. The rider's full standing position importantly aids low speed control and balance.

course of action. A motorcyclist planning to pursue this option should remember, however, that he will be carrying along the trail or cross country more weight and more horsepower than need or prudence dictates.

Regardless of size, the modern off-road motorcycle is a sophisticated piece of machinery. With sophistication has come specialization. Some dirt going motorcycles are designed to meet the needs of a statistically "typical" off-road rider. Yet even this typical rider, whoever he may be, has specialized

BUYING AN OFF-ROAD MOTORCYCLE

needs that differ from the performance requirements of an enduro rider, the motocross enthusiast or a trails specialist.

In order to fulfill as many of these different needs as possible, some of the larger motorcycle manufacturers produce a dozen or more different dirt going motorcycles. Just as we have grouped the various kinds of road-going motorcycles into three broad categories, so too can we classify off-road motorcycles into three groups based on the uses for which each group is intended. For the sake of convenience, we will refer to these three groups as trail bikes, dirt racers and roughriders.

Trail Bikes As the name suggests, a trail bike is designed for use on back country trails. It is also intended for nearly every other kind of off-road riding. A trail bike is happy not only on trails, but also cruising across open rangeland, fording streams or climbing hills. The weekend motorcyclist in search of off-road recreation, the professional cowboy with many miles of fenceline to patrol and a hunter intending to travel deep into the back country would all find a trail bike ideally suited to their needs. In other words, a trail bike is an all-purpose two-wheeler, the off-road equivalent of a plain jane road-going motorcycle.

Like a plain jane, the trail bike has a mildly tuned engine. Peak horsepower is not its forte. Instead, a trail bike will pull strongly and evenly at low speed and prove to be an altogether reliable, forgiving mount. Ease of starting, tractability, stable low speed handling and economical operation are all virtues of the trail bike. To be sure, the trail bike is not likely to win any races. Yet it will almost always reach its destination without fuss, bother or

Kawasaki's 175 cc enduro is an excellent example of the many lightweight trail bikes presently available to the off-road rider.

mechanical problems. More than any other two-wheeler, the trail bike is a mechanical workhorse able to take on most any task assigned to it.

What trail bikes lack in the way of style or pizzaz they make up for in practicality. The trail bike has little to offer riders seeking sleek lines, dashing performance, exotic design and superlight construction. But for motorcyclists in search of dependable, economical and versatile off-road transportation, the trail bike is an ideal choice.

Dirt Racers The dirt racer is available in many different forms. It might be a flat track or scrambles racer, a motocross machine or a large capacity desert racer (readers unfamiliar with these forms of motorcycle competition should refer to Chapter 8). Regardless of its disguise, a dirt racer is the off-road equivalent of a hot rod. Large carburetors, high engine compression, efficient though noisy exhaust systems and performance oriented valve timing enable it to produce gobs of wheel spinning power. Dirt racers are intended for hard, fast riding over nearly any kind of off-road surface. All except the most highly tuned dirt racers will chug along slowly if called upon to do so. But they are unhappy at low speeds. It is only when a rider points his front wheel toward a winding fire road, a steep hill or a long sand wash and opens up the throttle that the virtues of a dirt racer become apparent. In the hands of an experienced rider, the dirt racer will drift through hairpin turns, conquer nearly vertical hills and blast through sand washes with the greatest of (apparent) ease.

The sight of a rider cruising through deep sand at 70 MPH or leaping two or three car lengths off the crest of a small hill is a stirring sight. Yet it should not prompt an inexperienced rider to attempt duplicating these feats with his own trail bike or to rush out and purchase a dirt racer. In either case, it is

The Suzuki 400 cc dirt racer packs enormous power into a lightweight package designed for the serious enthusiast who intends to go racing with the big boys.

likely he will soon come to grief. For few dirt racers are forgiving of human error. Because of their quick handling, light weight and massive power output, dirt racers must be ridden well to be ridden at all. Balance, coordination, strong kidneys and a healthy measure of raw courage are important attributes for dirt racing.

Put simply, a dirt racer is the two-wheeled equivalent of a thoroughbred race horse. In both cases, an owner must pay a heavy price for classic looks and stunning performance. The initial purchase price is high and it is an expensive beast to maintain, prone to all manner of maladies, temperamental by disposition and ill-suited to perform more than one task. But that single task—to go quickly—it will carry out with graceful abandon.

Roughriders Roughrider motorcycles are like trail bikes, only more so. Their design emphasizes maneuverability, dependability, low speed pulling power and precise, controllable handling. Roughriders are built exclusively for off-road riding and largely for competiton. The kind of competition event in which the roughrider excels is not a contest of speed. Rather, the contest is a matter of getting there, wherever *there* may be, at a precisely determined time or with faultless style. The end point can be as near as a hundred yards away or as far as one hundred miles from the starting point. In between are obstacles that will challenge even the most experienced rider. Steep rock inclines, off-camber footpaths around a mountain (both preferably covered with water) and knee deep mud holes are but a few of the hurdles that a roughrider must overcome in the course of an afternoon's entertainment.

A perfect roughrider motorcycle would offer the power of a locomotive, the traction of a bulldozer, the durability of a sledgehammer and the weight

A full size roughrider. The Bultaco Sherpa T offers a classic blend of low overall weight, precise handling and tractor-like pulling power.

of a feather. Modern technology has not yet matched these requirements, yet the better roughriding motorcycles combine an outstanding balance of power, traction, reliability and lightness. Not every rough country motorcycle exhibits each of these features in equal measure. One model may emphasize traction and precise steering above all else while another model is perfectly suited to the rider who demands low overall weight and maximum reliability. Yet every roughrider is light, strong and durable.

Since roughriders are more specialized than the ordinary trail bike, they are more expensive and less versatile. Many roughriders are not even equipped with the lights, horn and other equipment required to license a vehicle for use on public roadways. Those roughriders that include the full complement of street legal accessories do so on the assumption that a rider might have to operate his motorcycle briefly on a public road that adjoins or cuts across a back country riding area. Consequently, the lighting and other street going equipment attached to a roughrider are not intended to inspire a rider's confidence; they are only sufficient to comply with minimum state licensing requirements.

Roughriders usually make extensive use of lightweight materials and receive special attention to design and construction details, so they carry a high price. For the competition rider or experienced off-road motorcyclist who demands the best equipment available, this additional premium matters little. The casual or occasional off-road rider should think carefully, however, before buying a roughrider. It is unlikely that he will take proper advantage of the special capabilities that a roughrider offers. Indeed, cruising a high quality roughrider down a well cultivated trail is equivalent to using an IBM series 360 computer to balance your checkbook. It will do the job, but it is much more machine than the job requires.

Some Purchasing Considerations

So far, we have identified two sizes and three different types of dirt going motorcycles. As in the previous chapter, the relationship between these various sizes and types are shown here in diagram form.

On which category should a shopper focus his attention? The answer is that it all depends. Specifically, it depends on his needs, his experience and his budget. Thus, an experienced motorcyclist searching for a high performance dirt bike that he can use for cruising the wide open spaces of the high desert or western rangeland will want a full size dirt racer. A low budget

A TOPOLOGY OF OFF-ROAD MOTORCYCLES

	Lightweights	Full-Size Models
Trail Bikes	Lightweight Trail Bikes	Full-Size Trail Bikes
Rough Riders	Lightweight Rough Riders	Full-Size Rough Riders
Dirt Racers	Lightweight Dirt Racers	Full Size Dirt Racers

BUYING AN OFF-ROAD MOTORCYCLE

This Honda 125 cc Trials cycle is a lightweight roughrider able to negotiate nearly any terrain.

rider who plans to try his hand at enduro riding in Vermont or New Jersey would restrict his attention to lightweight roughriders.

A lightweight off-road motorcycle is an excellent size to begin with as it will do most anything a larger machine is capable of doing, yet it will be easier to manage and more forgiving of rider error. Then, too, a lightweight motorcycle offers no handicap to a prospective racer if he decides to try his luck—and skill—at competition riding. Most competition events are organized by engine class, so that big bore machines compete against each other and the lightweights (generally 125 cc or less) battle it out among themselves. Although most experienced riders elect to participate in the 250 cc or 500 cc classes, competition in the lightweight categories is fierce. Indeed, lightweight motorcycles have become so sophisticated that except in events requiring sheer horsepower and speed, they can compete nearly on a par with full size dirt bikes.

Most motorcyclists, however, do not have interests as specialized as the ones discussed above. Instead, the majority of riders require a general purpose off-road machine designed for at least occasional pavement use. Motorcycle sales reflect the needs of this majority. Trailbikes outsell all other categories of off-road motorcycles by a wide margin. Not only does the trail bike take more kindly to pavement riding than other dirt going motorcycles, but it also is the most flexible and forgiving of all back country cycles. Of course, a trail bike rider must sacrifice certain features. It is unlikely that he

Buying the proper size dirt going motorcycle (in the case pictured here a Hodaka Dirt Squirt) is the key to enjoyable off-road riding.

could lay claim to having the fastest, the most exotic or the most expensive off-road motorcycle in town. Nor would his motorcycle handle as precisely as a trials bike, accelerate as rapidly as a flat track racer or ford deep streams as readily as an enduro machine.

In return for these shortcomings he would own an economical, rugged and versatile two-wheeler with years of off-road recreational use built into it. Like the hunter who goes in search of rabbits with a .22 caliber rifle, our hypothetical motorcyclist would be properly armed for the task at hand. He could, of course, indulge himself in the motorcycling equivalent of hunting rabbits with a 30-06 high power rifle. But why bother with such overkill? Many persons derive a certain satisfaction from owning the fastest or most exotic motorcycle (or car or boat or whatever) around town. Yet there exists an equal satisfaction in knowing that your motorcycle is perfectly suited to performing its appointed task.

Like a well fitting shoe, the proper size motorcycle is neither too big nor too small. As is the case with road-going motorcycles, dirt bikes should be big enough in size that a rider will not soon grow bored with the model he has selected. Since a beginning motorcyclist will grow quickly in experience, it may make sense for him to buy a somewhat larger size motorcycle than he can comfortably handle now. He should not, however, go overboard. An oversize motorcycle is no more comfortable or sensible than an oversize shoe.

Most everything previously said concerning the purchase of a road-going motorcycle holds true for off-road motorcycles, too. But the prospective owner of a dirt going motorcycle should bear in mind a few special considerations.

First, there is the matter of test riding. For customers shopping the road bike market, a test drive presents no problem. Since the pavement begins at curbside, a prospective buyer can readily sample a motorcycle's handling

BUYING AN OFF-ROAD MOTORCYCLE

and performance. A customer is usually free to test drive a dirt going motorcycle in the same fashion. Unfortunately, he will learn far less of what he needs to know about its handling and all around performance. A spin along the pavement may yield valuable information regarding the suitability of that motorcycle for use on public roadways. It will prove nearly useless, however, as a guide for evaluating a motorcycle's off-road capability.

How can a rider overcome this problem? In the first place, he should ask the salesman, the motorcycle's present owner (if it is a used vehicle) or an experienced off-road rider a variety of questions: How does it handle at low speeds? Does it display any unusual handling characteristics at high speed? How reliable has it proven? What components are most likely to fail? How has it fared in competition events? What do you believe are its strong features? What are its liabilities? Would you own one (or buy another one for yourself)?

The response to these and related questions can yield a wealth of useful information. A customer should bear in mind, however, that he has collected what the courts would classify as hearsay evidence or, in other words, information that requires confirmation from another source. One such additional source is the monthly motorcycle enthusiast magazines, which conduct knowledgeable and thorough road tests of nearly every make and model motorcycle imported into the United States. Since these road tests represent the considered judgement of specialists in the field, they provide an invaluable and largely impartial source of expert testimony. A few hours of library research or even a letter to the editor may be necessary to obtain the back issue containing the road test report(s) a shopper is searching for, but his time so invested will yield ample dividends.

Even expert testimony is, however, no substitute for direct observation. So a customer should make every effort to test ride a motorcycle in the environment where he plans to use it. Motorcycle dealers who are firmly convinced of a customer's good intentions will often allow him to spend an afternoon sampling a demonstrator vehicle's performance in the nearest available patch of off-road terrain. Then too, many suburban and small town dealers maintain a few acres of raw land next to the showroom as a test facility for the benefit of their staff and customers. A couple of telephone calls will usually prove sufficient to locate a motorcycle dealership with the appropriate facility and demonstrator models on hand.

Should an off-road motorcyclist buy a new or a used vehicle? Obviously, the rider who can afford to purchase a fresh, unused motorcycle ought to do so. Riders who are considering the purchase of a used cycle should bear in mind, however, some special considerations that apply to the purchase of an off-road motorcycle.

Motorcyclists who sacrifice the joys—and pains—of buying a factory fresh, dirt going cycle should shop the used machine market with special care. In the first place, indicated odometer mileage is a poor guide to vehicle condition. Ten miles of abusive back country riding will more quickly deteriorate a motorcycle than 500 miles of hard street use. Low odometer readings are a more valuable guide to selecting a road-going motorcycle than an off-road motorcycle—and this is especially the case in light of the fact that some riders detach the instrument pod to protect it from damage. Tire condition, the shape of the rims and spokes (how many are loose or bent) and signs of damage to the underside of the motorcycle will prove far better standards than odometer mileage for judging the condition of a used off-road motorcycle.

Nicks, scratches and an occasional dent are the natural consequence of normal wear and tear on a dirt going motorcycle. A new off-road vehicle will quickly acquire the war weary look of every other dirt going motorcycle that has been campaigned in the back country. But dented wheel rims or badly gouged lower frame rails suggest that the vehicle has received more than its proper share of back country abuse. If the wheel rims and spokes seem wobbly, perhaps the suspension and transmission components are tired, too. Signs of heavy use and even a fair measure of abuse may not be sufficient reason to overlook a used dirt bike. Nevertheless, evidence of abuse should prompt an alert buyer to expect a correspondingly reduced price tag and firm assurance in writing that mechanical failure will receive quick and cost-free repair.

Dirt bike shoppers should especially beware of the danger of buying a former dirt racer or a stolen motorcycle. Ex-race machines are offered for sale when they have become so tired that they are no longer competitive. At that point their reliability, which never was much to write home about, has deteriorated still further. To rebuild an ex-racer can cost as much as the initial purchase price. If a customer suspects that a used motorcycle may be an ex-racer, he should firmly inquire whether that was in fact the case. If the answer he receives still leaves him in doubt, it is advisable to solicit the opinion of an experienced mechanic. A man who purchases a used racer at least knows what he is getting for his money. But the unknowing buyer does not even have the advantage of this knowledge.

The subject of stolen motorcycles will be dealt with more thoroughly in the following chapter. At this point, however, it is worthwhile to point out that dirt bike buyers should be especially aware of the danger of buying a stolen motorcycle. Off-road motorcycles that are not equipped or licensed for use on public roadways make an ideal market for vendors of stolen merchandise. Since the buyer of a pure dirt going motorcycle would not normally undergo the title search and serial verification procedure required to obtain license plates, he is a more likely target for the merchant of stolen goods. Consequently, the buyer should satisfy himself that his prospective purchase does not still belong to someone else. Simply claiming ignorance of the facts is neither ethically nor legally sufficient to get him off the hook.

Most everything that has been said so far argues against the purchase of a used dirt going motorcycle. Actually, however, the case against buying a used dirt bike is not the least bit one sided. The world of off-road motorcycles also includes some outstanding two-wheeled bargains.

These bargains, or creampuffs as your friendly used car salesman might call them, take the form of dirt going motorcycles that have never or hardly ever left the pavement. Fortunately for the astute shopper, each year a legion of motorcyclists buy dirt going motorcycles simply for reasons of styling and fashionability. Or a would-be dirt rider buys the newest Guzzlefire Mudslide Special only to discover that off-road riding is not for him. So what happens to his carefully designed dirt pounder? More often than not, it receives a few thousand miles of city riding and then is offered up for sale. Because these off-road motorcycles have never suffered the agonies of back country riding, their mechanical innards are usually still fresh. Simply because they are used, such motorcycles command only a modest price. True, they may cost a few dollars more than a two-wheeler well on its way to a deserving rest in motorcycle heaven. The extra cost, however, is well justified by the additional life left in these cycles.

How to identify a creampuff? Again, the condition of the tires, rims and lower frame rails are a useful guide. Look also at the paint and chrome. Is it unscratched? Are there no signs of mud underneath the engine or inside the fenders? Are the ends of the footpegs, the tips of the control levers and the side of the muffler unmarked? If the answer to all these questions is yes, then it is likely you are looking a creampuff in the eye.

Before Closing the Deal

An astute shopper can often save himself many dollars. The temptation of bargain hunting should not, however, cause him to lose sight of his initial objectives. The search for bargains is not a goal in itself, but only a method of achieving that goal. Like the buyer of a road-going motorcycle, the dirt bike purchaser should remember to stop, look and listen before he closes the deal. Precisely what kind of motorcycle is he seeking and how closely does his number one choice conform to that ideal motorcycle? Is he making a rational choice or simply satisfying his impulses? Should he act now or wait a bit longer?

Consideration of these and related questions cannot guarantee a shopper the right decision. But a bit of forethought will enhance the likelihood that he can live comfortably with the decision he has made. Moreover, the pleasure of that satisfaction is sufficient reason for him to buy with all due care and consideration.

Chapter 3

Motorcycle Ownership

Owning a motorcycle is more than a matter of polishing the fenders, tuning the engine periodically and riding it forever—or at least until the weather turns cold and wet. Motorcycle ownership usually requires that an owner entangle himself in the red tape of financing, licensing, insuring and safety inspecting his cycle. A rider may find to his surprise that state law requires him not only to obtain a cycle operator's license and to wear a safety helmet of approved design, but he may also discover that his state insists on the daytime use of a headlight too.

Few motorcyclists can free themselves from this burden of red tape. Off-road riders or racers who pay cash for their motorcycles need not concern themselves with the details of financing, license plates, safety inspection or a state issued operator's license. Yet even motorcyclists who plan to operate a vehicle only on private property or the back stretches of public land, far from the nearest roads, run the risk of accidentally purchasing a stolen motorcycle or sustaining damage to themselves, a passenger or their vehicle. Backwoods riders and the racer can benefit substantially from a vehicle registration title search and the proper insurance coverage. These and related precautionary measures are usually not required by statute for off-road motorcycling, yet they certainly are dictated by the laws of common sense.

No sane human being enjoys wading through an endless swamp of red tape in pursuit of the paperwork required to keep straight with the law. Anyone who has done frequent business with large organizations—like motor vehicle departments—knows well the old song and dance routine called the bureaucratic shuffle. It usually opens with the refrain: "Sorry, this is the wrong department. Why don't you try room 1426 C." Then once you arrive at that well hidden location, a clerk politely informs you that Room 1426 C never did, does not now and probably never will have authority to deal with your problem. So you shuffle off to a third location only to receive the same old song and dance routine once again.

Unfortunately, there often exists no surefire method of avoiding the bureaucratic shuffle. Like leprosy and the plague, it simply happens and often without prior warning and for no apparent reason. A well intending citizen takes the appropriate documents to the motor vehicle bureau (or tag office or whatever your state calls it) in anticipation of receiving that precious rectangle of stamped steel we call a license plate. But lo, our citizen did not bring along an MV 77 Form. What is an MV 77 Form? It is a notarized certification that the motor vehicle in question bears the serial numbers listed on the registration. How does one obtain an MV 77 Form? By having the vehicle inspected at a local police station. How does one drive an unlicensed motorcycle to a police station? "Well, dearie, can't your borrow a dealer plate?" Of course you cannot since you bought the motorcycle from a private party who kept his license plates. "Well dearie, I can't help you. Why don't you call the police and ask them?"

Scenes like these are sometimes inevitable. No amount of good advice can guarantee the consumer free passage through the administrative jungle of forms and procedures most states require of anyone wishing to license a motor vehicle. Nor can a prospective buyer hope to understand all the intricacies surrounding finance loans. This chapter promises no easy detours around the administrative chores connected with motorcycle ownership. Instead, the following pages are simply intended to provide readers with an introduction to the legal and economic aspects of owning a motorcycle. Along with its other roles, a motorcycle also represents an important economic investment and its operation requires a rider to assume various legal obligations. It is the objective of this chapter to examine the economics of motorcycle ownership and to outline the legal responsibilities of a motorcycle operator.

The Economics of Motorcycle Ownership

It is a basic fact of life that motorcycles, like other consumer goods, cost money. Once purchased, either outright or by installments, they represent an investment of depreciating value that can be cashed in or traded off as an owner sees fit. The rate at which a motorcyclist's investment depreciates will depend on a variety of circumstances. How well an owner cares for and maintains his vehicle certainly helps determine its cash value when the time comes to trade or sell it. Those fortunate few for whom money is no object need not concern themselves with the economics of owning a motorcycle. For the majority of us, however, a motorcycle is an important enough investment that we must carefully consider how much it will cost to buy, how best to pay for it, what it will cost to maintain and how to reap the maximum return when selling or trading it. We will look at each of these issues in turn.

How Much Does It Cost? As we have already discussed, every motorcycle (and in this respect motorcycles are no different than other motor vehicles) has two prices. First, there is the price tag of the vehicle itself which is often negotiable. Then, and more importantly, there is the price of the vehicle ready to ride. These two prices can differ from as little as a few dollars to well over half a thousand dollars. Why so vast a difference? Here are some of the extras that can quickly inflate the initial price of a motorcycle:

accessories added to the basic vehicle
a safety helmet and other protective equipment
final price bargaining with the seller
sales tax (from none to 7%)
one-time financing costs and fees
interest costs
insurance premiums
registration and licensing fees & property taxes

To these items the buyer of a used motorcycle may wish to add the cost of any indicated repairs and the replacement of parts.

The price tag of the Guzzlefire V-3 a shopper is lusting after may be marked $1499 and the dealer may be willing to cut as much as $100 off his price, depending on the season, the model in question and a host of other considerations. A prospective owner should count himself lucky, however, if he is not $2000 poorer by the time he has put a set of license plates on the motorcycle. A buyer who is prepared to spend an even thousand dollars to go motorcycling has two choices. Either he can purchase a motorcycle in the range of $750 and spend the remainder of his funds on the various "hidden" costs listed above. Or he can buy that thousand dollar motorcycle and plan to finance about $200 to $400 of the purchase price.

Which route a buyer selects is entirely a matter of personal preference. Regardless, it is important that he calculate in advance the hidden cost of getting his motorcycle on the road. Commodore Vanderbilt reportedly said of his yacht that if you have to ask how much it costs, you cannot afford to own it. The same is fortunately not true of motorcycles. Nevertheless, a prospective motorcycle buyer should ask how much it costs in order to find out if he can afford to buy it without undue financial strain.

Motorcycles, like automobiles, are not of course always sold at the price indicated on the tag or first mentioned by the salesman. How much it costs is to some extent a function of how hard a bargain the customer can drive and how much room the seller has to maneuver. A newly introduced motorcycle in great demand will usually carry a firm price tag. Especially in spring and early summer, motorcycle prices tend to be non-negotiable. On the other hand, models in low demand or high supply, models left over from the previous year and post-season (after September in colder climates) motorcycle sales are susceptible to considerable negotiation. Since motorcycle dealers reap their greatest profit on higher priced models and on accessories, the prospective buyer of a full dress heavyweight has more room to negotiate price than does the shopper for a lightweight plain jane.

Prospective buyers considering a trade-in should bear in mind that the actual price of any motorcycle is a function of the price tag on that new motorcycle and the trade-in offer they receive for their present mount. The practice of offsetting a favorable price tag with an undervalued trade-in offer leaves a rider no better off than if the salesman had offered him fair market value for his present motorcycle in return for the indicated price of a new motorcycle.

A shopper who wants to know the score can satisfy his curiosity in two different ways. First, he can obtain from whomever is selling the motorcycle, two separate offers: a straight cash price and the price with a trade-in. Then he should consult with the "blue book" of prices to determine the industry standard wholesale and retail price of his own motorcycle. Nearly every motorcycle dealership and most loan officers keep a copy of this book handy for quick reference.

More often than not, a shopper will discover that the trade-in offer he receives is lower than he expected or even a bit below the average wholesale price of his motorcycle. In that case a would-be buyer has two choices. He can accept the offered trade-in price and attempt to bargain for a lower price on the motorcycle he is hoping to buy, or he can decide to sell his current motorcycle himself.

This second option will require some time, a bit of expense perhaps (for a classified advertisement in the newspaper and some tune up work), and a fair measure of inconvenience. But in return an owner can expect to unload his motorcycle at a significantly higher price than its trade-in value. How much higher depends on several considerations. As a rule of thumb, however, a private transaction should yield at least 10 to 15 percent more than the offered trade-in price for a used motorcycle. A dealer's gross profit from the sale of a used motorcycle is largely consumed by the labor and overhead costs involved in selling that motorcycle. By providing his own time and effort, a customer can save himself much of this expense, which would otherwise be passed on to him in the form of an apparently low trade-in price. For buyers short on cash but long on time, the private sale route is a handy way to reduce the actual price of buying another motorcycle.

Paying For It   Once a prospective owner has decided to buy a motorcycle, he must pay the agreed upon price. This can be done in one of two ways: either by paying the full cash price or by securing a loan for a portion of the cost. Outright purchase offers a number of advantages:

> the buyer immediately obtains full legal ownership of the vehicle
> in the event of financial need his motorcycle can serve as collateral against which to borrow money

Financing also offers advantages of its own:

> the buyer can ride now and pay later
> he need not commit his funds to a single large purchase
> in a period of rapid inflation future dollars are cheaper than present currency

Installment purchasing is a form of renting money on condition that a renter will return the money and rent charges—known as interest—at certain intervals over an established period of time. The English appropriately call loan financing "hire purchase": a buyer agrees to hire or rent a sum of money in order to pay the price of an item he wishes to buy.

Financing, however, is not without its disadvantages. First, motorcycles are financed in accordance with a conditional sales contract. Money is loaned to a purchaser on the condition that the lender retains legal control over the title to the vehicle until he has received full repayment of his loan. The vehicle usually cannot be sold, traded or taken out of the country without written permission from the lender. The vehicle becomes collateral that is subject to confiscation in the event a borrower does not fulfill his portion of the financing contract. Late payment of installments is usually sufficient grounds for repossession of a vehicle.

Second, a borrower pays and indeed pays dearly for the privilege of renting money. The apparent interest charge on motorcycle loans ranges from about 10 percent upward. But even a "10 percent" loan usually yields a true interest rate of nearly 20 percent. The finance charge is computed on the full value of the loan and tacked on to each monthly installment despite the fact that the balance of a loan declines with each monthly payment. Halfway through a 12 month loan the borrower has already repaid half the money he borrowed. Yet he is usually still paying a finance charge calculated on the full face value of the loan—half of which has already been returned to the lender. Since finance charges are computed on an annual basis, the longer a borrower rents his money, the more he must pay for the privilege of doing so.

To make matters worse, some lending institutions deduct their first finance charge off the top of a loan. A borrower who contracts for a 10 percent loan of $1,000 may discover that he receives only $900 of working capital. A number of financing contracts also provide the borrower with a life insurance policy naming the lender as beneficiary for the unpaid balance of the loan in the event that the lender dies before he can repay his loan. The insurance policy is purely for the protection of a lending institution, yet the cost of the policy is charged to the borrower as a fee tacked on to the front end of his loan. In other words, a loan applicant must often buy a short term life insurance policy for himself—and sometimes pay for his own credit investigation—before the lending organization will issue him a loan.

Credit organizations insist that motorcycle loans are a risky business: the high finance charges they levy are dictated by the rapid depreciation rate of most motorcycles and a tradition of non-payment on motorcycle loans. Regardless of whether this is so, motorcyclists must usually pay a steep price for the privilege of borrowing money toward the purchase of a motorcycle.

The price of commercial credit is high enough that a prospective borrower should first explore all other sources of paying for a motorcycle before he seeks the assistance of a finance company. Does he have savings he can draw upon? The loss of these savings may cost him 5 percent interest. Yet this is a cheap enough price to pay for avoiding an interest charge of 25 percent or more per year. Many motorcycle shoppers can also borrow money from an employee credit union where they work or against a current life insurance policy. In either case they will be money ahead. Few banks look forward to the prospect of writing a motorcycle finance loan at favorable interest rates. Nevertheless, a well established customer can sometimes convince his loan officer to write him a motorcycle financing loan at rates much lower than those available from a finance company on the basis of his good name and clean credit record at the bank.

Most motorcycle dealerships also have available a credit financing plan for their customers. A shopper should carefully inspect these gift horses before signing on the dotted line. In too many cases, the dealer's eagerness to provide financing is not only a function of his desire to sell motorcycles. He may also be receiving a kickback or "finders fee" from the finance company for each contract he brings them. This finders fee, which can amount to 3 percent or more, adds considerably to a dealer's profit on every cycle he finances. It may also mean the dealer is doing business with a finance company that pays its finders fees from the steep finance charges extracted from the customer. In that case, the customer will end up paying three bills: first, for the motorcycle; then, for the money to buy that motorcycle; and, finally, for the kickback that got him the money to buy the motorcycle.

Riding Costs How much does it cost to operate a motorcycle? The answer is that it depends on many considerations such as:

the size of the motorcycle
the kind of motorcycle
how much use it receives
the price it brings when sold or traded

The larger the size of a motorcycle, the more expensive it will be to operate. Moreover, off-road motorcycles are usually more expensive to operate per mile of travel than are road-going motorcycles.

The care with which a cycle is driven and maintained will also have a bearing on the cost of its operation. Hard riding coupled with infrequent maintenance is a surefire route to expensive repair bills in the future. The rider who flogs his cycle like a jockey on a reluctant race horse must expect to pay more in the way of maintenance, repairs and even depreciation than a rider who treats his mount kindly. Frequent use of a motorcycle, however, makes good economic sense. All other things being equal, the more a rider uses his cycle the less per mile it will cost him to run it. The reason is simple enough. Insurance premiums, licensing fees and depreciation rates represent fixed costs that a rider must pay regardless of the use his cycle receives. Assuming that these three costs are $500 for the year, a motorcyclist who travels only 2,000 miles during that year has fixed operating costs of 25¢ per mile of use. If that same rider had accumulated 10,000 miles of travel, his fixed operating expenses would decline to a much more economical 5¢ per mile.

Selling It Periodic maintenance, careful operation and an occasional cleaning enhance the cash value of a motorcycle when the time comes to sell it. No amount of spit and polish will make that 1953 Peerless Special look like a factory fresh model. But a careful cleaning brings out the best in every motorcycle. And when a cleaning is combined with a general tune-up, an owner can present his motorcycle at its best.

How and when to sell a motorcycle is a problem that confronts most riders at one point or another in their cycling careers. Obviously, the best time is when the demand is high or when the supply of motorcycles is low. In most parts of the country, demand is seasonal. In spring and early summer, many a person's thoughts turn to cycling. Demand, in turn, goes up and with it the price of used motorcycles begins to climb from their cold weather levels.

Classified advertisements, bulletin boards and a circle of friends are all potential marketplaces for a used motorcycle. Which one should an owner pick? Probably all three, if possible. One never knows where he will find a customer willing to pay his price. Owners who want to obtain the maximum price for a cycle will generally have to sell it themselves. Riders who wish to save themselves the time and nuisance of dealing with a parade of potential customers have available two alternatives. An owner can either trade his motorcycle for credit on the purchase of a new cycle or he can request a motorcycle dealer to place his motorcycle for sale on a consignment basis. Under this agreement, the owner and dealer agree that the dealer will act in the capacity of an agent, using his staff and facilities to sell the owner's motorcycle. The owner and seller agree upon a minimum sale price and when the sale is consummated, the owner pays his agent a commission, generally in the form of a percentage of the sale price. Assume a rider decides his motorcycle is worth at least $900 on the open market. He puts his cycle up for sale on consignment and it is sold for $1,050. The seller charges him a 15 percent commission, leaving a net return of $891. Perhaps our rider could have sold the motorcycle himself for $900 or even $1,000. But how long would it take him to do so and at the price of how much aggravation? The consignment sales route makes sense for an owner short on time or unwilling to involve himself in the details of selling his cycle.

Motorcycling and the Law

Buying, selling and operating a motorcycle—in short, motorcycle ownership—is a freedom available to most of us. It is a freedom that must be practiced, however, within the framework of numerous legal constraints. The rider who decides to sell his motorcycle does not simply hand over his vehicle in return for the agreed upon price. He must also produce the appropriate ownership papers, affix his signature to them and obtain the services of a notary public who can attest to the validity of his signature. The buyer of a motorcycle must comply with even more regulations than the seller. For it is the buyer who will be required to show proof of ownership, obtain an insurance policy, register the vehicle and, if he has not yet done so, obtain for himself a motorcycle operator's license.

Neither buying nor selling a motorcycle requires the services of a lawyer or a degree in public administration. The key ingredients needed are simply patience and a knowledge of the system. No book can teach a motorcyclist—or anyone for that matter—patience. That every person must learn for himself. Nor is it possible to explain precisely how the system works. For each of the fifty States has issued its own laws and regulations. New York, for example, requires all motor vehicle operators to present proof of insurance before they are eligible to receive a license plate. The State of Oklahoma, however, places no such restriction on motor vehicle owners. Nevertheless, there does exist sufficient uniformity from state to state that once an owner has grasped how the system works in one state he will experience little difficulty learning what to do in any other state. The principles that enable him to avoid bureaucratic bother as much as possible are perfectly simple and self-evident. By applying common sense and a bit of forethought, anyone can learn how best to sidestep the legal snafus and administrative boondoggles that may otherwise befall him. It is the objective of this section to outline just what a motorcycle owner needs to know for his own protection from the law, from bad luck and from those who would do him harm.

Buying It Legally A motorcyclist who purchases his vehicle new from a dealership can usually assume he is getting what he pays for. Even in the best of dealerships, however, mistakes happen. So before leaving the premises an owner should confirm that he has received precisely what he ordered. Is it the exact model he specified and is it in genuinely new condition? Are the proper accessories installed on the vehicle? Is the proper paperwork prepared and properly filled out? Do the serial numbers on the engine and frame match the numbers typed onto the bill of sale and the other papers that come with the motorcycle. If the serial numbers do not match, the reason is usually a matter of clerical error. Do not assume, however, that the matter can be cleared up at a later date. If you have any doubts or questions, now is the time to ask and now is the time to get the problem remedied.

These recommendations for the buyer of a new motorcycle become doubly important when shopping for a used motorcycle. Many of the 300,000 or more motorcycles stolen each year return to the marketplace from whence they came, to be offered for sale to a new—and often unsuspecting—owner. Motorcycles that still belong to someone other than the party selling them are never branded "HOT" or "STOLEN" along their gas tanks. Nor is it always possible to prove that a given motorcycle is definitely hot merchandise. But anyone shopping the used motorcycle market should beware of various signs that point to the possibility of a stolen motorcycle.

The first and most obvious evidence of a hot motorcycle is the price. Private party sales offer the astute shopper an opportunity to buy a bargain priced motorcycle. Beware, however, of cycles priced far below their market value and be especially suspicious of attractively priced cycles that carry out of state registration, that show signs of being repainted and that are not accompanied by the proper papers. Check also the frame identification and engine serial numbers. Not only should those numbers match the registration papers but they should also bear no evidence of file work, welding, grinding or restamping. The numbers should be even in size, uniform in depth and perfectly legible. Beware the seller who claims that a used motorcycle he is offering for sale has "special" or replacement cases or a frame that the factory never numbered or numbered in an unconventional manner.

If he is in doubt, a shopper should carefully quiz the seller regarding any irregularities he observes. Under no circumstances should he buy the motorcycle in question immediately. Instead, his best course of action is to copy down the identification numbers and place a call to his local police department and motor vehicle bureau. One or both of these organizations can trace the serial numbers in question to determine whether they lead to a motorcycle listed as stolen. Numbers that come back with a clean bill of health do not prove that a motorcycle is legally owned by the party listed on the registration or bill of sale. They may only indicate that the thief and his accomplices covered their tracks well. So check also with a dealer who sells that make of motorcycle and explain the situation to him, giving a full account of the particulars. Request him to verify the year of manufacture of the motorcycle based on the serial identification numbers. Stolen motorcycles have a habit of lying about their age. A motorcycle equipped with a 1968 frame, a 1972 engine and titled as a 1971 may not be stolen. But a prospective buyer certainly has good reason to question its parentage and career.

As a final precaution, anyone buying a used motorcycle should insure that he knows who the seller is. A motorcycle dealership will usually stand behind a vehicle it sells, but a private party will rarely do so and may have reason to misrepresent himself. In the interests of self-protection, a buyer needs evidence of who sold him a motorcycle. A name scribbled on a bill of sale and a street adress from a newspaper advertisement may not prove sufficient to trace the seller. Consequently, a buyer should try to obtain positive identification such as a driver's license number in order to protect himself from future problems. Anyone accused of buying a stolen motorcycle will want to know who sold it to him and where the seller can be located.

Getting It on the Road Buying a motorcycle is only the first step in getting it on the road and legally licensed in your own name (or the name of your finance company). Riders who buy from a dealership will usually find the dealer prepared to guide them through the registration process. In fact, such service should be expected from the dealer's staff.

Cycle owners who have to go it alone will not find their job difficult as long as they know what they need to do. A few quick telephone calls or a visit to the office that issues license plates should prove sufficient to learn just what papers and procedures are necessary to keep within the law. Once an owner prepares himself a checklist—either a written or mental one—of the steps he must follow and the papers he must have in his possession, getting his motorcycle on the road becomes a relatively painless process. The secret lies simply in planning enough in advance, knowing what needs to be done and patiently going about the job of doing it.

Protecting Yourself Now that you have purchased a motorcycle and licensed it to operate on public roads, you need only concern yourself with the joys of motorcycling. Of course, there is always the chance that someone out there may wish to steal your pride and joy. Or perhaps a drunken driver will sideswipe you and your passenger. How likely are these occurrences, you ask. Frankly, both theft and accidents happen, and happen often. A motorcycle owner can go for years, as did the author, without experiencing the theft of his motorcycle. Then one evening—it's gone. Perhaps the police can recover it for you. But do not count on it. The recovery rate among stolen motorcycles gives nobody except motorcycle thieves reason to rejoice. Even if somebody merely borrowed your cycle for a few hours of joyriding, you have no guarantee it will be returned intact. Perhaps the police will recover it on the other side of town. Your cycle may be so badly damaged, however, that it will cost nearly as much to repair as to replace it.

Those persons who trust in the powers of divine protection and other heavenly agents may prefer to pray hard and leave it all to faith. For the rest of us, insurance is the best available answer. Nobody, of course, enjoys owning insurance. Motor vehicle insurance is a form of betting that the worst will happen shortly. You place your bet (in the form of insurance premiums) on the possibility of theft, bodily harm, fire or some other calamity. The best that can happen is to lose the bet each year, in which case your premiums reimburse somebody else for his misfortune.

Motorcycle insurance may indeed be a dismal subject to contemplate. It is nowhere so dismal, however, as the prospect of not having it in the event of

MOTORCYCLE OWNERSHIP

A case study in why every rider needs a good insurance policy. (Photo—John Chew)

a misfortune. In recognition of this fact, many states require every motor vehicle owner to insure himself (or post a substantial bond in place of taking out insurance) against the possibility of inflicting personal injury or property damage. Traditionally, a motorist insures himself first and foremost against the personal and property damage he might inflict on others and secondarily against theft, damage to his own vehicle and reimbursement for his accident-related medical expenses. Some states, however, have instituted no-fault insurance laws. No-fault insurance largely erases the distinction between liability protection and the protection of oneself. Each motor vehicle operator simply insures himself against the personal and property damage he might suffer regardless of who is at fault.

Motorcyclists residing in a state that requires all motor vehicle owners to obtain insurance obviously have no choice in the matter. They must comply. Riders who finance the purchase of a motorcycle must also insure the vehicle in order to protect their lending institution's investment against a loss of economic value. In neither case, however, can a rider assume that the mandatory insurance he receives will provide him with the coverage best suited to his needs. The six basic forms of insurance coverage (except under no-fault coverage) available to an operator are:

personal liability
property damage
medical payments
uninsured motorist
collision
comprehensive

Most state laws requiring motorists to obtain insurance specify only that the coverage include mimimal personal liability and property damage coverage. If a motor vehicle operator wishes to insure his vehicle against fire, theft and collision, he must add this coverage to his basic policy. Whether a motorcyclist decides to obtain complete or only minimal coverage is entirely a matter of personal preference. But it is important that he understand the alternatives available to him and how much they will cost. Collision and comprehensive (which includes theft, fire, vandalism, hail and other sources of loss) coverage rank high on every cyclist's list of desired insurance protection. A rider may discover, of course, that the cost of such coverage is simply too expensive. Especially in large metropolitan areas like New York, Boston, Chicago and San Francisco, the cost of liability, collision and comprehensive insurance for an unmarried male under 25 years of age can equal or exceed the market value of his motorcycle. In that case, a rider must decide just where his priorities lie. Can he afford to lose the motorcycle through theft? Or is it worth $250 per year to protect from theft and collision a financial investment of $1,000 with a current market value of $750.

A motorcyclist faced with such decisions should have all possible information at his disposal and he should obtain that information as soon into the game as possible. Consider, for example, the case of a shopper struggling to decide between the purchase of a 250 cc class lightweight and a 400 cc middleweight. Might the cost of insurance have a bearing on his decision? Most likely it would. Many insurance companies scale their rates for personal liability coverage on under 300 pound motorcycles at 50 percent less than the rate for automobiles and motorcycles weighing 300 pounds or more. In addition, the cost of collision and comprehensive coverage is often lower for small, light motorcycles. Depending on his age, driving record and place of residence, the rider in question could reduce his insurance bill by as much as several hundred dollars simply by selecting the smaller motorcycle. Moreover, this reduction represents an annual savings that occurs each year. An insurance saving of $100 per year may not seem substantial, but over a five year period it amounts to $500, or fully half the cost of a motorcycle in the range of 250 cc to 350 cc.

Where does one go to obtain insurance information? First, though not necessarily foremost, is a motorcycle dealership. The staff should be thoroughly familiar with the details, if any, of the insurance laws prevailing in that state and how best to comply with them. In fact, asking around at a dealership often yields some helpful leads on where and from whom to obtain motorcycle insurance. A number of motorcycle dealerships even provide vehicle insurance themselves in cooperation with a specialty underwriting firm. But the same warnings that apply to dealership financing also apply to insurance plans offered by cycle dealers. A customer rarely knows for certain whether the dealer is providing his clientele with a valuable public service or simply seeking a supplementary source of income from the insurance outfit that promised him the most lucrative arrangements. A rider's best bet is to investigate the terms of any dealer sponsored insurance and compare them with two or three other insurance estimates for the same level of coverage.

In checking out other sources of insurance, a shopper may discover that the dealer's insurance plan, like that offered by other specialty insurance firms, is much less expensive than the rates quoted by local agents of multipurpose insurance companies (such as State Farm or Allstate). Moreover, a customer may encounter agents unwilling to insure a motorcycle at any cost. Or an agent may prove willing to write only a partial coverage policy—one that provides personal liability and collision protection, for example, but that does not include theft or comprehensive coverage. Perhaps the dealership sponsored insurance plan *is* a rider's best bet. Yet the decision should not be made only on the basis of cost. Few specialty motorcycle insurance companies maintain offices or field representatives in any but a small number of principal cities. A motorcyclist may live a thousand miles or more from the nearest representative of the firm. So long as no misfortune occurs, such distances do not matter. But what happens in the event of an accident? How does a motorcyclist obtain prompt service and fair treatment over so great a distance? If the firm is reputable and the agent sympathetic, mail order insurance can prove to be a bargain, but an insurance company that pulls a disappearing act when its services are needed is no bargain at all. Insurance companies that refuse to pay up or that pay only partially on a claim are worse than no coverage at all. For the rider who carries no insurance at least knows the risk he is taking.

High price insurance is worth the price only when you need it. Then it suddenly becomes a bargain. Accidents, theft and the diverse other misfortunes that can befall a motor vehicle operator always cause hardship. But prompt, courteous and fair compensation serve to lighten the hardship and anguish that result from an accident or similar misfortune. Even more than a good mechanic, an honest insurance agent can prove a motorcyclist's best friend in time of need. Expensive insurance is no guarantee that a cyclist has bought himself good service when he needs it. Yet a local insurance agent sympathetic to your problems and backed by a reliable underwriting firm, is like money in the bank. Those of us who can afford it should not be without it.

Keeping Out of Trouble For most purposes, the law defines a motorcycle as a subcategory of motor vehicles and subjects it to the same regulations as private automobiles and trucks. Motorcycles must be registered, licensed and insured in the same fashion as other motor vehicles. And their operators must obey the same rules of the road.

Nevertheless, motorcycles represent a specialized category of motor vehicle the operation of which is governed by some special regulations. Thus, a number of states require the use of a safety helmet (see map, Chapter 5) and the daytime operation of cycle headlights. Other states require that a motorcycle operator obtain a separate driver's license to operate his vehicle on a public road. A few states prohibit the operation of motorcycles on certain roads (for example, the Garden State Parkway in New Jersey) while other states restrict the off-road use of motor driven cycles. Moreover, state and local governments enforce their motor vehicle laws with less than perfect uniformity. In some areas (for example, Connecticut and Nebraska) the mandatory helmet law is not (or once was not) enforced. Elsewhere, motorcycle related regulations are enforced on a selective basis.

It is the legal responsibility of every motorcyclist to know his obligations both as the operator of a motor vehicle and as a motorcycle rider. If he is to keep out of trouble with the law, then he must first know what the law requires of him. Moreover, it is directly in his interest to learn whether local law enforcement officials practice selective enforcement of the motor vehicle regulations and under what circumstances selective enforcement commonly occurs.

The nearest branch of a state motor vehicle department or a local law enforcement agency can provide information regarding the provisions of state and local motor vehicle regulations. Riders seeking less formal information must, however, look elsewhere. Excellent hunting grounds for additional information include local motorcycle shops, cycle related sporting activities and nearly any place where two or more riders congregate. Riders hoping to shortcut the law should beware of freely offered advice from fellow cyclists, however, as it is not admissible court evidence. The best available advice is to know the law and obey it.

Chapter 4

Knowing Your Motorcycle

One fine summer afternoon, Henry Brakebender was touring along a deserted fireroad back in the hills. As he gunned his motorcycle over the crest of a small jump, Henry observed the road veering off to the left. In anticipation of the corner he turned the handlebars in that direction while the motorcycle was still in mid-air. The motorcycle immediately banked to the right and Henry, who was not anticipating so untoward an event, found his motorcycle heeled over in the wrong direction for the approaching turn. Because nothing in Henry's previous motorcyling experience suggested any other course of action, he decided to "ride it out," attempting to negotiate the corner. It was the last decision Henry ever made. He and his motorcycle skidded off the road and into the trees. The motorcycle survived but Henry, who neither rolled on wheels nor had bones of steel, was less fortunate.

A post-mortem investigation of the accident showed Henry to be a victim of Newton's Revenge, which is a fate that befalls those of us who fail to heed the basic laws of motion. Henry's demise resulted from a phenomenon known to physicists and engineers as "gyroscopic precession." Though gyroscopic precession may sound like a mysterious and forbidding notion, its consequences are perfectly simple and straightforward. When a rotating wheel is turned to the left, a force is created which tends to bank the wheel and anything attached to it toward the right, or in a clockwise direction when viewed from behind. This force is at work everytime a spinning wheel is turned. It becomes significant—and dangerous—only when the wheel is free from the ground, as happened when the late Mr. Brakebender rode rapidly over the crest of a hill.

If Henry had known of this effect he could have done one of two things.

He might have remembered not to turn the handlebars while his motorcycle was in the air, or realizing his mistake, he would have turned the handlebars in the opposite direction (to the right), thereby returning his motorcycle to an upright position and preparing to bank it into the left-hand turn. Alas for Henry, he did not understand the physics of motorcycling.

Perhaps this tale of the fate that could befall an unsuspecting motorcyclist sounds rather farfetched. If so, consider the story of another motorcyclist who was called Jack Warmshoe. One warm and sunny day Jack and his motorcycle were at a stoplight waiting impatiently for it to turn green. To occupy himself in the meantime Jack was, as they say, "winging it." In other words, he was periodically revving up his engine to enjoy the melodic sounds issuing forth from the exhaust pipes and also, he told himself, to insure that the spark plugs did not become fouled with soot during his brief intermission at the light. Just as the engine was rising to another crescendo of flashing pistons, the motorcycle and its rider leaped forward across the intersection and into the path of an oncoming truck.

Jack's untimely departure from the world of motorcycling was the consequence of his forgetting that when a motorcycle is in gear with the engine running, only the thin metal strands of the clutch cable separate rest from motion. If those strands are pulled taut, the motorcycle will remain motionless at a stoplight. But when the pressure on the clutch cable is released, either accidentally or intentionally, the vehicle commences to accelerate at an alarming rate. Had Jack known his clutch cable was frayed, perhaps he would have remembered to place the transmission shift lever in Neutral while waiting for the light to turn green. Unfortunately, we all tend to overlook the nagging details of life—which is why an intelligent motorcyclist will place his machine's transmission in Neutral when that machine has stopped. The late Mr. Warmshoe paid dearly for his mistake of forgetting that anything subject to stress, from the human heart to a motorcycle cable, is likewise subject to failure, which will usually occur at the most inopportune moment possible. Preventive maintenance (the subject of Chapter 6) such as checking and lubricating control cables, will help delay mechanical failure or detect potential points of failure resulting from normal wear and tear. But it will not eliminate unanticipated mechanical breakdowns or the consequences of human error.

A wise philosopher once remarked that to err is human. Engineers, in turn, have observed of mechanical things that nature always sides with the hidden (from us) flaw. So what is to be done? Should we allow the sad tales of Mr. Brakebender and Mr. Warmshoe to inhibit us from owning and operating two-wheeled motor vehicles? Not a chance. This book is dedicated to the proposition that motorcycling is the only—or at least the best—way to go if you believe that getting there is at least half the fun of traveling. To get there in a safe and enjoyable manner, however, it is necessary to know your motorcycle. The sole mistake of our two sadly departed friends was not that of climbing astride their respective motorcycles but in not understanding the characteristics of the machines they were attempting to operate.

Federal law requires that airplane pilots exhibit a modest understanding of motor coordination skills and aircraft design characteristics. For various reasons, our present motor vehicle laws require of a legally licensed operator not much more than minimal vision and a passing acquaintance with the functions of the steering wheel, foot controls, shift lever and turn signals. Many automobile drivers know little or nothing at all about their vehicles—which is one important reason why nearly fifty thousand automobile caused deaths occur every year in this country. The average motorcyclist understands substantially more about the operation of his two-wheeled vehicle than the normal driver knows of his car. Yet each year many persons climb aboard a motorcycle with no more introduction than a brief lesson to the effect that "Here's the throttlegrip, that handle over there operates the clutch and the little lever by your foot is for shifting. Remember to give it enough gas so the engine doesn't stall." Only later, after he is rolling down the street, does our intrepid cyclist recall that nobody told him which controls activate the brake system.

Perhaps you are already familiar with the various controls on a motorcycle. But understanding which controls do what on a motorcycle is only a small part of the injunction: *Know Thy Bike*. More specifically, you should also know something about the engineering principles of two-wheeled motor vehicle design, the mechanics of a motorcycle and the psychology of safe and enjoyable motorcycling. In the remainder of this chapter we will look briefly at each of these subjects.

Motorcycle Engineering

An engineering description of a motorcycle would define it as a self-propelled single track vehicle capable of maintaining auto stability when in motion. A motorcycle is an inherently unstable vehicle when at rest, but beyond a certain minimal speed it will remain upright either through the efforts of the rider or on its own accord.

When compared with the automobile, a motorcycle appears to be a much simpler vehicle. It *is* simpler in the sense that it has fewer moving or stationary parts and it is not enclosed by the expanse of glass, plastic and painted or chrome plated metal with which auto makers wrap their products. Yet the engineering design and construction details of a modern motorcycle, whether it is a 100 cc motorbike or a 1200 cc King of the Road touring machine, are every bit as sophisticated and complex as those found on the latest automobiles.

Despite vast differences of size, virtually all motorcycles have a similar appearance. These similarities of design and construction are less the result of unoriginality or imitation on the part of manufacturers than the fact that well over 50 years of trial and error experimentation—which in days gone by yielded some truly bizarre configurations—have shown the present motorcycle design to be nearly ideal for the purposes of most riders.

What does this modern configuration look like?

Nearly all motorcycles are built around a sturdy central frame of single or parallel tube construction. The tubing is generally formed from mild steels for strength and resistance to fracturing under abrupt loading, and it is brazed together with relatively heavy steel lugs. In some designs the engine assembly is suspended beneath a single large top tube and short connecting struts so that the engine itself becomes an integral load-carrying portion of the frame. More commonly, the engine/transmission assembly rests in the center of a triangular or box shaped frame. This frame consists of the horizontal top tube(s), one or two down tubes reaching from the steering head to beneath the engine and a connecting center tube which joins the back end of the top tube(s) to the down tubes.

The basic engine/frame assembly is used to house the battery and ignition components, the oil tank (except in the case of motorcycle engines that include an oil supply system in the bottom of the engine crankcase), the footrests, exhaust pipe supports, a tool kit and the gas tank.

Because nearly all motorcycle engines employ direct air cooling, there is no need for a radiator, water pump or cooling fan assembly. Extensive finning in the cylinder barrels and the aluminum head allow the engine to dissipate the heat of combustion directly into the air. Motorcycle engines are of two or four-stroke design, with from one to four cylinders. Nearly all engines have their cylinders arranged in line and mounted transversely to the frame in order to simplify the problem of insuring an adequate flow of air and to allow for the transmission of power via a chain and sprocket drive to the rear wheels. A single set of engine cases is usually used to house the engine, clutch and transmission assembly in order to simplify construction and insure a rigid power train package. Often, but not always, a wall separates the transmission from the crankshaft components, thereby allowing each portion to enjoy an independent oil supply. The clutch unit is generally a multiple plate wet unit (the clutch runs in an oil bath) rotating on the transmission input sprocket and driven by a chain connected to an engine crankshaft sprocket.

Four-stroke motorcycle engines employ either a pushrod and rocker arm assembly to operate the valves or an overhead camshaft layout with the camshafts chain driven and located in a compartment above the top of the valves. Most two-stroke engines use piston controlled ports, whereby the top and bottom edges of the piston act as valves, allowing the intake and exhaust gases to enter and exit the engine from ports cut in the cylinder walls. But some two-stroke motorcycles use a rotary valve layout. This design employs a thin circular blade rotating on an end of the crankshaft. The blade includes a cutaway portion that periodically exposes a port through which the fuel/air intake mixture enters the engine from the carburetor.

A motorcycle's ignition and other electrical needs are usually satisfied by a crankshaft mounted AC generator, which consists of a magnetic core assembly rotating around fixed electrical coils. Most motorcycles still use a mechanical breaker point system to regulate the ignition timing, but solid state electronic ignition systems are becoming increasingly widespread on account of their greater stability and reliability.

Each cylinder of a motorcycle engine is usually equipped with its own exhaust pipe and muffler assembly and with an individual carburetor that supplies a fuel/air mixture to that cylinder alone. The majority of motorcycle carburetors are constructed with a tubular slide valve assembly to regulate the flow of air rather than the rotating butterfly valve design used in automobile carburetors. The simple and rugged design of most motorcycle carburetors includes no more than three or four moving parts and allows for quick, simple servicing.

The front suspension and steering system of a motorcycle is attached via a tubular head lug located at the junction of the top and front down tubes of the frame. The topmost portion of the steering assembly consists of an upper yoke or crown. The handlebars are attached directly to the crown, which also serves to hold in place the upper ends of the twin fork legs. These fork legs extend downward at a shallow angle to the middle of the front wheel and brake hub, where they are joined together by an axle shaft that holds the brake and wheel assembly in place. Slender coil springs and hydraulic damping system inside each fork leg assembly allow the lower portion of the legs to slide or telescope through a range of approximately half a foot. The deflection rate of the springs, the weight of the hydraulic fluid and the size of the openings through which the fluid is forced, serve to govern the characteristics of the front suspension system. The different uses to which motorcycles are put dictate whether the front suspension should be stiff or soft, of long or short travel and how much damping should occur on the compression and rebound strokes.

The angle of the fork legs and the relationship of the tire contact point to the axis of the steering lug determine in large measure the handling characteristics of a particular motorcycle. These two properties, known as *rake* and

RAKE AND TRAIL ILLUSTRATED

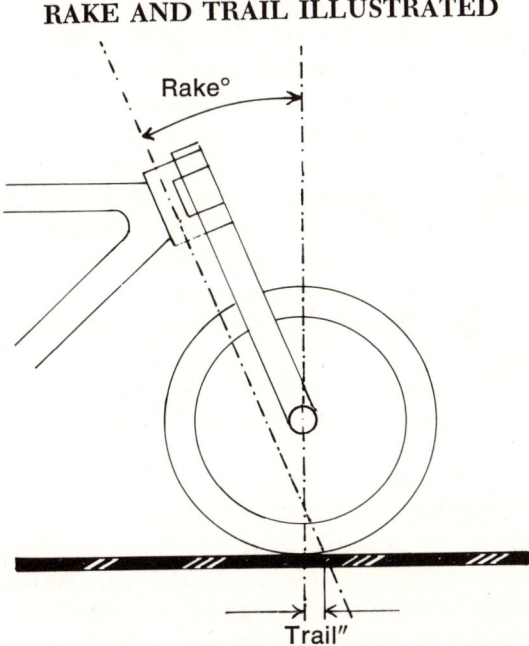

trail, are frequently misunderstood but they are actually quite simple concepts. Rake refers to the angle formed by the fork legs and an imaginary vertical line through the center of the front wheel axle. The more the front forks are tilted forward, the greater the rake becomes. Trail is the distance in inches between the tire-ground contact point and the point where an axis line drawn through the steering lug would touch the ground. Generally, the contact point of the tire rests about three inches behind this imaginary line. This distance places the point where the tire strikes road irregularities far enough to the rear that the entire front wheel assembly will tend to realign itself in the original direction of travel after striking a small obstruction. In other words, trail helps a motorcycle continue traveling in a straight line and also tends to align the front wheel when the motorcycle is banked over. The proper combination of trail and rake enables a motorcycle to steer in the intended direction at low speeds (where the gyroscopic force created by the wheels is small) and to travel smoothly through corners and over obstructions at high speeds.

No single combination of rake and trail will produce the best possible handling characteristics at all speeds and under all circumstances. For example, a relatively small amount of rake and considerable trail enable a motorcycle—such as a specialized trials competition machine—to steer with enormous precision at low speed over a rough field or a boulder strewn river bed. Yet that same motorcycle will not handle well when racing through a downhill stretch of road at high speed (nor is it even capable of high speeds). By the same token, a high performance heavyweight touring motorcycle which has the necessary amount of rake to remain stable at speeds well in excess of 100 MPH will not accurately negotiate a rough trials course at 4 or 5 MPH. Most general purpose highway motorcycles and dual purpose road and dirt bikes come equipped with a carefully engineered combination of rake and trail that enables them to travel comfortably along a wide variety of road surfaces at nearly any speed above a walk. Specially engineered single purpose motorcycles will do a better job of negotiating one particular kind of terrain but at the cost of handling rather poorly under any conditions other than the special ones for which they were designed.

The rear portion of a motorcycle's engine/frame unit contains a welded or bolted-on subframe assembly consisting of a pivoting swing arm and a rigid upper support structure. Hydraulic shock absorber/spring units (much like those used in automobiles to control excess weight loads) are connected at their base to the far end of each swing arm and at the top to the rigid upper supports. The swing arm assembly holds the rear brake, drive chain and wheel assembly in place laterally, so it resists any side-to-side motions. But the swing arm can pivot through a vertical arc along a distance of three to five inches in response to any bumps or other irregularities in the riding surface.

The Physics of Motorcycling

Although a motorcycle is unstable at rest, it is in equilibrium at nearly all other times. In fact, a motorcycle becomes increasingly stable as its speed increases (up to a limit of course, at which point aerodynamic problems can quickly create a lack of stability). The reason is quite simple. A motorcycle remains upright while in motion as a result of the gyroscopic force generated by its turning wheels. This force increases with the *square* of the velocity of the wheel assembly. Therefore, the force acting to keep a motorcycle upright and moving in a straight line at 60 MPH is about four times as great as the force acting on the same motorcycle traveling at 30 MPH. This does not mean that a motorcyclist is four times safer or even as safe when traveling at 60 MPH than at 30 MPH. At 60 MPH his tires will be nearer their limit of adhesion when rounding corners, it will take him longer to stop and he will have less time to dodge obstacles like a beer bottle in the roadway. What it does mean is that a fast moving motorcycle has a strong tendency to continue traveling upright in a straight line, unless acted upon by one or more deflecting forces.

Once a motorcycle has entered a curve and is moving at a steady speed, it is also in a state of equilibrium. The tendency of a motorcycle to fall inward while rounding a corner is exactly balanced by the centrifugal force acting outward through the center of gravity of the machine and its rider. (See figure) The vector sum of these two forces (the downward gravitational pull

THE PHYSICS OF CORNERING

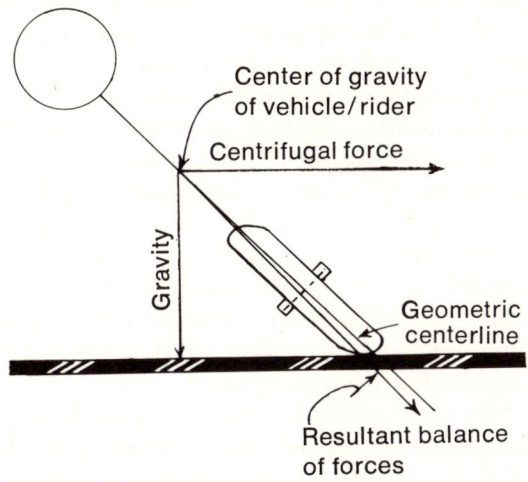

and an outward centrifugal force) passes in a line from the center of gravity of the rider and his motorcycle through the point where the tires contact the road. So long as tire adhesion is equal to or greater than the vector sum of these two forces, there is no chance that the motorcycle will tip over or slide out of its path around the corner.

Beginning motorcyclists, passengers and motorists assume that the banking of a motorcycle as it rounds a corner is a potentially dangerous situation. This is not necessarily true. Specially prepared road racing motorcycles can exceed a 50° inward bank in sharp turns and even at this point enjoy a near perfect balance between the downward gravitational pull and the outward centrifugal force. Motorcycle cornering becomes troublesome only under two circumstances. First, a motorcyclist may round a corner with such speed that the resultant forces when combined together exceed the adhesive force generated at the tire-ground contact area. Second, the adhesion of the tires to the road may decrease for some reason, such as a patch of oil or a bump in the pavement, to the point where the frictional force holding the tire to the ground becomes smaller than the vector sum of the gravitational and centrifugal forces generated while turning. As soon as either of these two events occurs, the rear wheel of the motorcycle (and sometimes the front wheel, too) will begin slipping outward and the rider must take immediate corrective measures to stop his machine from going over on its side.

Contrary to popular myth, once either or both wheels of a motorcycle starts sliding, all is not lost. Professional dirt track and road race riders can slide or drift their machines at over 100 MPH with no ill effects other than rapid tire wear. Once either wheel begins to slide, a motorcycle is no longer in equilibrium, however, and its rider must act quickly and surely to keep it upright. Beginning riders should remember that although it is helpful to know how an operator can control or correct a skid, the learning process is usually long and often painful.

The Mechanics of Motorcycling

Once you have digested the theoretical aspects of motorcycling, the rest of what you need to know will come easily. But do not assume that just because you understand the physics of motorcycling, all you need do is hop onto the seat and ride off. Although a motorcycle contains many of the same controls as a car, these controls are located in a different pattern than automotive controls and there is considerable variation from one brand of motorcycle to the next. Moreover, most motorcycles include controls and adjusting devices that simply do not exist in the world of passenger cars.

Handlebar Controls

The following controls are usually located on the handlebars of a motorcycle. Those controls and other devices preceded by an asterisk (*) exist only on some motorcycles, while the remaining items can be found on nearly every motorcycle currently in production.

Clutch Lever   The clutch lever is invariably positioned on the left side of the handlebars. As the name implies, the clutch lever activates the clutch. Pull the lever in and the clutch is disengaged; release it and the clutch is engaged, thereby allowing the engine to transmit its energy to the transmission. Motorcycle clutches vary considerably in the abruptness with which they begin to engage and the length of pull on the lever needed to engage them. If you are preparing to ride a bike you have not operated before, find out by careful experimentation in Low gear whether you are dealing with a gentle "sweetheart" clutch or an abrupt racing style item.

Regardless of the kind of clutch, the lever should pull easily and smoothly, with about 3/8 in. of free-play before you begin to feel tension on the lever. If a clutch lever does not exhibit these characteristics, see Chapter 6 of this book on preventive maintenance or have a competent mechanic remedy the problem.

Compression Release Lever   This handy device is found on some older, large displacement four-stroke motorcycles and on an increasing number of two-stroke dirt motorcycles. The compression release lever, which is always shorter than the clutch lever and located just to its right, is connected via a cable to a valve in the cylinder head of the engine. Pull the lever and the cable opens the valve, releasing the compression pressure from the cylinder. Why, you may ask, would we want to release the pressure, since it is the very force of compression that makes the pistons go down and the wheels go around? There are two reasons. Large capacity four-stroke engines are often difficult to start, due to the effort necessary to kick the piston past all that compression to the point where it rests near the bottom of its power stroke, ready for the (hopefully) final kick back to the top of the compression stroke and ignition. A compression release valve allows a rider to gently ease the piston over the top of the compression stroke and thereby simplify the starting process.

On two-stroke engines (those without camshafts and valves, the kind of engines that sound like a nest of angry wasps), the compression release serves another function. For reasons that are not worth explaining here, a two-stroke engine exerts little braking effort while a motorcycle is coasting with the throttle off and the transmission in a lower gear. But a compression release, when fitted to a two-cycle engine, allows that engine to develop a substantially increased braking effort that is roughly equal to the deceleration force exerted by a four-cycle engine. This braking force on the rear wheel is especially helpful for slowing down a motorcycle on a dirt surface.

Throttle Twistgrip The throttle twistgrip is always located on the right handlebar. Turn it toward you and the carburetors open, feeding progressively larger amounts of fuel and air to the engine. But turn it carefully. Most motorcycles employ a quarter-turn twistgrip, which means that a quarter-turn of the wrist is the only thing separating an engine from idle and 7,000 to 9,000 RPM. In high gear, this quarter-turn makes the difference between idle and top speed. So treat that little rubber covered handle with respect. Too much flexing of the right wrist can prove injurious to a rider's health and to the welfare of his motorcycle.

While you are looking respectfully at the throttle of a motorcycle you already own or intend to purchase or ride, also try twisting it. Is there more than a fractional amount of slack before the cable catches? Does the twistgrip seem to bind or catch as it turns? Does the twistgrip fail to snap back smartly as soon as you release it? If the answer to any of these questions is yes, you are dealing with a bike that will prove uncomfortable or dangerous to operate. You should remedy the problem yourself (refer to Chapter 6 of this book, on preventive maintenance) or request that the owner of the bike remedy the problem. Be especially aware of a sticking throttle. Manufacturers never "call back" their motorcycles to remedy such problems and motorcycles are more prone to sticking throttles than are automobiles. So keep in mind where the ignition switch or kill button (see below) is located and remember to reach for one or both of these controls if the throttle ever jams in the wide-open position. *A Special Note:* A few brands of motorcycle come equipped from the factory with a "suicide" throttle twistgrip that remains in whatever position you leave it. If you turn the throttle full open it will remain in that position forever more unless you or somebody else closes it. No, the engineers employed by these factories have no desire to see you dead or see their engines destroyed. In fact, they dearly love you and the sturdy engines they manufacture. They simply assume that you will appreciate the convenience of their throttle design and always recall its habit of not returning itself to idle position. If you have an opportunity to ride one of these machines, remember well its special habit and if you ever chance to own one of these motorcycles, consider changing over immediately to a more conventional throttle system.

Brake Lever The lever attached to the right front handlebar activates the front brake. Contrary to another old myth, that lever is not there as an ornament nor will its use, even when applied with vigor, catapult you over the front handlebars (stopping on gravel, mud and other slick surfaces does, however, require a delicate touch with the front brake lever). Because of a phenomenon known as "weight transference," the front brakes on a motorcycle—or a car for that matter—generate well over 50 percent of the stopping effort. Ignore the front brake and you have sacrificed somewhere over half the stopping power of a motorcycle. The trick is to apply the front brake lever and rear brake pedal in tandem with a gradual increase in pressure.

Since the average motorcycle can be brought to a halt in less distance than most cars require to stop and because a motorcycle is prone to skidding if the brakes are improperly applied, they must be used with care. But it is important to learn how to apply maximum braking effort to a motorcycle. Perhaps you will never need to employ this knowledge, but it could prove lifesaving.

Light Switch As the name suggests, this switch turns on the tail light, headlight and any other running lights. The switch is generally located on the handlebars or on the headlight housing.

High Beam Switch This switch turns on the high beam filament in the headlight. It functions in exactly the same way as its automotive counterpart and is usually accompanied by a highbeam indicator bulb.

Kill Button This control serves to interrupt the flow of electricity to the ignition system. Pressing the button is a convenient method of quickly stopping or "killing" the engine. Some riders use the kill button in place of the clutch to simplify shifting. This practice is ill-advised, however, as it creates increased wear and tear on various transmission and engine components. Nor should a rider use the kill button in place of the ignition switch to stop the engine routinely. On battery equipped motorcycles, it is all too easy to forget that the ignition is still on, thereby draining the battery and inviting the theft of your motorcycle.

Starter Button When the ignition is on, this handy little button activates the electric starter. Since motorcycle batteries are small, they provide only limited starting capacity. So remember to use the starter judiciously, allowing at least five or ten seconds to elapse between each starting interval. Your battery will appreciate the rest.

Choke Lever The choke lever is either attached to the handlebars (on most English motorcycles) or located directly on the carburetor body (on most Japanese motorcycles). Since motorcycles have a much larger relative carburetor venturi area than do automobiles, it is especially important for quick starting to apply the choke whenever the weather is cool and the engine has not warmed up. It is also important—and difficult for most of us—to remember that the choke lever should be released once the engine has warmed up.

Other Controls and Devices

Most motorcycles also include the following additional controls, devices and adjustment levers:

Brake Pedal The rear brake is activated by means of a pedal located about six inches in front of the right or left footrest, depending on the country in which the motorcycle was manufactured. The pedal should travel only a fraction of an inch before the brake light goes on and resistance to further pressure occurs. The pedal should travel easily through its arc, be capable of locking the rear wheel, and return immediately to its original position when released. If it fails to meet any of these standards, the brake mechanism requires inspection and repair.

If you are accustomed to a motorcycle with the brake lever on one side and find yourself about to ride a machine with the lever on the opposite side, be prepared to experience the coordination problems mentioned under the *shift lever*, below.

Steering Lock When a key is inserted in the steering lock and turned, the front forks are locked in place and cannot turn. Although a steering lock will rarely deter an accomplished motorcycle thief, it will slow him down a bit and discourage pranksters who wish to roll your motorcycle off to some inconvenient location. The only problem with steering locks is that a rider must remember to unlock them before he rides off. The author recalls an occasion when he attempted to drive his motorcycle before unlocking the steering head. The result was a short, swift, circular trip into a parked car. Only ego damage resulted, but it could have been worse.

Steering Damper Some brands of motorcycles employ a short hydraulic shock absorber mounted between a fork leg and the frame. Other manufacturers include an adjustable damper located inside the steering stem. A knurled knob protruding from the middle of the fork crown just in front of or behind the handlebars serves to tighten or loosen the damping mechanism. The damper should be tightened down when riding on rough roads or any other surface where the front wheel is easily deflected from its intended path. Otherwise, the damper should remain loose or under only slight tension to insure a quick, light steering response.

Gas Taps Before starting a motorcycle the gas tap(s) must be turned on. Large capacity engines generally have two taps located on each side of the bottom of the gas tank; other motorcycles have only one tap. On machines with two taps it is important to turn both on to insure an adequate fuel flow at high speed. Most fuel taps (the exception being the second tap on motorcycles equipped with two taps) have two open positions. The second position is for "reserve," which will give a rider between an extra thimblefull and a pint of reserve gas for getting to the next service station. Turning the fuel tap to the reserve position regardless of the amount of gas in the tank will deprive a rider of the invaluable sputter-sputter sound that warns him to turn on the reserve supply and begin searching for a gas station.

Because motorcycle gas tanks are notoriously difficult to "eyeball," (the gas cap is usually in the middle, over the hump) and because few motorcycles have reset odometers, which can be used like a gas gauge, the reserve position on the gas tap is a handy device.

Carburetor Tickler Motorcycles employing English carburetors have a small plunger protruding from the top of the carburetor float bowl. This plunger, which is known as a tickler, should be depressed for a few seconds until gasoline begins flowing from it. Once the gasoline has become visible on the float bowl or your thumb, the engine is primed and ready to start.

Ignition Switch Each manufacturer has his favorite location for the ignition switch. The owners manual, visual inspection or hints from a friend will guide you to where it is located. If the switch has more than two positions, be certain you understand the function of each different position before operating the motorcycle.

Kickstart Lever The kickstart crank may be located on either side of a motorcycle and it may engage by traveling forward, backward or sideways, depending on the make of the motorcycle. The secret to kicking over an engine is not weight or brute strength. It is a matter of balance and timing. So do not come down on the lever with all your strength. A friend of the author who was prone to do so, once had his foot slip off the lever and come crashing to the ground, which caused his kneecap to fracture. His mother laughed at him and his friends refused to speak to him for a month. To avoid this kind of embarrassment, try developing a smooth, balanced stroke. Also, make certain that the ignition is on and the handlebars are turned out of the way so that if the engine backfires, your leg will not collide with an unforgiving bit of steel. It is nearly impossible to be thrown off a motorcycle if the engine "kicks back." You can, however, get a nasty bruise when your leg comes shooting upward. Also, check whether the kicklever has a rubber cover around it. If not, exercise caution when cranking over the engine and get a cover as soon as possible, for boot leather and bare steel are a very slippery combination.

If you have an electric starter, store this information away in the back of your mind and simply push the little button on the handlebars when you wish to start the engine.

Shift Lever The transmission shift lever is traditionally located on the right side of nearly all English, Spanish, Swedish and American motorcycles manufactured before September 1974. Most other nations, including the Japanese, place the shift lever on the left side of the engine case, as is now required by Federal law. To further complicate matters, some transmissions have four speeds and others have five speeds; on some motorcycles the transmission shift lever must be depressed to change into a higher gear, while on others it must be moved upward. Be certain that the owner of a motorcycle you intend to ride tells you the shifting pattern and number of gears in that transmission. If you are used to a different pattern, exercise caution. Otherwise you may find yourself stepping on the brake lever when you wish to accelerate into Second gear or attempting to go from Third gear into Second gear as you are pulling away from a stop sign.

Shift levers sometimes refuse to do their job smoothly when a motorcycle is at rest. Do not force the lever. Instead, gently rock the machine back and forth or slip the clutch a bit and the lever will promptly engage the gear for which you have been searching. Even the best transmissions have a habit of developing a "false Neutral" somewhere in their shifting pattern. If you encounter one of these phantom Neutral gears, simply engage the lever once more and the transmission should shift into the proper gear.

In addition to the controls and other items listed above, every motorcycle comes equipped with a host of adjustment devices and inspection caps, so that a rider can keep the external parts operating properly and check on what is happening inside. The items a rider should be familiar with include the following:

Shock Absorbers Motorcycle rear shock absorbers are adjustable through a range of three or more positions. By placing the shock absorber adjusting tool in the matching holes at the bottom portion of the shock absorber or by giving the unit a firm twist, it can be placed in a soft, medium or firm position. The higher a shock absorber is placed on its locating cam, the firmer will be the ride. The bottom position is intended for solo riding with a light load. When carrying a passenger or any substantial amount of baggage, the shocks should be placed in the middle or top position. If you are unusually heavy or if for any reason you prefer a firm ride, you should raise the shocks to their middle position.

Remember to make sure both shock absorbers are always adjusted to the same position, so that the legs of the swing arm assembly receive an equal distribution of force.

Chain Adjusters The back end of each swing arm leg carries a screw or eccentric cam adjuster, which is used to maintain the proper amount of free-play in the rear chain. An owner's manual or any experienced mechanic will illustrate how to adjust the rear chain (and the primary chain also). Chain adjustment requires little mechanical aptitude. A rider need only remember to move the two adjusters an equal amount, so that the rear tire alignment remains unchanged. (See the appropriate sections of Chapter 6, on preventive maintenance)

Inspection Caps The primary engine case, the transmission case and the main engine case (or the auxiliary oil tank) all contain removable caps for checking the oil level in each of these compartments. Whenever you purchase a motorcycle, even if it is new, or use someone else's motorcycle, first check the engine oil supply before starting the engine. Take the same precautions with your own motorcycle, even if you change the oil regularly yourself.

The Psychology of Motorcycling

A long time motorcyclist, who I chanced to meet one afternoon a few years back, remarked that if you have seen one automobile you have seen them all, but each motorcycle is different from the next. Perhaps this gentleman was biased. He did have a point, however, for there is an enormous range of variation in the performance and "feel" of different motorcycles. Motorcycles as a class of vehicles require a very different kind of coordination than is necessary to operate an automobile.

The best way of acquiring the hand, eye, foot and body movements necessary for skillful motorcycling is to ride a motorcycle as much as possible and under as many different circumstances as possible. But first, especially if you have not previously owned a motorcycle, go to a large deserted area such as a shopping center parking lot and practice turning, accelerating and braking in as many different patterns as you can think of. Go as slowly as you can. Drive as fast as your confidence and the area available permit. Do figure eights forward and backward. After an hour or so of practice, stop and come back a few days or a week later and practice again. The gasoline invested in these sessions will yield a dividend of increased riding skill, confidence and pleasure.

Learn also to hear your motorcycle and understand it nut by bolt by washer. Listening to your motorcycle requires no mystical skills of communication or meditation. It is simply a matter of picking out the individual noises in the concert of sound produced by the drive train, then becoming familiar enough with the sounds so that you can tell what is normal and what is a new and possibly troublesome noise. An experienced observer can learn much about a motorcycle—or any other piece of machinery—simply by looking at it and listening carefully to it.

The knowing process should begin as soon as you get a new or used motorcycle home. Pull out the owner's manual and your tools, then sit down with the motorcycle. Familiarize yourself with the manual, keeping the bike in front of you for reference and for inspiration. Then check all the controls, make whatever minor adjustments are necessary (such as handlebar angle, idling speed or tire pressure) and check each nut and bolt to insure that it is properly tightened. By the time these get-acquainted procedures are done, you will be well on your way toward a lasting and faithful friendship with your bike.

Chapter 5

Motorcycling Safety

MOTORCYCLING MISHAP SERIOUSLY INJURES AREA YOUTH. James T. Barrinton, 18, of 1256 Logan Lane, Julesberg, suffered serious injury yesterday when his motorcycle left the highway three miles east of Eckley and plunged down a steep embankment. The State Highway Patrol and Morgan County Sheriff Department officers are investigating the cause of the accident.

Each year many thousand such stories appear in newspapers across the country. Mothers, wives and many reasonable men conclude that motorcycles are harmful to life and limb. Motorcyclists, in turn, conclude that the press is singling them out for discriminatory and prejudicial treatment. In fact, motorcycles do not "cause" accidents any more frequently than guns, themselves, kill people. The problem is simply that motorcyclists cause themselves to become involved in accidents with alarming frequency and the press believes the public is interested in the morbid details of who suffered bodily injury on any given day of the year.

On rare occasions a mechanical or structural failure is the source of an accident. Almost invariably, however, excess speed, carelessness or lack of experience are the prime contributors to motorcycling accidents. Often, of course, it is not a motorcycle rider but a passing automobile driver who is guilty of the carelessness, lack of caution or excess speed that causes an accident. The point remains, however, that it is usually people, not vehicles, who are the principal cause of accidents. It is equally true that from the viewpoint of an accident victim, who caused the accident matters little. A broken leg hurts just as much whether it is self-inflicted or the result of negligence by someone else. Being in the right legally or ethically counts for very little from the perspective of a motorist resting in an early grave. The concept of no-fault motor vehicle insurance expresses well this modern thinking on accidents: the issue of liability is difficult to determine in most accidents; therefore, each individual (and his insurance company) must bear the responsibility for any damage to himself and his vehicle.

Since people cause accidents, only people can prevent accidents. Motor vehicle manufacturers, traffic safety engineers, highway department road crews, and legislators must all contribute their share to the prevention of accidents. The person controlling the throttle, however, must take final responsibility for preventing accidents. He is the one who has the most to gain by driving so as to protect himself from injury.

The study of traffic safety and accident protection has in recent years become a respected field of scientific inquiry and analysis. Entire journals are devoted to examining the cause of motor vehicle accidents and proposing methods to prevent their occurrence. Within the pages of these journals learned specialists earnestly debate the dismal facts of vehicular injury. As in most matters, however, common sense and a modest measure of experience will better fortify a motorcyclist for the real world than will a month's faithful study of traffic safety journals. An understanding of the science of traffic safety is no substitute for instinctively recognizing and avoiding situations likely to cause injury.

The situations likely to cause injury include a host of obvious road hazards such as potholes, drunk drivers and icy roadways. The circumstances that can contribute to the occurrence or avoidance of an accident and personal injury also include a rider's dress, the condition of his motorcycle and his state of mind. A deep pothole obscured by the shadows of late afternoon represents a hazard that might prompt one rider to take early and successful evasive action, cause another rider to suffer a nasty spill and prompt a third rider nearly to lose his balance. Why these three outcomes in response to the same situation? Simply because no two riders are equally prepared by reason of equipment, experience and state of mind to deal with the unanticipated hazards of motorcycling in town, on the open road or in the dirt. No book, pamphlet or instructional guide can teach a rider experience nor instill in him self-confidence and an alert mental outlook. This each motorcyclist must learn to do for himself. Nevertheless, a rider can learn how to recognize and, whenever possible, avoid or overcome most of the obvious causes of motorcycling mishaps. It is the intent of this chapter to help riders learn to recognize in advance and prepare for these impediments to happy motorcycling.

Safety First

As a precondition to safe motorcycling, a rider must be entirely familiar with the operation of his motorcycle. The location and function of a motorcycle's controls, its braking and cornering characteristics, its handling limitations and its current state of preparedness must become second nature to a rider. Not only, for example, should a rider memorize the gear shift pattern of the motorcycle he is operating but he must also know instinctively on which side of the vehicle that lever is located and in which direction to move it in response to an emergency situation. A safe motorcyclist must concentrate his conscious attention not on operating the controls of a motorcycle but in sensing the constantly changing environment about him. In order to focus the proper level of attention on his environment, he must treat his motorcycle and its controls as an extension of himself and his reflexes.

Motorists stopped next to a motorcycle rider often wonder how it is that when the signal turns green, a cycle smartly accelerates away from the signal with no apparent effort on the part of its rider. The disappearing act routinely performed by every motorcyclist results from the smoothly orchestrated movement of the clutch lever, throttle twistgrip and gearshift lever. Not one motorcyclist in a thousand can describe precisely how he coordinates the movement of these three controls. Yet every experienced rider knows that his safety and security depend on swiftly yet smoothly translating his intentions into the appropriate motions. No matter how honorable his intentions, a motorcyclist cannot ride safely without the knowledge and experience to master the operation of his motorcycle. The rider who cannot readily coordinate the controls of a motorcycle is a menace to himself, his passenger, pedestrians, passing motorists and to the sport of motorcycling itself.

Research studies have shown that limited riding experience is a chief cause of motorcycling accidents. A survey of 123 motorcycle accident patients in two Minnesota hospitals revealed that 20 percent of the patients were using the motorcycle for the first or second time. A study conducted by the Vermont Department of Motor Vehicles reported that 21 percent of motorcycle accident victims had held a driver's license for less than one year. The Minnesota hospital study revealed that 70 percent of the patients had either rented or borrowed the motorcycle on which they were injured. A study of motorcycle accident victims conducted in the Charlottesville, Virginia area showed that 12 percent of the operators had received no instruction in operating motorcycles.

Lack of experience plays a far more important role in contributing to motorcycle accidents than to automobile mishaps. A California Department of Motor Vehicles study indicated that four times as many motorcycle accidents involved operators with less than a year of driving experience. The authors of the study concluded, in part, that:

> the most important finding of this study concerns the role of age and experience in motorcycle accidents and traffic conditions. . . . the data indicates that a person who can drive a car safely may not always be able to drive a motorcycle safely.

The preceding statistics and findings, which were collected by the National Safety Council, argue strongly for extreme caution on the part of recent converts to motorcycling. The old sink or swim method of learning to ride has obviously produced too many drowning victims. Extensive driver education training by schools, by motorcycle dealers and by independent public agencies is obviously needed if we are to reduce the high toll of accidents among newly initiated motorcyclists. Special license tests, though unpopular among some motorcyclists, are presently required by more than 42 states in an effort to upgrade the minimum skill level of beginning motorcyclists.

Objective Hazards

A motorcyclist's world is constantly bombarded by a flood of sights, sounds and other sensations. Some of these sights, sounds and sensations are a source of joy to the beholder. Others, however, represent warning flags that indicate impending problems. Just as the ancient mariners watched the skies and the water for signs of change in the wind or weather, a motorcyclist is obliged to watch the roadway ahead and behind for indications of trouble. The road surface on which he travels is the single most important object of a rider's attention, but he must learn to scan both the road itself and the adjacent right of way, including sidewalks, driveways, cross roads and roadside ditches—where little children and their beloved pets sometimes lie in waiting.

What manner of objective hazards lurk along the road and in the backcountry? The number of hazards one may encounter sometime in his motorcycling career is nearly endless. But here is a partial listing:

Road Holes Chuckholes, potholes, animal burrows (on dirt roads) and washouts can prove a bone jarring experience to the rider who does not see them approaching. The California Department of Motor Vehicles' study of cycle accidents reported that defective road conditions, such as holes or loose material, contributed to 5 percent of all motorcycle accidents included in the study. This figure is nearly twice as high as the proportion of non-motorcycle accidents in which defective road conditions played a part.

Whether to ride out or to swerve around a road hole is a perennial question confronting motorcyclists (and auto drivers too) who have not been devoting their full attention to the road ahead. No single course of action works equally well in every situation. But as a rule of thumb a rider should take evasive action whenever possible and as long as the road surface is hard and dry. The only alternative is to hold on tight, shift your weight rearward, keep your eyes open and hope for the best.

Drainage Troughs Concrete drainage channels that cross intersections, galvanized culverts across country roads, natural drainage ditches and similar water channels can prove an exciting experience for the rider traveling too fast or looking in the wrong direction. The secret here is to traverse such obstructions at a modest speed or, if that is not possible, to keep one's weight rearward and resting on the footpegs (not on the seat).

Railroad Crossings Railroad crossings, cattle guards and trolley tracks do not mix well with motorcycle tires. Especially when steel becomes wet, it provides a treacherous surface that can suddenly divert a rider from his intended course. The answer is to proceed with caution and cross such obstructions at as close to a right angle as possible. The steel tubing used in the construction of cattle guards is especially treacherous. A difference of only a few degrees from perpendicular can, at the wrong speed, cause a motorcycle's front tire to drop instantly between the rails.

Litter City streets and highways accumulate an astonishing amount of litter ranging in size from nails and bottles up to tire bodies, animal carcasses and mufflers. As in the case of road holes, litter should be avoided whenever possible as it can puncture a tire or upset an entire motorcycle.

Road Debris Except for newly built or recently cleaned roads, most streets and highways are prone to carry a coat of oil, sand, gravel or wet leaves. A curve that was clear of debris only a few days ago and safe at 50 MPH can become dangerous to take at 30 MPH in the event a passing truck has deposited a patch of sand or oil. Those crisp fall leaves of yesterday might today be wet and as slippery as ball bearings on a plate of glass.

Rain slicked roads present a serious hazard not only on account of the moisture accumulated on them but because the water loosens accumulated oil, which rises to the surface of the water. Beware in particular of heavily trafficked roads after a dry spell. The first few minutes of a downpour can loosen enough oil to turn the roadway into a warm weather skating rink. After sufficient rain has fallen to dissolve the oil and wash it away, the traction will return to something like its normal rain soaked state. Until that time comes, however, beware!

Motorcycle riders should also beware of the aquaplaning phenomenon. When rainwater has pooled on a roadway, there exists an ever present danger that the tires of a motorcycle traveling at high speed will float or aquaplane onto the surface of the water. Aquaplaning lifts a motorcycle out of direct contact with the road and opens the door to a disastrously sudden spill that can occur without prior warning. Tires in good condition, with plenty of tread life left, are one form of insurance against aquaplaning. The best prevention is greatly reduced speed and keeping to the far right side of the road where the passage of many million tires has not created shallow ruts in the pavement.

Road Surfaces Motorists rarely think of the roadway itself as a potential hazard, yet many roadways in this country are highly dangerous. Ordinary road going tires usually obtain optimal traction on an open grained asphalt surface. Concrete, though long wearing, is often so smoothly surfaced that it affords only marginal traction—and this is doubly the case when the concrete is wet and curvy. A motorcyclist operating his vehicle on a road surface with which he is not familiar should always assume the worst unless he has irrefutable evidence to the contrary.

Bridges Bridges in all their varied forms present a scenic break from the monotony of the highway. Bridges are not, however, without their dangers. In cold weather they often freeze over well before the highway becomes slick. The reason for this phenomenon is simple enough. Since they are elevated above the ground, bridges radiate their heat faster than the surrounding earth and more quickly drop below freezing temperature—at which point slush, water and patches of snow freeze solid.

Many bridges exhibit a different and more hazardous surface than the adjoining road. A few older bridges, for example, employ an open mesh steel grating that causes the front tire of a motorcycle to swerve back and forth in a most alarming fashion. Many other bridges are equipped with one or more expansion joints, which themselves represent a hazard and which can also collect sand, gravel, nails or like forms of road debris. Still other bridges, because they are humpbacked, curved or narrow, present additional hazards to the unsuspecting cyclist.

As a final word of warning, two-wheeled riders should bear in mind that bridges, because they are elevated above the ground, occasionally expose a motorcyclist to sudden and surprisingly strong gusts of wind that can catch him unprepared. Like the massive grain storage elevators that dot the side of

Midwestern roads, exposed bridges are susceptible to wind conditions strong enough to cause a sharp heel or bank in a passing cycle and cause a moment of panic in an unprepared rider.

Stationary Vehicles Parked cars and temporarily stopped buses are an everpresent danger in city riding. The majority of drivers will signal their intentions and pull out slowly. But every so often a motorist simply charges into traffic with nary a thought to the consequences. As bicycle riders know all too well, parked cars present an additional hazard for two-wheeled riders traveling in the adjacent lane. When a motorist carelessly opens his door in the face of oncoming traffic, a cyclist can find himself trapped by a wall of cars on each side and a barrier of steel and glass before him.

Extreme caution coupled with a watchful eye on stationary vehicles is a motorcyclist's best protection against the risk of being sideswiped by larger vehicles. Riding in a traffic lane next to parked vehicles is an inherently risky activity. Only by keeping a weather eye peeled for parked vehicles occupied by drivers can a cyclist prepare himself for problems before they cross his path.

Animate Objects Every motor vehicle operator must beware of dogs, cats, children, cattle and pedestrians near the roadway. Motorcycles, however, have always held a special attraction for dogs and especially those varieties of the canine species that stand tall and enjoy the taste of human flesh on the run. No simple solution is guaranteed to solve the mad (or overly playful) dog problem. Simply running over the poor beast is no answer, for it is both inhumane and dangerous to a rider. Likewise, water pistols filled with ammonia, though perfectly effective as a method of punishing errant dogs, are dangerous to operate while riding a cycle and capable of causing an animal to endure long term suffering.

Riders who see an approaching dog at some distance down the highway are advised to slow down well in advance and allow the dog to approach them. Since it is largely the motion of a motorcycle that excites an animal (the noise helps too, of course), once the motorcycle has come to a halt the animal will usually mill around waiting for something to happen. Once the animal has wandered to the side of or behind a motorcycle, that something should happen; namely, a quick departure by our ingenious rider. For all but the very smallest motorcycles can out-accelerate nearly any dog alive. What, a reader may ask, if the operator of a small lightweight motorcycle and his passenger encounter a large and fleetfooted dog? In such cases the only expedient is prayer and a tight grip on the handlebars or, if the dog is spotted well in advance, a hasty retreat and a detour around the potential disaster area.

Motorcyclists riding in rural areas occasionally come across rabbits, deer, cattle and various other four-footed animals attempting to cross in their path. So long as the road is free of traffic and other hazards, a rider should attempt evasive action whenever possible to avoid hitting an animal. A high speed collision with even small game animals is often sufficient to upset a motorcycle while larger animals pack enough bulk to seriously damage even a colliding car and its passengers.

Traffic Markings Contrary to the opinion of some motorcyclists, state and local highway departments rarely intend to kill off cycle riders. It is simply that these public employees purchase and use their traffic marking devices with only four-wheeled vehicles in mind. Consequently, they fail to appreciate that plastic marking tape, which is often used to delineate pedestrian cross-walks, and traffic safety yellow lane marking paint can, when wet, act like chicken fat between a motorcycle tire and the road. The raised lane delineators along California freeways and the sand filled barrels and metal saw horses stationed at highway construction sites can prove equally disastrous to unsuspecting riders. A cautious motorcyclist must assume that any traffic marking device applied to the road or resting on its surface is a hazard to his health and welfare.

Off-road Hazards Off-road riding presents a unique set of hazards to the unprepared rider. Discarded glass hidden in the dirt can puncture his tires, tree branches reach out for his face and limbs, protruding rocks can pitch his cycle off its course, and barbed wire fences or a chain stretched across the road can unseat him in an instant.

Short of staying at home, which is not much fun, the best defense against these and a dozen other off-road hazards is a watchful eye coupled with a cautionary hand on the brake and clutch levers. A relaxed riding style is the key to enjoyable off-road riding. But a rider must never become so relaxed that his mind begins to wander from its appointed task of guiding him safely along his chosen course.

Protective Cycling

Whether or not a rider falls victim to these and related hazards will depend less on luck or even skill (once he has acquired a modest amount of experience) than his state of mind. Avoiding accidents is largely a matter of anticipating problems before they occur and knowing what action to take. Fast reflexes are no substitute for the kind of thinking that allows a rider to avoid situations that require him to depend on the speed and sureness of his reflexes.

What kind of thinking is at issue here? It is a preventive mentality that constantly observes and analyzes the environment in which a motorcyclist is traveling. That environment is assessed in terms of the hazard that it does now or could shortly present to the operator of a two-wheeled vehicle. Smart riders depend on a variety of defensive riding techniques to protect themselves from upset or injury. No single way of thinking and acting will guarantee a rider safe passage along our highways. Nor do any two riders depend on precisely the same method of keeping themselves out of trouble. Experience and research have shown, however, that certain techniques can significantly enhance the likelihood of avoiding accidents. Listed below are a few of these techniques.

The Exposure Concept Mountain climbers and technical rock scramblers refer to the danger of falling as exposure. A narrow ledge or a smooth face of rock many hundred feet above the ground is an exposed location because it opens a climber to the danger of a serious fall. As exposure increases, a climber will call upon various protective techniques, such as roping up or placing steel pitons in the rock, to protect himself from bodily harm. Experienced climbers insist that exposure itself is not dangerous so long as a climber is adequately protected by a rope anchor and other techniques of rockcraft. Exposure becomes dangerous, however, when a climber fails to note his exposed condition and take the appropriate protective measures.

Motorcyclists also endure varying degrees of exposure. Consider the case of a rider traveling at moderate speed along a well surfaced and lightly traveled road. So long as the weather remains mild, that rider is exposed to little danger. But assume that the road becomes winding with steep embankments on each side and a cold rain begins to fall. That same rider should recognize that his exposure to injury has increased and protective measures are in order. He should put on his foul weather gear, reduce speed appropriately and maintain a light touch on the controls of his motorcycle. Perhaps he should even consider the possibility of finding shelter until the rain slackens or turning around and heading home.

Most important of all, however, a rider must learn to recognize when his exposure has increased. Nearly always, the proper protective measures are simple and straightforward. But first a rider needs to recognize that those measures are in order. To do so he must perceive that for one reason or another, none of which is his fault, the likelihood of a serious injury is substantial. The source of the increased exposure may be as simple as heavy traffic or it may result from the complex interplay of several less than obvious factors. Regardless of its source, however, exposure spells danger to the rider who has not tuned in to the environment about him.

Worst Case Thinking Planners and public policy specialists know from experience that the best way of preventing a disaster is to anticipate it in advance. If the disaster never occurs, then nothing has been lost save a bit of time and money. If the disaster seems likely to occur or has already happened, then the appropriate steps can be taken either to prevent it or to lessen its impact. Flood control efforts take exactly this form. Most communities likely to suffer flooding maintain contingency plans to deal with the problem of high water. If a flood does not occur, then so much the better. In the event of rising water, already existing plans can be readily implemented to protect the community from flooding or to soften the impact of a major flood.

Motorcyclists can also benefit from worst case thinking. The object is not to think of the worst disaster that could possibly befall a rider. That kind of thinking is sure to drive a motor vehicle operator back into bed where he can hide beneath the covers. Worst case thinking is not a matter of wondering what to do if the sky falls in, which is known as the Chicken Little Syndrome. Instead, it is a method of anticipating likely problems before they occur. Consider, for example, the case of a rider who pulls up to a traffic signal. A bolt of lightning could descend from the sky and strike him dead. However, the chances of being struck by lightning are remote and there is little a rider can do anyway to protect himself from lightning.

Nevertheless, there does exist the possibility that a daydreaming motorist could run into our rider as he is waiting for the signal to turn green. Knowing that this possibility exists, a rider can take various precautions. First, he should keep well to the right side of the lane and mentally lay out an escape path in the event it is needed. Second, he should keep an eye fixed on the rearview mirror in anticipation of an approaching vehicle that fails to slow down as it nears the signal. A motorcyclist may repeat this routine a thousand times to no avail. Yet the next time could prove to be the "worst case" that makes all his efforts worthwhile. If worst never does come to worst, then a rider can be grateful for his good fortune. But in the event that the worst case does materialize, he will be prepared.

Fancy riding techniques are well and good—but they reduce even an experienced rider's margin of safety.

A Margin of Safety A motorcyclist is blasting along a deserted cow pasture late in the afternoon when suddenly he spies a mound of dirt lurking directly in front of him. Before he can hit the brakes our rider sails over the mound, parts company with his motorcycle and tumbles along the ground for a short distance before coming to a painful stop in the tall grass. Why did this accident happen? One observer might attribute it to excess speed; another to the mound of dirt hiding in the grass; a third to the lack of sufficient daylight.

Each of these answers is partially correct. Yet each one fails to explain fully the circumstances surrounding the mishap. As long as our rider did not encounter a hidden hazard, he was probably traveling at a reasonable rate of speed. Yet he was already *at* the limit of safety for the terrain. Because this rider allowed himself no extra margin of safety, any hazard would have placed him in jeopardy. A motorcyclist might travel many miles without encountering such hazards. Then again, he might travel only a short distance before finding an unexpected obstacle. In the long run, however, it is statistically inevitable (or nearly so) that sooner or later he will come face to face with a hazard like the one described above. It is equally inevitable that the rider who fails to allow himself a wide margin of safety will eventually come to grief.

Professional motorcycle racers must often operate their cycles with no margin of safety at all. Since they are professionals, these riders usually know just where the line between victory and disaster lies. Moreover, they are fully prepared to suffer the consequences of misjudging or exceeding that thin line. Casual riders, however, have less to gain and more to lose by traveling about town or across the countryside at the narrow edge of disaster. For nearly all of us, maintaining a margin of safety is not a luxury but a responsibility to ourselves and to others. A rider may travel for many hundreds of miles with no margin of safety. Eventually, however, he will pay the price of failing to allow sufficient leeway for the unexpected.

The Invisible Rider A number of years ago Ralph Ellison wrote a book called *The Invisible Man.* Although motorcycle riders are not invisible in the sense that Mr. Ellison meant the term, they are indeed often invisible to other highway users. Failure to see an approaching motorcyclist is a frequently cited cause of accidents. Other motor vehicle operators do have a point. A motorcycle rider and his vehicle are a small and often swiftly moving point of reference that can easily become lost in the glare of moving traffic and roadside distractions.

A motorcyclist rarely knows for certain—until it is too late—whether other motorists have observed his existence. The safety conscious rider should therefore think of himself and his machine as wholly invisible to larger vehicles. This pretense of invisibility will prove especially valuable to a rider at intersections, driveways and alleyways, where a statistically high proportion of car/cycle accidents take place. By thinking of himself and his vehicle as invisible, a rider will have little need ever to place himself in a position where his health and welfare are dependent on the perceptive skill of other drivers.

The rider who thinks of himself as invisible will also recognize the importance of enhancing his visibility by way of his horn, lights, turn signals and brightly colored or reflective clothing. In an effort to increase the visibility of motorcyclists, a number of states require the daytime use of a headlight by all riders. Extensive research conducted on contract for the U.S. Department of Transportation has shown that the daytime use of a headlight increases the visibility of a motorcycle by 44 to 142 percent, depending on the traffic conditions. Cloudy weather conditions produced an even more significant increase in the effectiveness of cycle headlights. Analysis of the motorcycle accident rate in four states with mandatory daytime headlight laws suggested that daytime use of headlights can reduce daytime motorcycling accidents by nearly four percent. When this reduction rate in accidents is projected onto a national scale, it represents about 7,000 fewer motorcycle accidents and nearly 100 fewer fatalities each year.

Defensive Dress

Despite the well intended effort of most motorcyclists, accidents do happen. And when a motorcyclist is involved in an accident, he runs a greater chance of dying or suffering serious injury than does the victim of an automobile accident. The reason is simple enough. Automobile riders are surrounded by a more or less protective cage that can withstand a substantial impact before collapsing. The motorcycle rider, however, is largely unprotected from the consequences of an impact with solid objects. Once an impact dislodges him from a motorcycle, the rider travels out of control through an environment filled with telephones poles, passing cars, fence posts and other equally dangerous obstacles.

Since a motorcyclist is not surrounded by a steel cage, his only alternative, short of constant exposure to the cold, cruel world, is to wear a protective shell around his body. Like the tortoise, who has survived for untold millions of years, motorcycle riders need to carry a protective environment on their backs for use in the event it is needed. The National Safety Council warns, and for good reason, than an improperly dressed motorcyclist is increasing the risk of serious injury in the event he becomes involved in an accident.

It is not known for certain just how much safer motorcycling becomes when riders equip themselves with a helmet, face protection, boots, gloves, a sturdy jacket and heavy pants. All available evidence, however, points to the fact that protective dress makes a difference, and a big one at that. Chapter 10, on the accessory market, considers the virtues and vices of various kinds of rider apparel. Yet a few pieces of rider protection are sufficiently important that they also deserve special mention in this chapter.

Approximately 10 percent of all motorcycle accidents cause injury to a rider's eyes or face. Protective face gear, especially in the form of a plastic shield, will not only help reduce the severity of eye and face injuries, but by keeping foreign objects away from a rider's eyes, face gear can prevent accidents from occurring in the first place. Motorcycle riders must, however, select their facial protection with extreme caution. Prescription eye glasses, for example, even when equipped with tempered or safety hardened lenses, apparently provide inadequate eye protection under certain circumstances. Traffic safety research conducted under contract for the government produced the tentative conclusion that corrective glass lenses "are unsuitable for protection on motorcycles." Likewise, this same research contract (Contract No. FH-11-6940, NHSB No. HS-800-168) revealed that some "flip-up face shields may flip down and strike the vulnerable area of the neck upon application of a relatively small force to the frontal area."

Motorcycle windshields can prove an equally hazardous form of facial protection. Although windshields offer the touring rider a heightened level of comfort, they are reportedly capable (according to the research cited above) of "causing vehicle instability, glare and reflections and may act as an agent of injury in a crash." A research report summary issued by the National Highway Traffic Safety Administration warns:

> Plexiglass is a poor material [for the construction of windshields] since it fragments into sharp lacerating pieces. Laminated glass flies off without shattering but flies like an aerofoil or winged missile capable of slitting throats. Toughened glass shatters and disperses apparently innocuously and appears to be the best current proposition.

Important technological advances in the plastics industry and the increasing availability of highly impact resistant plastics have enabled some manufacturers of protective facewear to overcome the dangers described above. But the consequences of buying the wrong product can prove sufficiently dire that a motorcyclist should shop carefully and conservatively for eye and facial protection. How much facial or eye protection equipment costs or in what colors it is available should matter far less than its resistance to impact, penetration and fragmentation.

Analysis of motorcycle accidents repeatedly demonstrates that the parts of a rider's body most often injured are his head, arms and legs. Head injuries, however, are the single leading cause of death in motorcycle accidents. Somewhere on the order of 60 percent of riders killed in cycle accidents die as the result of head and skull injuries. Data gathered by the National Highway Traffic Safety Administration indicates that at speeds below 35 MPH unhelmeted riders are about three times more likely to receive a fatal head injury in a crash than are helmeted riders. At speeds above 35 MPH unhelmeted riders appear to be seven times (700%) more likely to receive a fatal head injury. On a national scale, the universal use of safety helmets can be expected to produce about 1.5 fewer deaths per 10,000 registered motorcycles for a net saving of about 600 lives a year.

If a reader does not consider these findings to be sufficiently compelling evidence in favor of using a safety helmet, then he had best check the laws of his state. As of May 1973, 46 states had enacted mandatory helmet legislation. Only California, Iowa, Illinois and Mississippi do not require motorcyclists to wear a safety helmet of approved design. (See the accompanying map) A number of motorcyclists have argued that mandatory helmet laws are unconstitutional under the Fourteenth Amendment. One State Supreme Court, in Illinois, has declared that state's mandatory helmet law to be unconstitutional, thereby causing Illinois to repeal its motorcycle headgear legislation. A number of lower courts also declared mandatory helmet laws unconstitutional. However, the majority of court challenges to state and local helmet statutes have proven unsuccessful. As of January 1972, there were at least 48 court decisions on the subject of headgear legislation. In 38 cases the courts upheld the constitutionality of mandatory helmet laws. The United States Supreme Court has consistently refused to overturn cases upholding headgear legislation. The case against mandatory helmet laws is now largely a dead issue since the courts generally agree that such laws are a rightful exercise of the police power invested in state and local governments.

The question of what constitutes an "approved safety helmet" remains, however, the subject of lively debate. Since it was first issued in 1966, the self-imposed industry Z90.1 performance standard for safety helmets has un-

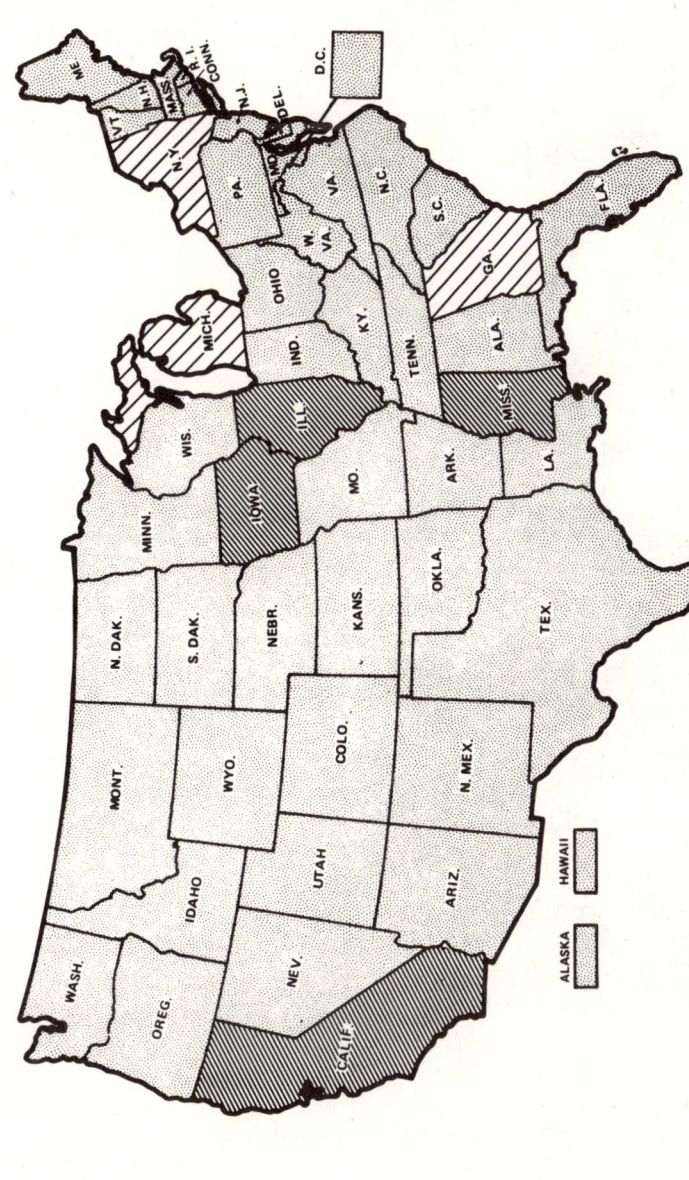

Youngsters especially need the protection of a high quality safety helmet.

dergone revision and refinement. In May 1972 the National Highway Traffic Safety Administration proposed that the minimum performance level for motorcycle helmets be upgraded (to the Head Injury Criterion required by Motor Vehicle Safety Standard No. 208) effective September 1, 1974. Then in August 1973, NHTSA underwent a change of heart and announced it would defer a final decision on the upgrading until further research was completed. Many independent observers believe that an upgrading of the Z90.1 standard is desperately needed. Although better than no standard, Z90.1 sets minimum performance levels that offer a rider less than the best protection available. Like most such standards, Z90.1 represents a compromise that takes into account the need of many different interest groups.

Upgraded performance standards, however, are only part of the answer to the problem of adequate motorcycling headgear. A considerable body of information indicates that many helmets fail to meet even the Z90.1 performance standards. In July 1971, the National Highway Traffic Safety Administration announced that it had received numerous reports indicating that:

- polycarbonate (moulded thermoplastic) helmet shells may be highly susceptible to common chemicals and cleaning agents, the use of which could degrade their protective ability
- quality control efforts on the part of many helmet manufacturers appeared to be producing minimal results
- helmets were failing without proper cause; that is, by cracking apart after falling off shelves or receiving other hard impacts

In response to these alarming reports the NHTSA issued an advisory warning and undertook an investigation of safety helmet performance standards. The advisory recommended the following precautionary steps until such time as a new federal standard could be implemented:

- safety helmet users should beware of the materials used in the construction of their helmets. Helmet shells are almost exclusively manufactured from fiberglass or polycarbonate materials. Polycarbonate helmets should be painted or decorated only with paints certified by the manufacturer as compatible with the helmet shell material. A wearer who cannot identify the material used to construct a given helmet should contact a retailer who sells that brand of safety helmet
- solvents and cleaning materials should not be used on any helmet unless certified by the manufacturer as compatible
- prospective owners should insure that a helmet they intend to buy is either approved by their state of residence or certified by label as meeting the Z90.1 standard
- if cracks or stress lines appear on the helmet shell, it should be replaced immediately

Preliminary results of the NHTSA sponsored helmet performance study were discouraging. Tests conducted in 1972 by an independent laboratory revealed that almost 90 percent of the helmets included in the performance study failed to meet one or more of the Z90.1 performance standards for shock absorption, penetration resistance to a pointed object and chin strap strength. Some helmets failed all three tests. The greatest number of failures occurred in the vitally important impact attenuation test for shock absorption. Polycarbonate helmets came out second best in the investigation. Test results indicated that fiberglass shelled helmets performed 22 to 45 percent better as a group than those made of polycarbonate material.

Passengers deserve equal headgear protection. A set of full coverage helmets represents the best protection available for an operator and a passenger.

For the motorcyclist striving to protect himself from the consequences of a motorcycling mishap, these findings will prove discouraging. How can a consumer know he is receiving a fair return of protection for his money? The answer is that in most cases he will not know for certain until—if even then—the moment of truth arrives. The chances are quite good, however, that a customer who takes the time to shop carefully and who is willing to pay for the best will not be disappointed by his purchase. The best safety helmets on the market may not offer dazzling metallic paint jobs nor will they be bargains, yet they are well worth their price. Unfortunately, the colorful helmets that some motorcycle dealers offer cyclists to sweeten the deal on a new motorcycle are rarely the best helmets available. Although the helmet market may include some good buys for the money, a customer needs a briefcase full of test data and the advice of a consulting engineer to know which safety helmets are indeed good buys and which ones may be worthless in the event of an accident. Shoppers lacking the time and money to research exhaustively the subject of helmet design and performance have no recourse except to seek the advice of a knowledgeable retailer and pay the price he is asking for the best.

Motorcycle Safety: An Overview

The preceding discussion of motorcycling safety issues may prompt a reader to ask just how dangerous are motorcycles. Is riding a motorcycle equivalent to running down the street with a loaded pistol pointed at your chest? Or, are motorcycles a perfectly safe and sane method of travel? Such questions do not readily yield simple answers. But a brief examination of the facts may help clarify a number of misconceptions held both by motorcycling enthusiasts and by those opposed to the sport of motorcycling.

All told, motorcycles, motorscooters and motorized bicycles represent about 2.7 percent of all vehicles registered in the United States. In 1971 these motor powered two-wheelers (over 90 percent of which were motorcycles) became involved in 1.2 percent of all motor vehicle accidents. In other words, motorcycles and related vehicles were involved in less than one half their fair share of accidents. Passenger cars, in comparison, included 80 percent of all registered vehicles, yet they produced 85 percent of all vehicle accidents. The proportion of commercial buses involved in accidents was six times greater than their proportion of total vehicles on our roads. From the standpoint of accidents among all registered motor vehicles, the motorcycle can boast of an enviable track record.

In the category of fatal accidents, motorcycles do not fare so well. That same 2.7 percent of total motor vehicles accounted for 3.4 percent of the motor vehicle fatalities in 1971. Motorcycles therefore produced somewhat more than their share of fatalities. Passenger cars may be more likely than motorcycles to be involved in an accident. But motorcycles, because they are smaller, lighter and offer less protection, are more likely to produce a fatal accident.

Motorcyclists, however, average fewer miles of travel per year than do other motorists. The average motorcycle accumulates perhaps 3,000 miles of use during the course of a year. Therefore, the rate of motorcycling accidents per mile traveled is somewhat higher than the accident rate among passenger car operators. The fatal accident rate among motorcycle riders in 1971 was estimated by the National Safety Council to be about 20 deaths per 100 million miles of motorcycle travel. One fatality for every 5 million miles of motorcycle travel is a more favorable rate than some foreign nations can boast of among their passenger car drivers and substantially lower than it was in years past. The licensing of motorcycle operators, mandatory helmet laws, periodic inspection requirements and related measures have all played a part in reducing the frequency of fatal accidents involving motorcyclists and their passengers. Nevertheless, the fatality rate among motorcyclists remains greater—in fact, about four times greater—than the rate rolled up by automobile drivers.

Part of the gap between the safety performance of motorcycles and automobiles is a function not of motorcycles themselves but of the age of their operators. The average motorcycle rider is a 22 year old male whose age places him in a high risk/high accident rate category of vehicle operators. Research reports examined by the National Safety Council indicate that for the most part from 40 to 66 percent of motorcycle accident victims are under 20 years of age. Since motorcycles are operated by a more youthful population than passenger cars, the motorcycle accident and fatality rate is inevita-

94 CHILTON'S COMPLETE GUIDE TO MOTORCYCLES

bly and artificially inflated relative to automobile accident and fatality rates. Just how much of the difference is attributable to the youthful characteristics of motorcycle riders is difficult to determine accurately. It is clear, however, that a portion of the blame placed on motorcycles should lie with the statistical accident that many motorcycles are operated by persons who by reason of their age are prone to become involved in motor vehicle mishaps.

Despite claims to the contrary, it is largely as a result of the government's effort to impose mandatory motorcycle safety standards that the fatality rate among cyclists has declined. Much of the improvement can be attributed to the near universal promulgation of safety helmet statutes. State laws requiring a special drivers license, eye protection, a passenger seat, passenger footpegs, a rearview mirror, periodic safety inspection and the daytime use of a headlight have also played a part in reducing the incidence of injury producing accidents. For one reason or another, some states have not adopted all the motorcycle safety standards advocated by the U.S. Department of Transportation/Federal Highway Administration. But enough of the states have adopted enough safety standards to put a substantial dent in the rate at which cyclists injure themselves. Readers who are curious to know which safety standards their state has adopted should refer to the following chart. This presents in scoreboard fashion the track record of each state, current to October 1973, in implementing motorcycle safety legislation.

State Implementation of the Motorcycle Safety Standard

State	Special Driver License	Safety Helmet	Eye Protect.	Passeng. Seat	Passeng. Foot-Rests	Rearview Mirror (1 or more)	Periodic Safety Inspt.	Daytime Use of Headlight 5
Alabama		Y	Y	Y				
Alaska	Y	Y	Y	Y	Y	Y		
Arizona	Y	Y	Y	Y	Y	Y		
Arkansas		Y	Y	Y	Y	Y	Y	Y
California	Y			Y	Y	Y		
Colorado	Y	Y	Y	Y	Y	Y	Y	
Connecticut	Y	1	Y	Y	Y	Y		
Delaware	Y	Y	Y	Y	Y	Y	Y	
Florida		Y	Y	Y	Y	Y	Y	Y
Georgia	Y	Y	Y	Y	Y	Y	Y	Y
Hawaii	Y	Y	Y	Y	Y	Y	Y	
Idaho		Y		Y	Y		Y	
Illinois	Y			Y	Y	Y		Y
Indiana		Y		Y	Y		Y	Y
Iowa	Y			Y	Y	Y		
Kansas	Y	Y	Y	Y	Y	Y		
Kentucky	Y	Y	Y	Y	Y	Y	Y	
Louisiana	Y	Y	Y	Y	Y	Y	Y	
Maine	Y	Y		Y	Y	Y	Y	
Maryland	Y	Y	Y	Y	Y	Y		
Massachusetts	Y	Y				Y	Y	
Michigan	Y	Y	2			Y		
Minnesota	Y	Y		Y	Y	Y		
Mississippi						Y	Y	
Missouri	Y	Y					Y	
Montana		Y		Y	Y	Y		Y
Nebraska	Y	1					Y	
Nevada	Y	Y	Y	Y	Y	Y		
New Hampshire	Y	Y	Y	Y	Y	Y	Y	

State Implementation of the Motorcycle Safety Standard (cont.)

State	Special Driver License	Safety Helmet	Eye Protect.	Passeng. Seat	Passeng. Foot-Rests	Rearview Mirror (1 or more)	Periodic Safety Inspt.	Daytime Use of Headlight 5
New Jersey	Y	Y	Y	Y	Y	Y	Y	
New Mexico	Y	Y	Y	Y	Y	Y	Y	
New York	Y	Y	Y	Y	Y	Y	Y	Y
North Carolina		Y		Y	Y	Y	Y	Y
North Dakota	Y	Y		Y	Y	Y		
Ohio	Y	Y	Y	Y	Y	Y		
Oklahoma		3	Y	Y	Y	Y	Y	
Oregon	Y	Y				Y		Y
Pennsylvania	Y	Y	Y	Y	Y		Y	
Rhode Island	Y	Y	Y	Y	Y	Y	Y	
South Carolina	Y	Y	Y	Y	Y	Y	Y	Y
South Dakota	Y	Y	Y	Y	Y	Y	Y	
Tennessee	Y	Y	Y	Y	Y	Y		
Texas	Y	Y		Y		Y	Y	
Utah	Y	4	4	Y	Y	Y	Y	
Vermont	Y	Y	Y	Y	Y	Y	Y	
Virginia	Y	Y	Y	Y	Y	Y	Y	
Washington	Y	Y	Y	Y	Y	Y		
West Virginia		Y	Y	Y	Y	Y	Y	
Wisconsin	Y	Y	Y	Y	Y	Y		Y
Wyoming	Y	Y		Y	Y		Y	Y
Dist. of Col.	Y	Y	Y	Y	Y	Y	Y	
Puerto Rico	Y	Y	Y	Y	Y	Y	Y	
TOTAL	42	48	35	46	45	45	39	12

Y = Yes
1 = The helmet law is not currently enforced.
2 = Required at speeds above 35 mph.
3 = The law applies only to operators and passengers under 21.
4 = The law applies only on roads with speed limits higher than 35 mph.
5 = Not required by the Motorcycle Safety Standard.

Source: Department of Transportation, National Highway Traffic Safety Administration. Revised 10-5-73.

These efforts toward decreasing the rate of motorcycle accidents, though they have been effective, represent only a portion of what many safety experts believe necessary to reduce further the incidence of injury among motorcyclists. What do these safety experts believe necessary for the proper protection of motorcycle riders? Here is a partial listing of the steps that some public officials and safety researchers advocate to protect motorcyclists from injury.

Foot Controls The lack of standardized motorcycle foot controls has proven a source of nuisance to motorcyclists for many years. It is also a likely source of accidents among riders who are changing from one system of shifting and braking to another system. Now government officials are standardizing the foot control position on all motorcycles offered for sale in the United States after September 1974, in an effort to eliminate this potential source of rider disorientation.

Gas Tanks Motorcycle crash tests performed under contract for NHTSA have demonstrated that fuel tanks are a hazard on two counts. First, a number of tanks, especially those made of fiberglass and aluminum, ruptured on impact, thereby creating a fire hazard. Monza type snap-open gas caps were found to open under impact, soaking riders and their vehicles with gasoline. Moreover, fuel tanks that rose abruptly from the seat, or that had raised seams or parcel grids attached to them, were prone to cause pelvic and groin injury to the instrumented test dummies. Steering head fixtures that rose above the tank top also proved a source of injury.

The remedy for these problems is simple enough. Fuel tanks should be sturdily constructed, perhaps with synthetic rupture-proof liners, threaded filler caps should be used and the tank surface should present a smoothly shaped contour that will not impact a rider in the event of a sudden stop. At the fore end, the gas tank should rise high enough to protect a rider from impact with the steering head fittings. Fuel valves should be located in such a fashion that they do not catch a rider's leg during an accident; and ignition coils should be placed not directly underneath the tank, as commonly happens, but well away from any location where they could ignite spilled gasoline.

Handlebars Though most motorcycles will never have the experience, a head-on impact can catapult the rider forward and over the handlebars. Many handlebar configurations induce injury even before a rider has left the motorcycle. High handlebars, especially those that rise a foot or more above their mounting point, can seriously injure a rider. So, too, can the various fittings on the handlebar, including protruding switches, choke levers and rearview mirrors, cause considerable damage to the body of a rider. Again, the cure is simple enough. Switches, control levers and other fixtures need to be designed so as to produce minimum injury. Smoothly rounded shapes and flexible or snap-off fittings have been recommended as methods of reducing rider injury. Handlebar and control lever ends should be fitted with ball tips to prevent the possibility of puncture wounds. Rigidly mounted instruments also present a hazard, which can be overcome by the use of a recessed mounting position and energy absorbing cases that will yield on impact.

Footpegs Test motorcycle crashes have shown that the fixed footpeg can protect a rider's leg from serious injury. In the event of a slide, folding footrests offer little protection. Indeed, they could conceivably crush or trap a rider's foot as they folded toward the engine cases or frame. Government sponsored research indicates that footrests should not fold and that they should be equipped with ends that slide readily across a variety of hard and soft surfaces.

Radical Cures Self-styled safety experts both within and outside government have at various times recommended much more drastic cures than those we have so far discussed. Pivoting handlebars, inflatable airbags, upholstered fairings and even restraining belts are among the devices that have been proposed to reduce the toll of motorcycling injuries. Whether or not such measures would actually protect riders and at what cost in dollars and convenience is not known. But it is clear that well intending non-riders will continue to press for equally or even more radical cures until the rate of motorcycle injury declines still further than it has to date.

Motorcycle riders, their organizational representatives and industry spokesmen would do well to undertake their own efforts at reducing the severity and frequency of cycling mishaps. Only in this fashion can motorcyclists and manufacturers ward off the spectre of massive government intervention in motorcycling activities. Many riders and their representatives have complained bitterly about the present level of federal interference. But this level of involvement, bothersome as it may be to some members of the motorcycling community, is only the lull before the storm of governmental intervention that could well result. Effective organization and industry-wide self-policing may not prevent this storm, but they can certainly soften its intensity and reduce the resultant damage to the sport of motorcycling as we know it today. There are various paths to the goal of motorcycling safety. It is the responsibility of every rider, manufacturer and representative to insure that the route followed is as smooth and short as possible.

Chapter **6**

Preventive Maintenance

Engineers and mechanics have learned from bitter experience that the stressed parts of any machine are subject to failure sooner or later. Several years ago, some genius by the name of Murphy codified this experience into a set of laws. The laws that bear his name describe the fate of most every mechanical device and human activity. Murphy's Laws state:

1. *In any field of endeavor, anything that can go wrong will go wrong.*
2. *Left to themselves, things always go from bad to worse.*
3. *If everything seems to be going well, you have obviously overlooked something.*

Motorcycles are no more prone to the consequences of Murphy's Laws than other high performance motor vehicles. But a motorcyclist must remember that his bike is not mechanically identical to a car, a lawnmower or any other piece of machinery he is likely to own. In the first place, modern motorcycle engines operate at very high speed. Maximum engine speeds in the range of 7,000 to 10,000 RPM are common. Many motorcycles cruise down the highway day in and day out with their engines rotating at 6,000 RPM. Most passenger car engines, in comparison, will self-destruct well before reaching 6,000 RPM. In addition, motorcycles employ sophisticated engineering designs of the sort commonly found in $15,000 European sports cars. Finally, motorcycle engines produce enormous amounts of power relative to their size. The industry average is in excess of one and one-half horsepower per cubic inch of displacement. This output is roughly equal to a

PREVENTIVE MAINTENANCE 99

Volkswagen producing 140 horsepower and a Buick sedan with a 600 horsepower engine under the hood.

The high power output and sophisticated engineering of modern motorcycles does not make them inherently unreliable or failure-prone. But motorcycles deserve more frequent and careful maintenance than the family car. Perhaps your Ford station wagon requires an oil change every 8,000 miles and an annual lubrication job. A motorcycle, however, deserves better treatment. Infrequent service intervals may prove adequate for a lawnmower or an American passenger car. But they will do irreparable harm to most motorcycles, just as they would to a Ferrari. To the extent that you treat any motorcycle, regardless of its size, not as a glorified lawnmower but as a miniature Ferrari, your repair bills will decrease proportionately.

This does not mean that a motorcycle must be driven gently and taken out of the garage only on warm sunny afternoons. Far from it. Most motorcycles are designed to be run, and run hard, in every kind of weather and over all kinds of terrain. But you should lavish upon a motorcycle frequent attention according to an established schedule. Routine servicing, or preventive maintenance, can be likened to birth control. Both are intended to prevent problems before they occur.

The owner's manual spells out the recommended intervals for performing service work and also lists the operating specifications (such as tire pressure and spark plug gap) for each model of motorcycle. Since these time intervals and operating specifications vary substantially from motorcycle to motorcycle, an owner must consult his handbook or a reputable dealer to obtain accurate information for his make and model of motorcycle.

Maintenance and Repair Tools

Despite these variations from one motorcycle to the next, any maintenance work requires certain basic tools and standardized procedures. Lets first look at the tools that are necessary. Perhaps you are not an experienced mechanic. Yet you are perfectly competent to learn how to do routine servicing work and you probably have about the house many of the tools needed to perform most regular maintenance chores. If you do not own the items listed below under the heading of "essential tools", it is important to get them. Otherwise, you cannot carry out many elementary service tasks. Or, in attempting to use the wrong tool, you may butcher the job. The items listed among the useful tools are still basic to maintenance work. But they fall more in the category of aids to speed the job or make it easier rather than items without which you cannot do the job in the first place.

Essential Tools:

a set of open end wrenches or a 3/8" socket drive set   Get a set to fit all the common bolt sizes on your motorcycle. You can get by without both these items. But it is necessary to have a socket drive set *or* a set of open end (or box) wrenches in the bolt pattern (English, metric or Whitworth) of your particular motorcycle.

two crescent wrenches   One wrench should have a 6 inch handle and the other an 8 or 10 inch handle.

three screwdrivers   Most motorcycles require both a phillips head (the x pattern blade) and a regular or single blade screwdriver. Get two regular screwdrivers: one with a long shaft and wide blade, the other with a shorter shaft and a narrower blade. Also get two phillips heads: one fine and one blunt.

needle nose pliers Get the kind with a wirecutter near the joint and tips sturdy enough so they will not bend out of alignment the first time you use them.

spark plug wrench If you already own a socket drive set, you need only purchase a spark plug socket. Otherwise use a cheap spark plug wrench until you can afford the real thing.

feeler gauges Make certain the set you buy includes the proper size for checking the spark plug and rocker arm clearances.

tire pressure gauge Proper tire pressure is essential for good handling and long tread life.

tire irons (2) and a valve stem puller If you ever need to remove a tire, spoon-shaped tire irons are essential. Screwdrivers may look like they will get the job done. But they have a habit of pinching holes in the tube, tearing the tire bead and bending the rim.

allen head or hex-head wrenches If your bike comes equipped with allen head bolts (the ones with a six sided insert in the head) you will need these wrenches.

plastic electrical tape This is probably the single most useful "soft tool" for motorcycle maintenance work.

penetrating oil Penetrating oil is much cheaper than the repair work required to fix a shredded screw head or a fractured bolt stud.

lubricating oil Lightweight motor oil works well. Be certain to get a dispensing container with a self-sealing tip. Old dish soap and toiletry bottles work well.

non-hardening sealer compound Sealer is invaluable for a dozen different tasks, from fixing leaky chaincases to securing screws and nuts that have a habit of vibrating loose.

hand cleaner and fresh rags Girl friends, wives and mothers do not appreciate dirty fingers in the kitchen and other places.

Useful Tools:

open-end wrenches or a socket set Now is the time to purchase the other of these two tool sets.

vise-grip pliers This is among the most useful of all tools in a mechanic's arsenal of equipment. It is also the most dangerous. A pair of vise-grip pliers can crush a penny, round off the end of a nut or snap off a bolt head with little effort on your part. So use them with discretion.

spark plug gap gauge This inexpensive device simplifies the task of checking and adjusting the plug gap.

a file Get a medium size general purpose example of the breed.

a soft headed hammer A hard plastic or copper headed hammer will wreak less havoc on motorcycle parts and will work as well as a steel headed instrument.

a torque wrench These strange looking instruments are necessary for tightening down the head and various internal parts of a motorcycle.

lube gun A small model with a flexible hose attachment is ideal for motorcycle work. Be certain the model you get has a fitting that corresponds with the fittings on your bike.

PREVENTIVE MAINTENANCE 101

silicone sealer This space age wonder material is an all-purpose soft tool that can do anything from seal a loose speedometer case to repair a cracked chaincase.

All the essential tools listed above can be purchased for as little as $35. By spending a few dollars more, however, (in the neighborhood of $50) you could purchase tools that will last for decades rather than a few seasons of use. It is wiser to put your money into a few good tools and wait for the rest or use what comes in the tool kit rather than buy a whole set of second or third rate tools.

A Few Rules of Thumb

Before taking your tools outside to attack the various parts of a motorcycle, it is important to remember the basic rules of thumb that apply to service work on any mechanical device. These rules are especially relevant to motorcycle maintenance and repair work.

1. Think before you act. When in doubt, do not begin by taking pieces apart. Read or ask first to learn what special problems you may encounter when disassembling the various components of a motorcycle. Thus you can avoid having fork springs pop up in your face and ball bearings by the dozen roll across the floor. These unhappy events befall every intrepid mechanic sooner or later, but better that they happen later rather than sooner.
2. In motorcycle servicing matters, cleanliness is next to godliness. Small even invisible bits of grime and dirt quickly combine with oil to form an amazingly effective grinding compound that will wear away, score or otherwise damage the multitude of moving surfaces found on every motorcycle. The soft alloys and close tolerances common to motorcycles demand clean tools, clean parts and a clean working area.
3. Working areas should be not only clean, but well illuminated, comfortable and hard surfaced. It is bad enough when those ball bearings go rolling across a concrete garage floor. But when they fall into a grassy area, you might as well give up all hope of retrieving them.
4. Motorcycle parts, although strong, are not unbreakable.

This is how the English language edition of a Spanish manufacturer's handbook puts it:

> *If you are a person of unusual strength, do not enter into a contest of will with the nuts and bolts on the motorcycle. The nuts and bolts are made of steel suitable for the purpose, but nuts and bolts do not have unlimited strength. Use discretion when tightening them.*

In other words, do not attempt to force parts. If a nut refuses to turn or a flywheel will not disengage from a shaft, the problem may be quite simple. Perhaps the bolt has a left-handed thread, in which case you were turning it the wrong way. Or the flywheel you were attempting to pull off is attached by means of a taper fit, requiring a gear puller to extract it. A bit of thinking about the problem or a phone call to someone who knows can save untold amounts of grief.

5. A rushed job usually becomes a slipshod job. Trite as it sounds, patience is a key virtue in any maintenance or repair work. You are not being paid on a flat rate basis to get the job done. So take your time. Allow a few hours for a stubborn nut to soak in penetrating oil and for your temper to cool down. You may save yourself the trouble and expense of having someone drill out and retap the bolt that snapped when you were giving it that one final try with the wrench.

Preventive Maintenance Chores

Much of the work necessary to maintain a motorcycle lies outside the realm of the usual tune-up work (such as checking the tappet clearances and setting the ignition timing) performed by dealers and outlined in the fine print of an owner's manual. Maintenance work is rarely difficult or complex, but it is a bit time consuming. Because time is money for a motorcycle dealership or repairshop, the price of routine maintenance quickly mounts up, which is one reason (along with knowing the job was done right) for doing the service chores yourself.

These servicing chores are arranged below in order of their importance from the standpoint of rider safety. Arbitrary decisions are an inevitable part of any such listmaking. A reader may question the placement of one item ahead of rather than following another item. Perhaps on the basis of his experience or from the point of view of his needs, he is correct. But there is a clear progression from items with a direct bearing on a rider's safety to items that are largely important for the welfare of his motorcycle's mechanical parts. When an engine's oil supply runs low, the pistons may seize and the rear wheel lock up. If the motorcycle begins to skid before a rider pulls in the clutch, then a situation potentially injurious to his health has resulted from neglect of the lubricating system. Yet this progression of events is less likely to happen than a snapped drive chain wrapping itself around the rear wheel (in this case, the clutch will not save the motorcycle from skidding) or a broken brake cable robbing a motorcycle of its stopping power at a critical moment.

Clean-up   Clean-up, as it is used here, refers not to the polishing that will make a bike gleam like the day it came off the showroom floor. Instead, it is the process of stripping away grease, road grime and dirt. These enemies of every motorcyclist cover up a multitude of possible problems and can themselves become a source of mechanical or electrical problems if left undisturbed. A high-pressure spray of hot soapy water and a healthy dose of degreasing liquid, if the engine area has a bad case of gunk, will pull off the grime and reveal what lies underneath.

The Frame and Fittings   Once the motorcycle is clean, put it in a warm, well lighted place where you and it can get together comfortably. Then take the appropriate size wrenches and go over the entire machine nut by bolt by screw, tightening what is loose and looking for signs of metal fatigue.

If you encounter a loose nut or screw that you recall having tightened down before, the problem usually lies not with your wrench work but with vibration. Remove the screw or nut and place a small amount of non-hardening sealer on the threads before tightening it down again. If the threads (such as those on an exhaust pipe clamp) are located in an area exposed to high levels of heat, you will either have to use a heat resistant gasket sealing

PREVENTIVE MAINTENANCE 103

compound or resort to the old but effective technique of drilling and wiring the part in place.

Modern motorcycle frames are sturdy, trouble-free units. But motorcycles subjected to hard use in the dirt or around town and motorcycles that have suffered even a minor accident at some time in the past should be checked for signs of stress failure. When examining the frame, look with special care at the natural stress points: near the steering head junction, the engine mounting points, and where the swing arm assembly meets the frame. Examine the tabs used to attach various components to the frame and inspect carefully the sheet metal or fiberglass around these tabs.

Hairline fractures in the metal or fiberglass can often be stopped with a bit of epoxy glue and the simple expedient of installing oversize metal washers and a rubber suspension system. Small rubber washers from a hardware store and hand cut discs from an old automobile inner tube make effective vibration insulators to protect fenders, side covers, license plates, gas tanks and other parts from the destructive vibration some motorcycles produce.

After frame and running gear have been examined for signs of stress failure, lubricate the swing arm and any other frame points that require routine greasing.

Cables The sad tale of Jack Warmshoe, told in Chapter 2, illustrates the danger of operating a motorcycle with worn or ill-maintained control cables. Mr. Warmshoe, you will recall, met an untimely fate when his clutch cable snapped while he was gunning his engine at an intersection.

If you know for certain that the clutch, brake, throttle and instrument cables were cleaned, inspected and lubricated at the last 1,000 mile service interval, the cables will require only routine maintenance. Detach the cables at the point where they join the control levers and inspect the ends at the top and bottom for signs of fraying or kinks. If the ends are in good condition, hold or tape the cables upright and drip lightweight oil inside the brake and throttle cable housings. Periodically move the cable up and down to speed the flow of oil down the housing. Speedometer and tachometer cables are best lubricated with light grease or special instrument cable lubricant. Remember to leave the top few inches of these cables clean to protect the instruments from damage.

Clutch cables should be lubricated with grease whenever possible. Some cables come equipped with a greasegun fitting to facilitate lubrication. If a cable you are working on lacks a fitting, the next best alternative is to use the oil drip technique mentioned above and to coat the ends of the cable with a film of protective grease. Before reinstalling the cables, place a drop of oil on the control lever pivots and fill the throttle cable housing (located inside the twistgrip) with grease. Also renew the lubricant on the right handlebar where the twistgrip slides over it. Once the cables are replaced in their fittings, check and adjust them for the proper amount of play or backlash (about $3/8$ inch).

If you are uncertain when the control cables were last serviced or if they look dirty and otherwise in doubtful condition, a more extensive maintenance job is in order. Remove the cables entirely from the motorcycle and wipe them down or better yet soak them in kerosene or another appropriate solvent. After the cable assembly has dried, inspect the housing for cracks and examine the cable itself for frayed wires, loose ends and sharp bends. If the cable shows signs of wear and tear such as a badly cracked housing, broken wires or misshapen ends, it is not long for this world. Obtain a high quality replacement immediately. Sure, the cable may have a few thousand more miles of life left in it. But even if you carry a replacement on the motorcycle, it is likely you will need to change over at an inconvenient moment, like during a rainstorm or on a busy expressway. And there is always the danger that the cable will snap at the moment when you most need it to brake, accelerate or shift quickly.

When reinstalling a cable, avoid any sharp turns or kinks. Wide radius bends may not look neat or orderly. They prolong the life of cables, however, and create the smooth, light action one finds on the controls of most professional racing motorcycles. If the cables are not connected to the handlebars and frame with cinch straps or a similar securing device, use a few winds of tape to hold them in place. This procedure will effectively keep them out of the way and give a more positive, direct feel to the controls.

After you have finished working on the cables, check each control to make certain it performs according to your expectations. If the motion is not light, even and smooth, examine the clutch, brakes or carburetor(s) to locate the source of the problem.

Brakes   Modern motorcycle brakes usually require little attention. Whenever the cables are lubricated, the front and rear brake cable adjusters should be reset for the proper clearance. At the same time, add a few drips of oil to any exposed points on the front brake linkage and the rear brake operating mechanism. Remember to grease the rear brake pedal shaft or spindle and check both the front and rear brake light activating switches to make certain the brake light is illuminated as soon as either brake control is activated.

Whenever the front or rear wheel is removed, the brakes themselves should be inspected and serviced. Note that hydraulic disc brakes do not require removal of the wheels for periodic checking of the hydraulic fluid level and pad wear. To service drum brakes, first remove the drum and wheel assembly (they are generally bolted or laced together) from the backing plate. Clean the accumulated dust from the drum and inspect the inside surface for scores or cracks. Check the backing plate for broken shoe retainer springs, cracked shoes and excessively worn linings. If any portion of the lining has worn to within $1/16$th of an inch of the rivet heads or, on bonded shoes, of the brake shoes, then it is high time to replace the brake linings. Riders who replace the brake linings themselves should take care to install the linings correctly. Most motorcycles use noninterchangeable leading and trailing shoe sets on both the front and the rear brakes, so it is important to avoid installing the shoes backward. To simplify matters, do not remove the old shoes until you have labeled the new linings as leading or trailing with an additional notation to distinguish top from bottom.

If an adequate amount of lining material remains on the present brake shoes, they may require light sanding with a medium grade sandpaper to remove the glaze (a hard glossy surface on the linings) and restore them to like-new operating condition. After the linings, springs and other parts of the brake mechanism have been serviced, place a small amount of high temperature grease on the brake cam pivot points. Since even a tiny amount of grease on the linings will destroy their effectiveness, be certain to wipe off any excess that could find its way onto the linings or the drum surface. Before the wheel and drum assembly is reinstalled on the backing plate, wipe the drum clean with a soft, dry cloth.

Before finishing the job, make sure that the axle nuts and the locking arms that hold the backing plate in place are securely fastened. Then double check your work by rolling the motorcycle along at a slow speed and applying the brake lever or pedal. This final step will prevent the embarrassment and panic that comes from discovering at the first intersection that you—or someone else who worked on the brakes—forgot to install the activating cable or some other equally necessary part.

Tires All too many motorcyclists disregard the subject of tire care. If there is a tread pattern showing on the carcass and it will still hold air, then they assume that the tire will roll along for a few more miles. Tire care usually consists of adding sufficient air to maintain a roughly circular appearance and occasionally using a garden hose to clean off the accumulated dust or mud. Proper tire maintenance and replacement requires, however, more careful consideration than many motorcyclists—especially recent converts—devote to the subject.

In the area of tire selection, brand choice is largely a matter of personal preference. Except when you have good reason for preferring a tire brand other than the one selected by the manufacturer, stick with his decision, unless you believe it was motivated largely by cost saving concerns. Tread pattern is usually a function of the use to which a motorcycle is subjected. Touring tires are designed for city and highway driving. The rib pattern front tire gives excellent steering, braking and cornering control on pavement, but it is unsuitable for use on dirt, sand and other loose surfaces. Universal pattern tires such as the Dunlop K-70 or the Pirelli Universal, give good performance on pavement, hard packed dirt or clay. When used with discretion, they allow adequate control in softer dirt and shallow sand. The universal tread pattern is the preferred choice of riders who generally follow the road signs but occasionally venture off the pavement into the woods.

"Dirt tires" include a variety of patterns ranging from those with relatively small and closely placed cleats to full motocross style "knobbies", which give superb traction in mud, gravel, deep sand and a variety of equally treacherous surfaces. Most cleat pattern tires wear rapidly, handle poorly around paved corners or in the rain and create a fearful vibration level that is sufficient to jar your teeth, undo the bolts that hold a motorcycle together and fracture fenders or a gas tank. The milder trials pattern tires are suitable for dual purpose motorcycles that live part of their life on paved roads. The more radical knobbie tires should not, however, leave the dirt.

The dictates of good sense and the principles of safe motorcycling, which were discussed at length in Chapter 5, require that a motorcyclist operate his machine only where it is properly equipped to go. True dirt tires are no more intended for use on the pavement than are touring tires designed for driving on soft surfaces. Proper tire care begins with a rider selecting a tire tread pattern consistent with the intended uses of his motorcycle.

Motorcycle tires are expensive, in some cases more expensive than a full size automobile tire. To preserve your investment and your life also, it is important to maintain motorcycle tires in the best possible condition. Frequent checking of the tire carcass and inflation pressure is the key to tire maintenance. Automobile drivers often replace their tires *after* the tread becomes thin. Motorcyclists should always purchase a replacement *before* the tread wears out. Do not save a tire just because part of the tread shows sufficient depth. Rear tires wear thin first in their center section and front tires wear more rapidly near the sidewalls, which absorb the punishment of high cornering forces. Since rear tires need ample tread depth in their center section and front tires require a full tread pattern along the sidewall, even partial tread deterioration is more than ample reason to obtain a replacement. Thin treads not only provide less adhesion with the road surface but they are more likely to become punctured or fail entirely. Any motorcyclist who experienced a flat tire in heavy traffic or during a rainstorm far from a service station appreciates the importance of preventing a recurrence of the problem.

Maintaining proper tire pressure is the most effective way to prolong tread life, prevent premature tire failure, and insure safe handling. Improper inflation destroys car tires and motorcycle tires alike. But motorcycles are more sensitive than cars to any variation in tire pressure. Changes in tire pressure alter the contour of motorcycle tires. Since motorcycles rotate around the contours of their tires when turning, different amounts of air pressure will produce altered handling characteristics.

There exists no single correct tire pressure. For nomral one-up touring, however, the inflation pressure specified in the owner's manual is your best bet to begin with. Increased loads and high speeds demand somewhat higher pressures, while dirt driving usually requires lower than normal tire pressure. After you become accustomed to the handling characteristics of a motorcycle carrying the recommended tire pressure, you may wish to vary the pressure two or three pounds on either side of the manufacturer's suggestion in order to tailor the handling characteristics of a motorcycle to suit your tastes. Experiment with caution, however, and watch carefully for signs of abnormal tire wear and unstable steering conditions (uneven tire wear patterns can often be corrected by the simple expedient of removing the tire and reversing its direction of rotation on the rim). When checking tire pressure, always use the same gauge and make certain the tires are cool. The gauge you use should not only be accurate, but it must produce consistent results if it is to be of any value.

Routine tire maintenance requires frequent inspection of the tire body for rips, bruises or bubbles and the prompt removal of any oil or grease from the tire. Also, check periodically to insure that the rear wheel is properly aligned. Many front end handling problems result from improper rear tire alignment. Motorcycles subjected to heavy acceleration and frequent dirt driving with low tire pressures tend to rotate their rear tires on the rim. As the tire begins pulling around the rim, the valve core will bend and then break. Chisel lines placed around the inside of the rim or sheet metal screws drilled through the rim into the tire bead will often prevent tire rotation. But the surest solution is to buy a set of bead locking pads and install them between the rim and the tire.

A motorcycle's drive chain is the most exposed and vulnerable part of the entire machine. The average chain contains hundreds of moving parts that must transmit abrupt power impulses without the benefit of a protective covering to shield them from the dirt, water, acids, sand, and other harmful substances lying in their path. A clean, well-lubricated chain and sprocket drive system is more efficient (nearly 98%) and quieter than a gear drive and nearly as trouble-free, too. But few motorcycle drive chains enjoy so comfortable an environment. Neglect and the ravages of time can quickly deteriorate a chain to the point where it suddenly changes from a faithful transmitter of power to a lethal weapon, able to hurl itself into motorcycle parts or human flesh with the destructive force of flying shrapnel. When a chain self-destructs at highway speed, it can wrinkle a license plate into crumpled tin foil, break spokes as if they were bits of straw, and carve deep gouges in the frame. Any motorcyclist who has chanced to observe the havoc wreaked by a flying chain instantly acquires a new-found interest in the care of that otherwise neglected motorcycle part.

The key to a long and trouble-free chain life is periodic lubrication combined with occasional adjustment and cleaning. A dry chain wears about 300 times more quickly than an adequately lubricated chain. Some motorcycles are equipped with automatic chain oilers, which are supposed to keep the links well nourished with oil. Yet few chains enjoy the luxury of an effective automatic oiler. Thus, it is usually the rider's responsibility to manually lubricate the links with medium weight oil or one of the commercial chain lubricant preparations available. How often should the chain be lubricated? It all depends. Any time the links look dry and clear of oil a rider must assume they have gone too long without lubrication. Frequent riding in the rain, at high speed or on dirt surfaces is sufficient reason to lubricate a chain as often as once or twice a week.

Whenever a chain is lubricated, and otherwise at intervals of about 1,000 miles depending on usage, it should also be checked for slack and adjusted as necessary, so that the total play at mid-chain does not exceed one inch. Before adjusting the chain, however, check whether it is covered with a grimy paste and examine the sprocket teeth for signs of wear. If either of these conditions exists, the chain drive components probably require more than lubrication and adjustment.

Begin by prying the spring clip off of the masterlink, removing the masterlink and then pulling the chain off the sprockets. Place the masterlink in a safe place (on the end of the chain) where it will not get lost. Then count the number of links in the chain, measure the overall length of the chain at full stretch (only light hand pressure is needed to stretch it), and compare this figure with the length of a new chain containing the same number of links. If your chain has grown by three percent or more, or if there is binding or excessive sideplay in the links, a high quality replacement should be obtained.

A well-worn chain generally means that the transmission and rear wheel sprockets are also damaged. Inspect the sprockets for chipped or rounded teeth and for uneven wear. The gap between each tooth should be a perfectly regular "U" shape. A lack of uniform slack in the chain as the rear wheel is rotated is one sign of sprocket wear. When worn sprockets are not replaced at the same time a new chain is installed, the chain will rapidly deteriorate as it runs over the deformed teeth. Moreover, the constant tensioning of the chain can place destructive loads on the rear wheel bearings and transmission components. New sprockets cost less than transmission repair work. Therefore it is a good practice to replace the final drive sprockets along with the chain. Remember also to lubricate a new chain before installing it. Chain oilers do not always do their job properly and some chains come from the factory with only a thin coating of preservative.

If the chain and sprockets on a motorcycle appear servicable, carefully clean the sprockets with a brush or rag dipped in solvent and soak the chain in a solvent bath. Rinse out and refresh the solvent (kerosene works well) as many times as necessary to clean the chain completely of abrasive particles that have worked their way into the rollers, bushings, and pins. Once the chain is clean, it should be dried and oiled thoroughly. Old-time motorcyclists cook their chains in a hot bath of grease, paraffin, graphite, and various other chemicals to obtain effective lubrication. A coating of SAE 20 motor oil or chain lubricating fluid also works well. It is best to soak the entire chain in the lubricant and wipe off the excess in order to insure that the inner surfaces of the chain get fully coated. When the chain is clean and well oiled, it is ready for installation on the sprockets. Even if the old masterlink shows no visible signs of wear, save it as an emergency spare and get a new masterlink, since this is the structurally weakest unit in a motorcycle chain.

After the chain is installed, check and adjust it for the proper amount of slack. If you did not replace the sprockets, be certain to measure the slack at the tightest point in the chain's travel around the sprockets. The tightest point can be determined by rotating the rear wheel through one complete cycle of the chain, checking every few inches to determine where the least slack exists. On many motorcycles, any adjustment to the rear chain will require recalibration of the rear brake light activating switch. After you have finished working on the chain, check and adjust the switch so that it turns on the brake light as soon as the rear brake pedal is depressed.

The final drive chain of a motorcycle requires more attention than the timing and cam chains (on four-stroke engines only) and the primary drive chain. But these other chains should also receive periodic inspection and adjustment according to the manufacturer's specification. Since most motorcycles use a unit construction engine/transmission design, adjustment of the primary chain (note, however, that some motorcycles use a gear drive to transmit engine power to the transmission) does not affect the tension on the rear drive chain. On older model motorcycles and those current makes utilizing a separate transmission, the primary chain must be adjusted (by moving the entire transmission backward or forward) before the rear chain is checked for the proper amount of tension.

Wheel Maintenance and Balancing Smooth tire wear and predictable handling require properly balanced and correctly aligned wheels. Motorcycle wheels are strong and light. But like any wire-spoked wheel, they require periodic servicing. Check occasionally for the obvious problems of broken or loose spokes and bent rims. To replace broken spokes, the tire and tube must first be removed from the rim before the new spokes are threaded into place. Loose spokes can be tightened by turning the flat sided portion of the spoke nipple, which projects through the inner circumference of the rim. Tighten the nipples by turning them clockwise until the offending spokes feel as tight—and produce the same pitch when struck lightly with a metal object like a screwdriver—as the other spokes. If the adjusters fail to turn freely, do not force them. Instead, remove the tire and tube, soak the threads with penetrating oil overnight, and try again in the morning. If the spokes still will not turn, try applying a bit of heat from a propane torch.

Small dents in the rim can often be removed by the judicious use of vise grip pliers, but remember to protect the rim by padding the jaws of the pliers. If the rim has any large deformities, do not attempt to repair them. Take the rim to a competent shop with the equipment and experience necessary to undertake such work and ask them whether the rim should be repaired or replaced.

Once all the spokes are in place and more or less uniformly tightened, you should determine if the rim runs true. To check for rim wobble, tape or strap an "L" shaped piece of wire to the fork leg or shock absorber and place the end of the wire at a point almost touching the *side* of the rim. Rotate the rim while watching for any change in the clearance between the rim and your makeshift pointer. Then remove the pointer from the fork leg and reposition it so that the end rests just above the *top* of the rim. Slowly spin the wheel again and watch for any change in the clearance between the pointer and the rim. Few motorcycle rims are in perfect alignment laterally (side to side) or radially (in a vertical plane) and you should expect to find some irregularity, especially on motorcycle wheels that have been subjected to hard use. But if the wobble exceeds $1/16$ inch in any direction, then the wheel needs to be trued. Properly aligned wheels are especially important for motorcycles subjected to high-speed driving. Spoke tuning is a fine art that requires considerable patience and much experience. It is a task best left to the expert, who knows which spokes to tighten and which ones to loosen.

If you insist on adjusting your own wheels, remember to work slowly, turning the spokes no more than one half turn at a time. Do not tighten or loosen just one spoke. Instead, think of a the problem in terms of a half dozen improperly adjusted spokes. Those spokes directly in line with the wobble will require the largest adjustment while the adjoining spokes should receive proportionately smaller amounts of adjustment. The object is to spread out the redistribution of tension as evenly as possible around the circumference of the rim. When spokes on one side of the rim are tightened, it is usually necessary to loosen the corresponding spokes located 180° away on the opposite side of the rim. Keep in mind that a gentle touch and gobs of patience are important assets in the trial and error process of obtaining anything near perfect alignment.

Specialized equipment is necessary to balance a motorcycle wheel dynamically. But a roll of solder or lead wire, some plastic tape, a piece of chalk and a bit of patience will yield a surprisingly accurate job of static balancing. First, back off the brake shoes, disconnect the rear chain and make certain the wheel and tire assembly is not rubbing against a fender, chain guard or other obstruction. Then spin the wheel and allow it to stop where it will. Place a chalk line on the tire at its low point and spin the tire twice more, placing additional chalk marks on the sidewall wherever the tire stops. If the chalk lines are more or less randomly distributed around the circumference, then the tire is usually well-balanced. You will probably find, however, that the three marks cluster in a single area. If this is the case, wrap about a half-dozen turns of solder around the spoke located 180° away from the center-point of the three chalk marks. Spin the wheel a few more times and add or subtract solder until the wheel is as likely to come to rest at one point as any other point.

The wheel is now roughly in balance. To refine the job a bit, cut in half the length of solder now on the wheel and tightly wrap each of the pieces around the two spokes adjoining the spoke from which you unwrapped the solder. Wrap a bit of tape around the solder and give the wheel one final spin for good luck before reinstalling the chain and adjusting the brakes. And remember when changing a tire, to mark the location of the tire against the rim and reinstall the tire at the same location in order to maintain the balancing job.

Lubrication and Suspension Systems The oil that circulates in a motorcycle engine serves a two fold function. First, it lubricates the moving parts. In addition, it is an important source of cooling. Oil draws the heat of combustion away from the various moving parts of an engine. Motorcycle engines, like other air-cooled motors, depend heavily on the cooling effect of oil and at the same time subject oil to higher heat levels than are common in water-cooled engines. Because motorcycle engines also operate at high speeds, clean fresh oil is critical to their survival. Infrequent oil changes and mediocre quality oil will quickly ruin most motorcycle engines—which require frequent replenishment with the proper amount and grade of high quality oil.

Motorcycles include as many as six different oil reservoir systems. Proper maintenance procedures require the periodic checking and refilling of each of these reservoirs. To service a motorcycle's oil supply systems, drain the engine oil (on four-stroke engines only) after running the engine to heat and circulate the oil. Then drain the primary case oil supply and the gearbox lubricant if the motorcycle in question has a separate transmission oil supply.

Check whether the transmission oil contains any residue or looks grimy. If it does, flush the transmission with kerosene and rinse out the solvent with light weight motor oil. Then top up the transmission with the proper amount and weight of gear oil. Some service shops suggest substituting motor oil or automatic transmission fluid for gear oil, but these procedures are of doubtful value unless specifically recommended in the owner's manual.

So long as the primary case oil flows freely and contains no solid matter, you need only replace the drain plug and refill the case with the recommended grade of oil. When the oil looks thick or excessively dirty, pull the chaincase cover and clean the inside of all the sludge, grime, and whatever else you find in there. This is a good time to check the primary chain for the proper amount of slack and to perform any needed work on the clutch mechanism. When replacing the primary chaincase, remember to clean the sealing surfaces thoroughly and use a new gasket. Motorcycles with a history of oil leakage in the chaincase area should receive a generous coating of non-hardening gasket sealer compound around the lip of the chaincase combined with a careful bolt or screw tightening sequence that develops gradual, even pressure.

If the engine oil looks free from residue, flows easily and has been changed frequently in the past, you need only clean out the oil filters (many manufacturers include two or more filters on each engine), replace the drain plug and refill the sump or oil tank with high quality oil. After pouring in the fresh oil, double check that the drain plug and washer are securely tightened down and not leaking. If the motorcycle has a visible oil return pipe or an oil pressure indicator, run the engine until you have evidence that the pressure system is working properly.

In the event that there is any doubt about the condition of the oil or if the motorcycle has an uncertain ancestry, more extensive maintenance is necessary. Particles of metal in the bottom of the drain pan indicate potentially serious problems. Take the evidence to a reliable repair shop and ask a mechanic or the service manager for his recommendation. Even if there are no bits of metal lurking in the old oil, motorcycles with a dry sump or external oil supply should have the oil tank and external oil lines removed for cleaning. After tagging the oil lines with coded tape or wires, use kerosene and a flexible brush to clean the inside of the tank and the oil lines. Then reassemble the tank, making certain that the oil supply and return lines are properly connected. For an extra measure of security, slip-fit oil lines should be secured in place with miniature hose clamps or sealer compound. Refill the oil tank with fresh oil as soon as possible to prevent the accumulation of moisture and rust inside the tank.

The front suspension system of a motorcycle requires occasional servicing. So long as the fork legs have suffered no injury and the dampening mechanism appears to be working properly, the front forks need only an occasional change of hydraulic fluid. Drain the fork legs by removing the drain plugs at the bottom of each leg and working the forks up and down to force out the old oil. Then remove the stanchion plugs at the top of each fork tube, remembering that on some motorcycles the plugs are under pressure when the fork legs are compressed. Refill the fork tubes with precisely the recommended amount of single-weight motor oil or hydraulic fork fluid. The special fork fluid is expensive, but it will not foam under pressure and it resists thickening in the cold.

The Fuel System Dirt and moisture are the principle enemies of the fuel system, which includes the gas tank, taps, lines, filters and the carburetor(s). The entire system should be serviced at routine intervals and whenever there is reason to suspect impurities in the fuel system.

Begin servicing by draining the gas tank and filling it with a quart of solvent. Slosh the fluid around and scrub the inside of the tank as best you can with a stiff brush. Then drain the tank with the taps removed and repeat the process if the initial cleaning produced more than a trace of residue. If the gas taps are equipped with mesh filters, clean the filters thoroughly and use new washers to insure a tight seal between the valve body and the gas tank seating surface. If new washers are not available or if the motorcycle has a history of gasoline leakage, place a small amount of non-hardening gasket compound on the threads of the tap body.

After the tank assembly has been cleaned, allow it to dry completely. Check the vent hole on the filter cap to make certain the passageway is clean and inspect the surface of the tank for signs (such as cracked paint near the mounting points) of metal failure. If the tank has already begun to crack, it must be welded before the damage worsens. A tank that is showing only the first signs of fatigue can often be saved by remounting it with new rubber suspension discs.

Routine carburetor maintenance includes the cleaning or replacement of the air filter and inspection of the float bowl. Unscrew or unsnap the lower float bowl housing, clean out the sediment or water and clean any mesh filters in the float bowl or banjo (gas line fitting) assembly. On motorcycles equipped with slide carburetors (the English Amal and Japanese Mikuni, for example), remove the top cap and pull out the slide mechanism. Clean the tubular slide body with solvent and apply a thin coating of oil before reinstalling the assembly. Before the cap is replaced, make certain the coil spring is positioned on its seat and the slide is installed with the cutaway (the side with the upturned lip) facing toward the air cleaner end of the carburetor. Tighten the top cap gently and evenly to avoid distorting the carburetor body. On multiple-carburetor engines, the slides must be properly synchronized if the engine is to operate smoothly. Check that the cutaways rest at an equal height and begin to move in unison as the twistgrip is turned.

The Electrical System Most motorcycle electrical systems require little preventive maintenance. However, it is important to insure that all bulbs and switches are in proper operating condition, that wires are not cracked or frayed, and that connections are tight and free from corrosion. Every week or so, and more often during periods of hard use, the electrolyte level in the battery should be checked and replenished as necessary. The cable connections to the battery also need to be examined for signs of corrosion and periodically cleaned. Since few motorcycles come equipped with a spare electrical fuse, it is important to obtain two spares and tape them in place where they can be easily reached as the need arises.

Engine Maintenance. Routine engine maintenance includes such tasks as cleaning and adjusting or replacing spark plugs, setting rocker arm clearances and ignition timing and the adjustment and synchronization of carburetors. Since these procedures are outlined in most owner's handbooks and service manuals, there is no need to describe them here. Suffice it to say that motorcycle specifications must be set with care. Errors on the order of a few thousandths of an inch in setting valve-to-rocker arm clearances or a few degrees in ignition timing, will dull the performance of a motorcycle and often compromise its reliability, too. There is no magic or mystery to tune-up work. It is necessary, however, to learn the proper steps and to have access to the right tools. But the rewards justify the effort. The motorcyclist who takes the trouble to learn how to tune his engine and otherwise service a motorcycle can reap a substantial saving of money, while taking pride in the fact that he has done the work himself.

Chapter 7

Bike Tripping

Imagine an endless ribbon of asphalt meandering across the countryside, bright sunshine streaking down from a crisp blue sky and the lush aroma of springtime. Add to this picture gently rolling hills and a few well banked curves. Off in the distance a faint hum deepens in tone and intensifies in volume. From around the nearest corner a high performance touring bike sweeps into view, its rider swiftly yet surely working his way down the road. The exhaust note rises in pitch and drops again as the motorcycle climbs a hill then vanishes across the horizon. The sound of its distant passage through the countryside lingers for a moment, then it, too, vanishes.

Visions like these form the stuff of which motorcyclists' dreams are made. If a motorcycle heaven exists, it must surely include a thousand such scenes. Motorcycle riders, however, are no more inclined than the rest of us to defer gratification until their uncertain arrival in a world beyond. Cycle touring has been an integral part of the sport since its inception. The motorcycles of half a century ago would hardly inspire a modern rider's confidence. Nor were the early roads conducive to smooth effortless travel. Gravel, dust and mud were the universal lot of old time motorcycle tourists. Yet open road motorcycling was nearly as popular an activity then as it is today.

In comparison with the tribulations faced by early day touring riders, the modern open road motorcyclist can indeed enjoy heaven on earth. A nationwide network of paved and well-maintained roads is at his disposal. Gas stations, roadside restaurants and sleeping accommodations are available everywhere to satisfy his material needs. Modern touring motorcycles enable him to travel swiftly, safely, comfortably and reliably to his destination. Fiberglass saddlebags accommodate his luggage, compressed air bottles ease the

The proper equipment (in this case a fairing equipped BMW 750) and clothing will enhance the pleasures of long distance touring.

burden of a flat tire and moulded fairings protect him from wind, rain and road debris.

Despite the creature comforts available to a modern road rider, motorcycle touring is not everyone's cup of tea. Travelers who value a temperature controlled environment and luxury above all else must rely on the beloved automobile. Come rain or sleet or bitter cold, a shell of steel and glass will insulate them from the outside world. Automobiles, of course, also insulate an occupant from the sights and smells of the countryside. The resulting loss of unity with the landscape is the price a traveler must pay to reach his destination without the slightest possible inconvenience or distraction.

Motorcycle touring, on the other hand, is for the person who believes that getting there is half the fun of traveling. Adventure, and misadventure, too, are still significant ingredients of long distance motorcycle travel. More often than not, bike tripping is an adventuresome experience packed full with discovery—and most long distance riders would not want it any other way. Discovery, excitement and adventure come, however, in two different varieties. First, there is the pleasurable kind of adventure that combines the excitement of open road cycling with the discovery of new people, new places and new activities. Then there is the kind of adventure—or perhaps more accurately, misadventure—associated with a broken clutch cable along a lonely stretch of road or a nylon wind parka that proves neither wind nor water resistant despite what the salesman said.

This second sort of excitement usually happens without apparent rhyme or reason. Flat tires, for example, occasionally occur even on the best roads and to the newest tires. God is not always our copilot. But just because good fortune does not always smile down upon us is no excuse for abandoning ourselves to fate. In fact, events that are conveniently attributed to luck often result for very good and simple reasons. Did a chance and invisible manufacturing defect cause that clutch cable to snap? Or was the failure due to a lack of periodic lubrication and infrequent or careless inspection which allowed the cable to deteriorate unnoticed? Flat tires do simply happen—sometimes. But they happen more frequently to worn tires. The cure is obvious. A rider should replace his motorcycle tires *before* the tread pattern wears thin.

Misadventures sometimes "just happen" despite our best laid plans. But planning is the best known method of reducing the likelihood of misadventure. We cannot entirely avoid the fateful consequences of Murphy's three laws referred to at the beginning of Chapter 6. Yet anticipating the worst and planning for the best allows us to minimize the chances of misfortune and maximize the possibility of good fortune. There exists no known method of guaranteeing a pleasurable bike tripping experience. We can, however, strive to nurture the possibility of adventure and anticipate the causes of misfortune, thereby doing everything possible to insure a successful trip.

It is the purpose of this chapter to suggest a number of practical measures to maximize the pleasure and minimize the pain of bike tripping. Motorcycle touring, unlike automobile travel, is an acquired skill. Riders who wish to learn the art of bike tripping entirely on their own may eventually benefit from the self-learning experience. But self-education is a slow and risky business. Since the wheel already exists, why bother to reinvent it? By learning from the mistakes made time and again by other riders, a motorcyclist can save himself much time and more than a little anguish.

So far, we have spoken of bike tripping as if it encompassed one single activity. All tripping does include some common features. A sudden afternoon thunderstorm can just as easily dampen the pleasure of a jaunt to a neighboring town as it can ruin an otherwise delightful day in a week long cross-country tour. More optimistically, the joy of the open road is a universal experience available to every highway rider, no matter what his destination. Nevertheless, long distance touring is a very different activity than the short haul trips that allow a rider to return home within a single day. To appreciate the difference we need to look at each kind of tripping separately.

Day Cruising

Far and away the majority of motorcycle travel involves a rider enjoying the pleasures of a day long spin through the countryside. His destination may be a state park, the beach or simply a scenic stretch of road within a day's journey of his starting point. Day cruising, as the name implies, is short distance highway motorcycling anywhere in the vast open space that surrounds our urban areas.

Successful day cruising requires a minimum of planning and preparation. Before setting out, however, a motorcyclist should ask himself four basic questions:

where am I going?
how do I plan to get there?
what conditions am I likely to encounter enroute?
what should I take along?

Let's examine each of these questions in turn.

Destination For the rider with a specific destination in mind, where to go is not an issue. Many motorcyclists, however, like to ride for the sheer pleasure of cycling; a destination is secondary to the fun of getting there.

Day cruising can be done alone or in pairs. Two-up highway riding requires, however, an appropriately large motorcycle (in this case a 500 cc Kawasaki).

Cyclists in search of an interesting destination can simply strike out blindly, allowing their judgement and intuition to guide them toward an unknown point on the map. Alternately, a rider might consult a map in search of a landmark that is itself of interest or that offers an opportunity to travel along a scenic route. Perhaps there is an abandoned mine located somewhere near the county line or a restaurant that lies at the head of a distant valley. Before a rider can expect to reach a destination, however, he must first learn where it is. Local residents may offer him an approximate description of where the landmark is located and how to get there. But a map will usually pinpoint the location of the site and its approximate distance from his departure point.

It may turn out that our intrepid motorcyclist never does reach his intended destination. Perhaps he took a wrong turn or a gathering storm forced him to turn back. An unreached destination should cause no concern, however. Like the summit of a high mountain, the day cruiser's destination is simply a point in space for which he was aiming. If a charming waterfall or an inviting sideroad distracted him from reaching his initial destination, then so much the better—that objective will still be there when he decides to try again.

Route No matter where a rider's destination lies, he must at some point decide how to get there. For the automobile driver, the issue of routing is usually straightforward. A driver simply calculates the shortest or quickest road and proceeds to point his car in that direction. The quickest route to any destination is, of course, usually the most heavily traveled and least scenic route. Day cruising motorcyclists rarely measure the success of their trip in terms of miles traveled per hour. Consequently, the fastest way is often the least desirable route for a two-wheeled vehicle.

Even though a cyclist may know the conventional route to a given destination, he would do well to consult a map in advance. What other routes exist? Are there secondary or county maintained roads that will brighten his trip with interesting terrain and novel sights? Can he find a hilly winding road to his destination and a high speed route home? Which highway offers the maximum scenery and the minimum likelihood of traffic? The answer to these and a dozen related questions will emerge only after our cyclist carefully examines a map and confirms his observations by talking with local residents.

Oil company maps—those that service stations give away to their patrons—are an excellent source of general information. But auto route maps yield precious little guidance for a rider in search of the most scenic route. Statewide road maps lack the scale and detail necessary to predict accurately what the landscape looks like. For this kind of information a rider must consult large format county maps on file in every county courthouse or the United States Geological Survey (USGS) National Topographic Map Series. Topographic maps, because they plot the contours of the land, are an invaluable aid to route selection. Does a particular road follow the valley or travel along the adjacent ridge? Which road offers the steepest hills and the most challenging curves? The USGS topographic maps (often referred to as grid sheets or quadrangles) will answer these and various related questions.

The USGS maps are available in a variety of scales from 1:24,000 (1 inch=2,000 feet) to 1:1,000,000 (1 inch=about 16 miles). Trail riders and off-road enthusiasts will appreciate the minute detail of the 1:24,000 scale or

7½ minute series maps, which present an area of 49 to 70 square miles. Road going motorcyclists would require a briefcase full of these maps to plot out a single day's journey. USGS fortunately offers a map series suited to almost every need. Day cruising riders can obtain the detail necessary for fine route planning on the 1:62,500 scale maps (1 inch=nearly 1 miles) which provide a large enough area—in the neighborhood of 4,500 to 8,500 square miles—for overall route planning.

Where can a motorcyclist obtain these topographic maps? Many sporting goods and outdoor equipment stores stock a selection of USGS maps for their area. Otherwise, a rider can order the individual maps and free index maps for each state directly from the Geological survey in Washington, D.C. 20242 or the Federal Center, Denver, Colorado 80225. County and municipal maps can be obtained at most courthouses and city hall buildings. County and state highway departments are an additional source of detailed road maps and up to date highway information.

Travel Conditions An afternoon spin in the countryside will prove more pleasant if a rider has taken the trouble to gather some elementary travel information. Which routes are the most scenic and which ones carry the least traffic? Are some portions of the route unpaved? If so, is the surface dirt or gravel, is it filled with potholes and a washboard surface? Is gasoline and food available on the route? What kind of weather is predicted? Will the wind pick up in the afternoon, are mild temperatures in store, will the skies be overcast or clear? Road maps and local residents will provide a rider with ample information regarding his route. A familiarity with local weather patterns and careful attention to the daily weather forecast are equally important sources of information for the day cruiser.

Preparation Destination, route and road conditions all play a part in determining the appropriate preparations for a day of motorcycle cruising. If a rider plans to ride in the mountains west of town, he had better be prepared for the chilly temperatures and afternoon thundershowers that commonly occur at higher elevations. Will our motorcyclist take the interstate or stick to the secondary roads? High speed riding requires heavy clothing and appropriate face protection. Obviously, a last minute weather report can have an equally significant impact on a rider's preparation. Overcast skies or the prediction of afternoon showers should prompt him to take a full complement of rain gear and keep an eye on the skies above.

Regardless of where a rider is heading or what route he plans to take, there are certain preparations he should make before departing.

First, he should go over his machine. Gas, oil, transmission fluid, air pressure and battery electrolyte should be checked and brought up to proper levels. Clutch and brake cables and the drive chain should be adjusted for free-play and adequately lubricated. Second, a rider should decide what he will need to take along. Has he packed the ten essentials? These include the following items:

a helmet and eye protection
foul weather clothing
a map of the area
a screwdriver
a crescent wrench

a pair of pliers
a tire pressure gauge
a roll of plastic tape
a spark plug wrench and a spare spark plug
sufficient cash to meet all reasonable touring contingencies

Does our rider intend to take his camera or some food for when the munchies strike? What other items will he wish to bring along? Once he has collected all these items, they should be inspected to insure that they are in serviceable condition (for example, is there film in the camera?). Then each item should be packed in such a fashion that it is as accessible as possible yet protected from vibration and the elements.

Third, there is the problem of coordinating arrangements with others. If a rider simply intends to motorcycle by himself then he is free to depart at his leisure and head directly for his destination. When he is taking along a passenger or traveling with other motorcyclists, he and everyone else must decide in advance when and where they will meet and what if any special equipment is required. These considerations, though seemingly obvious, can make the difference between a relaxing, pleasurable day of motorcycling and a frustrating experience. How many riders have had their plans completely disintegrate on discovering that they forgot to bring along a spare helmet for their passenger or that they forgot which gas station was the agreed upon meeting place? Adequate predeparture planning can eliminate these last minute emergencies that will delay or even destroy an otherwise well organized spin in the countryside.

Long Distance Touring

Motorcyclists bitten by the touring bug soon develop an irresistible urge to strike out beyond a one day radius from their home base. For those so afflicted, day cruising will whet but not satisfy the touring appetite. The magic of the open road beckons them to Alaska, New England, California Mexico or some other equally distant and exotic place. Stories of the hardships and difficulties encountered by previous long distance riders serve only to stimulate further the urge of an intrepid cross-country cyclist to ride off in search of his impossible dream.

On occasion, a budding long distance rider has simply strapped a few possessions onto a newly purchased motorcycle and set off successfully in fulfillment of his dream. Acting sheerly on the basis of impulse is an open invitation, however, to disappointment or disaster. A lucky motorcyclist occasionally gets away with departing on a moment's notice for a far off destination. Experienced touring riders wisely refuse, however, to place their trust in good luck—which has an unfortunate habit of running out at just the wrong moment. Instead, seasoned long distance motorcyclists depend on extensive research, meticulous mechanical preparation and careful preplanning to eliminate as much uncertainty as possible. Not all riders will wish to follow precisely these practices. Yet every touring rider can learn from motorcyclists who have developed the art of traveling long distances in style.

Like the day cruising motorcyclist, a long distance rider must concern himself with the issues of destination, route, road conditions and predeparture preparations. But the problems confronting a long distance rider are

Even high performance touring motorcycles—pictured here is a 900 cc Kawasaki—can average as much as 50 miles to the gallon at highway speeds.

more extensive and complex than those a day cruising motorcyclist must face. We will therefore re-examine these three subjects from the viewpoint not of an afternoon spin through the countryside but of an interstate journey that can take a rider to the far end of the continent.

Preliminary Planning Presumably the long distance touring rider has already selected his destination. Perhaps it is a specific geographic location such as Bangor, Maine. Or it may be no more definite than the West Coast. Regardless, our rider knows approximately what location on the map he wants to reach. His first step is to calculate the approximate mileage to his destination and determine how many days it would reasonably require—barring any unforseen delays—to complete the trip. The first three questions a rider must ask himself are:

will I have sufficient time for the trip?
will I have sufficient money for the trip?
will I have the proper vehicle for the trip?

If a rider must honestly answer any one of these three questions in the negative, he might as well readjust his destination to conform with the constraints imposed by time, money and equipment. So long as the response to these questions is either an emphatic "yes" or even a "maybe," a prospective bike tripper should continue his planning effort, bearing in mind how he can best overcome a possible shortage of time, money or equipment. Perhaps by sticking to the interstate highway system or eliminating a few anticipated side trips he can shave down the duration of his trip by a day or so. If he has available ample time but doubts whether his motorcycle can travel the distance at high cruising speeds, then he can select an alternate route that will permit him to travel at a more leisurely pace.

Road conditions and weather considerations must also enter into a rider's preliminary planning. What temperature ranges can he expect to encounter? Does there exist a chance of encountering snow, freezing rain or other adverse weather conditions? If there is a distinct possibility he will encounter extreme heat, severe cold or snow, then perhaps the trip should be postponed or advanced to increase the likelihood of better weather conditions.

Alternately, a rider can adjust his route to avoid the possibility of inclement weather. Consider, for example, a fall trip from the Midwest to San Francisco. The most direct route would carry a rider directly westward across the central part of the nation. But September and October often bring sudden, early season snow storms to the mountain areas of Colorado, Utah and California. A rider might manage to slip through the high country before or after the snows fall. Then again, he might not be so lucky. So long as a motorcyclist can afford the extra time and distance, he might select an alternate route to the south that would carry him over the low lying and temperate areas of New Mexico and Arizona, then up the coast of California to his destination. In return for the extra 500 miles required to travel the southern route, a rider exchanges the possibility of a frigid cycling experience for the prospect of balmy temperatures and excellent cycling conditions.

Once a rider has begun to consider his route, the length of his trip and the road conditions he can expect to encounter, he has available sufficient information to begin planning equipment needs. Does he own adequate protective equipment and sufficient rain gear? Or will he need to invest in a foul weather riding suit? If his motorcycle is not presently equipped with a fairing and saddlebags, will he need to purchase either of these items? How much additional strain can his budget withstand? If he cannot afford everything he needs, which items deserve the highest priority?

Like most consumers, motorcycle riders often think first of their potential equipment needs and only later—if ever—consider whether they truly require the specialized accessories they intend to purchase. Reasoning in this fashion places the proverbial horse before its cart. Equipment related issues are difficult enough to answer sensibly after a rider has tentatively planned the length of his trip, outlined his route and considered the road conditions he can expect to encounter. Attempting to anticipate major equipment needs as a first step in preliminary planning is not only time wasting but often proves cash wasting, too. Many a motorcyclist has purchased the full complement of lightweight camping gear only to discover at the last moment that he lacks the luggage capacity or the inclination to take along his newly purchased gear.

Preliminary planning is the appropriate time for a rider to sort out the various considerations on which his principal decisions will be based. Time, money, distance and equipment needs must be weighed and balanced as closely as possible. From the preliminary planning effort there should emerge an overall framework of decisions that will serve as the basis for a multitude of subsequent decisions. To the extent that a rider does his preliminary planning well, he will build a sound foundation on which to construct his secondary decisions. When the planning process operates correctly, his subsequent decisions should fit together neatly with a minimum of loose edges. Decisions that emerge only with difficulty and that do not feel or look right are a sure warning sign that a rider must rethink the considerations on which those decisions were based. An unsound foundation will invariably yield shaky and ill-fitting decisions.

Rider Preparation From the vantage point of a passing automobile driver, long distance motorcycle touring looks deceptively easy. The rider seems to sit comfortably in an upright position as the wind tugs gently at his clothing and his motorcycle effortlessly pulls him along the highway. Appearances, however, often prove deceptive. In fact, long distance touring requires considerable psychological and physical conditioning. Just as a motorcycle deserves careful tuning before a lengthy highway excursion, so must its rider start off with the proper state of mind and an adequately conditioned body.

Since a rider's mental state is the key to enjoyable open road motorcycling, the subject of mental conditioning deserves special mention. Many a would-be long distance rider has embarked on his first motorcycle trip only to decide that long distance touring is not for him. Perhaps the vibration, windblast and noise detracted from his pleasure, the cold and wetness of a rainy day dampened his spirits or his body became exhausted from remaining in the same position for hours on end. It may have been a flat tire that chanced to happen miles from the nearest service station. Or perhaps he simply became bored after a hundred or so miles of steady riding. More likely, it was a combination of circumstances that convinced him to forsake immediately the not so obvious joys of long distance motorcycling for surf boarding, ping pong or some other sporting activity.

The specific reasons cited by our disappointed rider may well be valid. Even experienced touring riders complain of the vibration, wind, cold, heat, mechanical bothers and boredom that can diminish the pleasures of long distance riding. Although they know well how to protect themselves from each of these misfortunes, experienced riders are by no means immune to heat, cold, vibration and the elements. The difference between these seasoned touring riders and our motorcyclist cited above is largely a state of mind. A seasoned rider knows what to expect enroute and is mentally prepared for the rigors of long distance touring. It is not simply that he has a higher tolerance for discomfort than most of us. Rather, he accepts the fact that a long distance rider must endure occasional hardship in return for the pleasures of his sport. He understands and accepts the fact that when motorcycle touring—like a well known fairy tale character—is good, it is very, very good. But when it is bad, it can be very, very bad. The latter case occurs only occasionally, but an experienced rider is mentally prepared to cope with most anything that happens on a long distance trip. In fact, what a novice might consider hardships are for him simply part of the adventuresome experience called long distance motorcycle touring.

How does a beginning rider achieve the mental perspective of an experienced bike tripper? Obviously, he takes every opportunity to expand his open road riding experience. But it is important that he obtain his experience gradually. Setting off for Alaska on a newly purchased motorcycle is a sink or swim experience that can quickly drown a recently converted rider's enthusiasm for long distance touring. A more sensible approach would begin with a month or more of day cruising followed by progressively longer overnight motorcycling journeys. Once a rider has put a few months of gradually more extensive trips beneath his belt, he will know whether long distance motorcycling is his game. Moreover, he will have acquired the self-confidence and mental conditioning so important to the enjoyment of a major motorcycling expedition. By the time our rider finally sets out for Alaska his state of mind will help rather than hinder his progress northward. The competence that comes with experience breeds self-confidence and an enhanced sense of motorcycling pleasure.

A regime of gradually more extensive touring experience aids not only a rider's mind but his body, too. In addition to his other roles, a motorcyclist is an athlete who must work to sharpen his reflexes and strengthen his body. Motorcycle riding is both a mentally and physically demanding sport. Passing motorists might assume that the motorcycle is nothing more than a lazy man's bicycle equipped with an engine, a suspension system and various additional vehicular luxuries. Compared to the motorcycles of a generation ago, modern touring heavyweights are sinfully comfortable. Never the less, any motorcyclist who has ridden eight hours at a stretch knows all too well the importance of physical conditioning. Blisters about the hands, a sore neck, aching muscles and a sense of overwhelming fatigue are the lot of a rider physically unprepared for the rigors of long distance motorcycling.

Vitamin pills, a high protein diet and daily exercises might conceivably enhance a rider's endurance. But frequent motorcycling is the key to physical conditioning. By riding as often as possible a motorcyclist can condition precisely those muscles and reflexes that bear the strain of long distance touring.

Proper physical conditioning is important not only for its own sake, but also because it bears directly on a rider's state of mind. Numerous studies have demonstrated that physical fatigue can lead to dulled sensations, sluggish reflexes, poor judgement and irritability. A properly conditioned rider remains alert and responsive to his environment, and he will be a safer, more contented motorcyclist, too.

Vehicle Preparation Frequent day cruising enables a rider to better know himself and his motorcycle. Before setting out on a long distance excursion, a motorcyclist should become thoroughly conversant with every aspect of his vehicle. He is advised to familiarize himself with:

 the gasoline capacity and maximum cruising range of his motorcycle
 the reserve capacity of his gas tank
 the normal oil consumption of his vehicle
 optimum front and rear tire pressures
 the approximate mileage on his spark plugs and ignition points and the proper air gap for these components
 the approximate condition of his rear chain and how frequently it requires adjustment or oiling
 the ideal cruising speed of his engine

any periods of vibration that occur in the power band
the proper rear shock absorber setting with and without a passenger
any and all mechanical peculiarities of his vehicle

The final item on this list deserves special mention. All motorcycles are presumably created equal by their respective manufacturers. For example, one Guzzlefire 350 should be exactly identical to every other model from the same production run. Two examples of the same motorcycle occasionally display different performance, handling or braking characteristics, however. These differences, most of which are minor, contribute to the unique personality that many riders attribute to each motorcycle. Whether or not a rider can detect signs of a distinct personality in his motorcycle will depend as much on the rider as on his particular vehicle. Every rider owes it to himself and to his motorcycle to look for evidence of a mechanical personality. If a rider understands his cycle well enough to identify its special habits, then he knows it well enough to detect the sound and feel of impending trouble. The motorcyclist who knows his vehicle can guess intelligently whether a noise that suddenly issues forth from the innards is simply a sound of contentment or a hint of bigger noises to come if the situation is not corrected immediately.

Short range motorcycle excursions also afford ample opportunity for a rider to contemplate which accessories will materially enhance his touring pleasure. Perhaps he may discover that the factory installed handlebars, though adequate for city riding, require a fully erect sitting position. In that case he may wish to substitute a pair of wind cutting low rise handlebars. Alternately, a rider may find to his surprise that the factory delivered gas tank yields sufficient cruising range between refills to eliminate the need for a larger tank. Or our rider may conclude after an hour of riding through the rain that a fairing is well worth the price. These and related discoveries should take place not on the open road a thousand miles from home but at a time and place where a rider can take the appropriate action.

Motorcycle racers who expect to win, tune their engines at home and go to the track fully prepared to race. Long distance touring enthusiasts should follow a similar course of action. That trip to Mexico is not the time and place to decide whether you enjoy long distance riding or whether you need a road fairing and safety bars. The open road is for riding, not for worrying about decisions that should be made weeks or months before a rider departs for his destination.

Before setting off for his destination, a rider needs to have at his disposal an adequate range of tools and spare parts just in case worst comes to worst. Specifically what a rider will need depends on the motorcycle he will use and where he is headed. Obviously, a solo trip down the off-road country of the Baja Peninsula or across Western Canada requires more spare equipment (and more know how, too) than a fair weather jaunt from Chicago to New Orleans.

When motorcycles fall prey to mechanical troubles, the cause is usually traceable to one or another of a half dozen sources. Fortunately, most of these problems readily respond to simple repairs that can be performed in a few minutes time with the proper tools and the appropriate spare parts. No rider can expect to carry the equipment necessary to repair every mechanical misfortune that might befall him. Yet for well less than fifty dollars he can assemble a basic survival kit that will enable him to overcome better than four out of every five mechanical problems that commonly occur on the road.

First, of course, a rider needs to get the job done. A basic set of emergency road tools include the following items:

   a six inch crescent wrench
   a ten inch crescent wrench or an appropriate range of open
   end or box end wrenches
   a straight bladed screwdriver
   a phillips head screwdriver
   a spark plug wrench
   a pair of needle nose pliers with wire cutting jaws
   two spoon-ended tire changing irons
   a valve stem puller, tire pressure gauge and tube repair kit
   a can of compressed air for tire inflation
   a roll of plastic tape
   baling wire (about three feet)
   electrical wire (about three feet)
   an emery file and gap gauges for plugs, points and tappets
   tubes of non-hardening sealer and epoxy glue
   a silicon based lubricant

A rider may want to add or subtract from this list as he feels is appropriate. Harley-Davidson riders know, for example, that not all the king's horses and all the king's men can remove a tire from an older Harley without the proper allen head wrench to extract the bolts holding the wheel hub to the brake drum. Various other motorcycles require one or another specialized tool to perform otherwise simple and routine repair tasks. Although the items listed above are sufficient to cope with literally hundreds of minor mechanical problems, they comprise only a basic tool kit.

Tools, however, are of limited value without the proper spare parts to substitute for components that require more or less routine replacement. A basic spare parts kit would include—but not be limited to—the following items:

   a spare set of spark plugs
   an extra set of points and a condenser
   an extra masterlink for the drive chain
   spare headlamp, tail light and turn signal bulbs packed to
   protect them from vibration
   two spare fuses
   a few spare nuts, bolts and lock washers ranging in size from $1/4$
   inch to $3/8$ inch
   spare throttle and clutch cables
   an extra inner tube
   a small supply of oil
   a spare ignition key

Tools and spare parts should be housed so that they are out of the way yet reasonably accessible in the event they are needed. A rider can store the first

Note the spark plugs, tube repair kit and spare masterlink stowed inside the headlight housing.

Spare cables can also be attached to the bottom of a seat.

Note the spare brake and clutch cables taped to the existing control cables. The wind cutting handlebars on this high performance heavyweight enhance rider comfort at high speeds. But the jeweled bicycle horn has no place on a motorcycle.

half dozen spare parts listed above along with various tools inside the headlamp housing, where they will be protected from the elements yet ready for immediate use as appropriate. Extra cables can be taped to the existing control cables in the style of an enduro or ISDT rider to facilitate a quick changeover in the event a cable snaps. Alternately, a rider may wish to wrap his spare cables in a loop and tape the loop to the underside of the seat or to the upper frame rails located beneath the seat. A compressed air can, spark plug wrench, tire irons and a number of other items can be taped to the frame rails, stored on the top of the rear fender or stowed at the bottom of a saddlebag. Ultimately, only a rider's ingenuity is the limiting factor in determining where and how he stores the tools and spare parts needed to render mechanical first aid.

Only a rider's imagination will limit the uses to which he can put these tools and parts. As every shadetree mechanic knows, there is the right way to do things and the way they sometimes must be done to get a vehicle running again. An inner tube, for example, is useful not only in the event of a flat tire but also because in an emergency it can be fashioned into strong elastic bands for fastening down loose parts or insulating a cracked gas tank or fender from further destructive vibration. Epoxy glue will overcome a multitude of problems ranging from loose electrical connections to a punctured primary chaincase. In an emergency the success of a repair job is measured not by its beauty or its conformity with established shop procedures but by whether or not it works.

A mechanical first aid kit can be likened to a medical first aid kit in that it may sit idle for months or even years before an emergency occurs. Once the need arises, however, the kit is suddenly worth its weight in gold. It is as true of motorcycling as of medicine that an ounce of protection is worth a pound of cure. In other words, careful attention to preventive maintenance procedures can save a motorcyclist from having to test his ability to diagnose and remedy mechanical ills that occur on the open road.

Motorcyclists planning to embark on a long distance tour need more than ounce of prevention. Their motorcycles deserve a thorough checkup to identify and remedy potential sources of mechanical failure. Here is a partial list of items that should be checked and adjusted or serviced:

    ignition timing—checked and adjusted
    spark plugs—checked and adjusted or replaced as necessary
    ignition points—checked and adjusted or replaced as necessary
    valve clearance—checked and adjusted
    carburetion—adjusted
    air filtration—checked and cleaned or replaced, as necessary
    fuel filter(s)—checked and cleaned as necessary
    engine oil—drained and refilled
    oil filter(s)—cleaned as necessary
    suspension oil—drained and refilled as necessary
    primary chaincase oil—checked and topped up or refilled
    transmission lubricant—checked and topped up or refilled
    primary chain—checked and adjusted as necessary
    final drive chain—checked, cleaned, adjusted or replaced as necessary

drive sprockets—checked and replaced as necessary
control cables—adjusted and oiled or replaced as necessary
chasis—lubricated
battery—checked and topped up
lightbulbs—checked and replaced as necessary
stop light switches—checked and adjusted as necessary
spokes—checked and tightened as necessary
tires—inspect carcass, check pressure and adjust as necessary
rear suspension—adjust for the proper load range
wheel alignment—check and adjust as necessary
all nuts, bolts and fittings—check for proper tightness

Attending to these maintenance chores may prove time consuming and bothersome for the rider eagerly awaiting the moment when he can set off for his chosen destination. Spokes and cables and gooey oil are not the stuff of which a touring rider's dreams are made. Yet some time spent with a tool box and owner's manual is excellent therapy for a rider whose head is in the clouds contemplating far off places. The rider who knows his motorcycle can travel confidently and secure in the knowledge that he has done everything possible to insure a troublefree journey. If mechanical problems do occur, he can take comfort in the fact that they happened sheerly by chance rather than by reason of his own negligence.

Final Preparation Final preparation for a long distance motorcycling trip consists of working out the bothersome details that are so easily put off until the last few days. These details include final route planning, packing and a few paperwork chores. We will look at each of these items in turn.

Once a rider has selected his destination and decided approximately how he intends to get there, a strong temptation exists to overlook any further route planning considerations. But knowing where you intend to go is only the first step in planning a trip. Detailed planning requires that a rider obtain a full set of maps and lay out his itinerary mile by mile. The American Automobile Association or another motorists' club is an excellent source of detailed road maps. Alternately, oil company maps provide sufficient detail to satisfy most overall route planning needs. Regardless of which maps a rider uses, he should, however, mark his route with a wide tipped felt pen of the sort that allows printing to show through beneath the ink. Where the opportunity exists, it can prove helpful to outline two routes: a through highway and a more leisurely scenic route. By marking out these two routes and designating them as the primary and alternate route (using, perhaps, two different colored inks) a rider need only glance at his map to decide when and where he can diverge from his basic route plan.

Once a rider has outlined his itinerary, he should calculate how many miles he can reasonably expect to travel each day and select appropriate overnight stops, which should be marked on the map with an alternate overnight stop in the event he makes less distance than expected that day. As a final precaution the intrepid tourer should confirm the feasibility of his route with a travel association or with someone who has taken the same journey recently. Are there scenic sidetrips our rider might not know of? Has he planned to use a highway that is undergoing extensive repair work? Or perhaps a new route will shortly replace a section of rough, obsolete highway. Road maps rarely convey this sort of information. First hand reports are therefore an invaluable aid in the final stages of planning an itinerary.

Properly detailed maps are of little use, however, unless a rider has ready access to them. Motorcyclists cannot rest their maps on the dashboard or unfold them on a car seat for convenient reference as the need arises. Nor can a two-wheel rider safely unfold a map or return it to his pocket without first bringing his vehicle to a complete stop. So long as a motorcyclist plans to remain on a single highway for an extended distance, route finding will present no problem to him. But when his route requires frequent switching from one highway to another, he will wish to check his progress frequently.

Experienced long distance riders faced with this problem often carry a plastic map case and cut or fold their maps into manageable sections before inserting them into a travel case. Some riders tape or strap maps to their gas tanks for quick reference as needed. Whatever method of handy storage and display a motorcyclist selects is largely a matter of personal preference. Yet it is important that he have some system of conveniently and safely referring to his maps.

A long distance rider's motorcycle is a mobile home. Since it is a small home with limited storage space, its occupant must decide carefully how he intends to store his possessions. In Chapter 9, on the accessory market, various alternative methods of storage are discussed in detail. Regardless of what method a rider decides on, he must pack his possessions carefully and insure that his luggage capacity is sufficient to handle the task at hand. As a rule of thumb, heavy items should be packed as low as possible and toward the front of a motorcycle in order to keep the center of gravity down and to prevent overloading the rear wheel. Moreover, luggage must be attached to a motorcycle as securely as possible if it is to resist the various forces working to pull it loose. Windblast and vibration can undo in a few minutes time what a motorcyclist has struggled hard to lash down.

Day cruising experience is one way to experiment with various methods of securing luggage. Riders who have not previously subjected their packing system to the ravages of the open road should pretest their fully loaded motorcycle before setting off for real. A brief dress rehearsal will enable a rider to check the balance of his loaded motorcycle and to troubleshoot any problems that arise. As in other matters, an ounce of prevention is worth the proverbial pound of cure.

Motorcycle touring, like other forms of travel, offers an opportunity to escape from the worries and concerns of our daily lives. Traveling, by whatever means, should be a liberating experience that refreshes the soul and invigorates the body. Successful traveling requires that a traveler devote his full attention to experiencing a new environment. He must free himself as much as possible from the petty problems that might otherwise detract from his traveling pleasure.

Most final planning is a matter of clearing away just those problems that might otherwise dampen the enthusiasm of even the most ardent long distance rider. Packing, route planning and last minute maintenance chores usually occupy a rider's mind as his departure time draws near. These concerns should not, however, cause him to overlook the financial and legal preparation necessary for a hassle-free travel experience.

Almost invariably, a rider ends up spending more money on his trip than he anticipated. Not only do planned costs mount up more quickly than a traveler expects, but unanticipated expenses further drain his wallet. Preparing a realistic budget is the first step toward estimating travel expenses. Each and every item for which a rider can reasonably expect to pay should figure into the calculation of his overall budget. Because unexpected costs inevitably occur, a rider should inflate his budget by 10 to 20 percent more than his anticipated costs. Good fortune or prudent spending habits may enable him to return home with a portion of his nest egg intact. More likely than not, of course, he will be grateful that he took along as much money as he did. To further protect himself, a motorcyclist might consider carrying a portion of his funds in some form other than cash. A checkbook works well enough, so long as the world includes trusting souls who accept personal checks from a stranger. A spare money order, or better yet traveler's checks, are near perfect methods of carrying money. Traveler's checks are especially handy in that they are protected against accidental loss or theft and can be cashed at nearly any commercial establishment in the country.

Credit cards present an alternative way to insure sufficient reserves for most unexpected expenses. Not only can a credit card owner go now and pay later, but in the event of theft he is protected by federal law for all liabilities in excess of fifty dollars. As an added bonus, the credit card route allows a traveler who is so inclined to total up his charges and discover just how much the trip did cost.

Motorcycle riders are no more prone to legal woes than any other category of traveler. Accidents do happen, however, and even the most cautious rider can run afoul of the law. In the event of an accident or a traffic violation, a motorcyclist must usually produce a variety of documents including a valid driver's license, his vehicle registration certificate, an ownership certificate, inspection sticker and insurance card with a current policy number. Failure to produce one or more of these documents can prove embarrassing and downright inconvenient. A rider may know that his motorcycle is properly registered, inspected and insured and that he is a legally licensed motorcycle operator. But law enforcement officers—and judges, too—will assume the worst unless presented with black and white evidence to the contrary. Given sufficient time, a law enforcement officer can usually verify that a rider is indeed the legal owner of a motorcycle and lawfully permitted to operate that vehicle. Verification, however, often proves time consuming and aggravating. Simply knowing that he remembered to bring along the proper documents can give a rider peace of mind and save him from an embarrassing predicament.

The Open Road

The emphasis of this chapter on planning, preparation and attention to a thousand details may prompt a reader to wonder if bike tripping is worth the effort. The answer is emphatically yes. Two-wheeled touring adds a whole new dimension to long distance travel. The tourist who switches from an automobile to a motorcycle can rediscover the sights, the sounds, the smell and the feel of the countryside. Predeparture planning will in no way inhibit a rider's enjoyment of the open road. In fact, careful planning and preparation allow a rider to concentrate his attention on the pleasures of long distance touring. Seen from this perspective, preplanning is the key to maximizing a motorcyclist's freedom on the open road.

Experienced long distance riders take to the highway not with the intention of setting new speed records or sticking inflexibly to a fixed schedule but in search of individual freedom and personal joy. Bike tripping is basically a leisurely way to travel. The rider who uses his motorcycle as the fastest method of getting from one point to another usually succeeds in his mission. But he must forsake the relaxed pace and sense of discovery that are the hallmarks of motorcycle touring. Riders who want to get there first or travel in the lap of luxury might just as well take the four-wheeled route to their destination. Like hiking, motorcycle touring is neither the most efficient nor the most comfortable way to travel. Both activities belong less to the realm of reason than to the kingdom of the spirit. Other methods of motorized travel may prove equally pleasurable, but motorcycle touring yields a unique sense of joy.

Chapter 8

Competition Cycling

The sport of motorcycle racing is nearly as old as motorcycling itself. Soon after the first motorcycles were produced, owners and manufacturers offered to match their machine against anyone who claimed to have a faster motorcycle. The early days of racing produced a number of remarkable records and various memorable personalities. But modern motorcycle racing has emerged only in the past two or three decades. Since it affords the spectator and participant alike a sense of excitement and satisfaction matched by few other sports, motorcycle racing has grown in popularity to the point where today a thousand or more race courses are scattered across the country.

According to myth, motorcycle racing is an insanely dangerous sport practiced by barrel-chested men with tattoos on their arms and dirt under their fingernails. Nothing could be further removed from the truth. Most forms of motorcycle competition are relatively safe and sane activities, boasting an injury rate record low enough to gladden the heart of any insurance executive. Ask a motorcycle racer about the dangers of the sport and he will probably tell you that the most hair-raising part of racing is not the actual event itself, but the drive along our highways to and from the track. The point is a valid one. Unlike highway driving, motorcycle racing involves skilled drivers, concentrating totally on the operation of carefully prepared machines that travel in a single direction. Is it any wonder that many racers are terrified at the prospect of being rammed head-on by a drunk or inexperienced car driver, operating an unsafe vehicle in the on-coming lane of traffic?

Motorcycle racing includes its share of daredevil types. Go to most any race track, however, and you will observe that the majority of competitors are quiet-spoken men, often thinly-built and even bespectacled. For the

COMPETITION CYCLING 133

Professional level dirt bike racing—demonstrated here by Jim Pomeroy—requires skill, courage and years of experience.

most part, they are knowledgeable mechanics and careful riders accustomed to rationally calculating every move they make on the race track or course. It could hardly be otherwise. Winning is a large part of what racing is all about, and to win, a motorcyclist and his machine must both cross the finish line in one piece. Having the fastest motorcycle helps, of course, but strategy and decision making are equally important. When a reporter once asked the prize winning skipper of a sailboat how he had beaten the opposition, the captain replied that he had made fewer mistakes than his competitors. Motorcycle racing is the same way: the rider who makes the fewest mistakes is most likely to win.

Without doubt, motorcycle racing is an exciting spectator sport. But is it a sport for the everyday rider, too? The answer is that it all depends on how badly a rider wants to go racing and in what kind of racing he wants to participate. We can draw a distinction between those persons who live *from* racing and those who live *for* racing. If a motorcyclist wants to fall in the first category; that is, if he hopes to make racing a professional career, then he had better trade in his car for a van or camper, pack his bags and begin moving full-time in road racing, motocross or whatever motorcycle racing circles are his special interest. He must read everything he can on the subject of racing, ask a thousand questions of experienced racers and race only to win. Perhaps, if he is lucky and patient, motorcycle racing will become his vocation.

Motorcyclists who wish to race as an avocation or hobby should first decide what form of racing interests them and how much it will cost to compete. The time and dollar costs of racing vary greatly, depending on the kind of events a rider wishes to enter. For example, road racing usually requires an expensively modified, single-purpose motorcycle, a large stock of spare parts and the time necessary to campaign the road racer at tracks located in widely scattered areas of the country. On the other hand, trials or enduro racing demands a smaller initial expenditure, lower upkeep costs and little travel, since trials and enduro courses are common in every part of the country.

A prospective racer must also know his own goals. If his sole interest in racing is to cross the finish line first, then he will need a motorcycle as fast and reliable—or faster and more reliable—than any other bike competing against him. A beginning rider may rest assured that he will pay and pay dearly for the privilege of owning such a motorcycle. Moreover, he will quickly learn that a fast, reliable competition motorcycle is time consuming and expensive to maintain. If a competition rider is equally interested in the fun of racing, if finishing first or even second or third is not his sole objective, than he can go racing for a substantially smaller investment of time and money. Typically, he would begin by obtaining a competition motorcycle that is not tuned to win or explode, whichever comes first. He would race in one of the smaller or middle-capacity classes in order to keep his expenses low and to make his mistakes where the speeds are not so great or the competition perhaps so fierce as in the larger-capacity classes. After a season or two of learning, he would trade up to a faster motorcycle in his present class or begin competing in larger-capacity events.

Before starting out on his weekend racing career, the prospective competitor should bear in mind that racing usually requires more time, more money and more skill than he anticipates. Paying the parts bill, doing the maintenance work and keeping in condition are racing related activities a spectator rarely observes. The dramatic activity that happens out on the race course is only the tip of an iceberg, the rest of which lies hidden from public view. From a racer's viewpoint, this submerged portion of the iceberg is equally important and far more time consuming than the hour or less actually spent racing his motorcycle each week.

Every competition motorcycle rider must also remember that in addition to whatever obligations he feels for his own self-preservation, he also carries certain obligations toward his family, friends and fellow riders. Most motorcycle racing associations require each rider to wear various forms of protective equipment. Any prospective racer should make certain he has the best possible safety equipment. This means he should not show up at the track with any old helmet that will sneak by the requirements, but with the sturdiest helmet, best riding leathers, and safest goggles that money can buy. The reasons for this policy are simple enough: a rider may sell or trade his motorcycle every season, but the protective equipment he begins with will last him (hopefully) for many years of racing. There is also a second and more important reason not to seek false bargains in safety equipment. When an engine fails because a rider lacked the money for the best possible parts or labor, the damage can be repaired and the parts replaced. Human heads and other body parts, however, are difficult to repair and usually impossible to replace.

Many motorcycle events require a rider to compete only against the clock. In these events a nasty accident may sadden a rider's friends, raise the sponsor's insurance rates, or generate unfortunate publicity for the sport. But the accident will rarely endanger anyone else. Much motorcycle racing, however, is a cooperative activity. It is cooperative not in sense that riders help each other win, but to the extent that riders are expected to avoid endangering each other—intentionally or through carelessness and lack of experience. A safe racer (which is no contradiction in terms) goes to the track on the day of a race not to learn the rules and techniques of racing, but to race. He has already learned from a rule book or from experienced racers what the different signal flags mean and he has learned how to control his motorcycle under the conditions he may reasonably expect to find at the track. He has also adequately prepared his motorcycle for the race and outfitted himself with the proper protective clothing.

To an inexperienced spectator, a motorcycle race may look like an out-of-control mass of riders battling unmercifully for first place. Good racers do battle and battle hard to win. Yet they rarely ride out of control. Instead, most racers operate their machines just inside the limits of control. When an inexperienced or careless racer fails to heed a warning flag, spills his machine in a corner or develops a major oil leak, he endangers not only himself, but other racers as well. Most competitors will spill their own motorcycles to avoid running over a downed rider, thereby throwing away their chances of victory and risking injury to themselves also. The riders involved in a pile-up as the result of another person's error have every right, therefore, to expect that the error resulted not from gross carelessness or inexperience, but from a reasonable mistake that they themselves might have made.

As a rule of thumb, the most dangerous moment in motorcycle racing

The action is intense and the pace fast at the front of the pack.

occurs when the riders in a curved track event enter the first turn. At that point, the contestants have not separated into small groups strung out along the track. Nearly the entire pack tries to rush through an area that lacks the space for everyone to pass at the same time. If one rider near the front goes down, he may carry with him various other competitors. Obviously, this is no place for the novice racer, who should begin his career remembering the biblical adage that someday the first shall be last and the last shall be first.

Every once in a while we hear or read about the novice racer who took his motorcycle to the track, put in a fresh set of spark plugs, cinched down his helmet, and rode off to victory in the first race he ever entered. If by reason of skill or good fortune a beginning racer should find himself at or near the front of the pack, the rules of charity and sportsmanship require only that he try to keep up the good work. Prospective racers should bear in mind, however, that success stories like this one are eventful only because they happen so rarely. The starting racer will generally learn more and last longer by staying well back in the pack, watching and profiting from the mistakes made by other riders. Up front, where the competition is usually sharpest, a racer has no time for anything but riding as hard as he can. Everything depends on intuitive judgements and reflex motions developed during the course of previous races. By hanging toward the rear, a novice rider will not win the race. Yet he can more readily acquire the reservoir of judgement and reflexes needed to win.

These words of caution are not intended to dampen the enthusiasm of a prospective motorcycle racer intent on winning. They are offered only to acquaint him—or a prospective spectator—with the realities of racing and especially those forms of racing that require a racer to negotiate turns rapidly in the company of other competitors. Obviously, competition motorcycling is a more dangerous and demanding activity than watching football on televi-

Following the leader is the way to learn the game of motorcycle racing.

sion. But an intelligent motorcycle racer, competing in amateur events, certainly exposes himself to less danger and discomfort than a big league football player. Modern motorcycle frame and suspension systems permit a rider to accurately control his motion while modern safety equipment affords him much protection from the results of a collision. The rest is up to the racer himself.

Motorcycle racing events are limited only by the different kinds of terrain a motorcycle can negotiate. Since properly equipped motorcycles can go most anywhere, racing events can take place through a swamp, up the side of a mountain, or along a paved stretch of asphalt. The following compendium of motorcycle racing activities is not intended to be an exhaustive description of every kind of motorcycle racing. Instead, it is designed to offer readers an introduction to the more popular forms of racing practiced in this country and abroad.

Road Racing In Europe, motorcycle road racing is a big-time spectator sport drawing crowds of 100,000 or more to watch professional stars battle it out. Road racing courses once followed country roads and city streets, but today nearly all road racing takes place on specially laid out circuits with smooth pavement and carefully engineered curves. Nevertheless, road racing requires great skill and courage. Grand Prix motorcycles are capable of speeds in excess of 150 MPH. Road racing motorcycles operate at engine speeds as high as 15,000 RPM and even 18,000 RPM; they transmit their power through complex and delicate transmissions, with as many as 8 or 10 speeds.

Amateur or sportsman class road racing is common in Japan, England, Europe and at various tracks in this country. Some racing associations maintain "production racing" classes that allow contestants to compete on more or less factory stock or production motorcycles. These machines differ from ordinary touring motorcycles only in minor respects like spark plugs, tires, handlebars, sprocket ratios, and the care with which the engines have been assembled. But most road racing takes place on extensively modified motorcycles equipped with streamlined fairings, extensive engine modifications and special frame components. A road racing motorcycle must accelerate quickly, brake rapidly and negotiate turns with great speed and precision. High power output, low weight and mechanical reliability are important attributes of a road racer.

Road racing is more popular in England and on the Continent than in this

The late Jarno Saarinen prepares to bank his Benelli 500 cc road racer into a turn.

COMPETITION CYCLING 139

This Harley-Davidson powered drag racer is a study in quality workmanship and functional design. The low handlebars and rear set foot pegs allow the rider to assume a wind cutting prone position.

country. But American fans of the sport, though few in number, claim with some justification that it is the most elegant and demanding form of motorcycle racing.

Drag Racing This American contribution to racing is a contest of straight line acceleration over a paved course, usually 1/4 mile long. The object is to travel that distance in the shortest possible time, starting from a standstill. Contestants race individually or in pairs and their performance is measured by precise electronic clocks, accurate to a one-hundredth of a second. Drag racing is among the most popular and exciting forms of motorcycle racing in this country. Racing classes vary in accordance with engine size, fuel used and the extent to which the engine and other components have undergone modification. Contestants race every kind of motorcycle from small displacement touring bikes to multiple engine dragsters that burn exotic fuels, containing their own built-in oxygen supply. These single-purpose dragsters generate tremendous amounts of power (in some cases 200 or more horsepower); they are designed from the wheels up for the sole purpose of accelerating as rapidly as possible from a standstill to the end of a quarter mile course. The quickest machines can cross the finish line in less than 8 seconds, at a terminal speed of above 160 MPH. Piloting a motorcycle dragster is a difficult and dangerous task, but the drag racing of production motorcycles is a relatively safe sport. The rider operates his bike along a wide, smooth lane of pavement at a relatively low average speed. During the period of greatest acceleration, near the start, he is traveling slowly and only for a brief interval of less than ten seconds does a rider travel in excess of normal highway speeds.

Drag racing, or sprinting as it is called in England, has acquired the reputation of a crude and simple-minded sport, requiring little skill or imagination on the part of a racer. The facts, however, fail to support this myth. Single-purpose drag racing motorcycles are elegant and sophisticated racing machines, constructed according to the same standards found on grand prix racing cars. Beneath the starkly functional simplicity of these motorcycles rest enormously efficient engines, specialized alloy frame components and highly efficient drive systems.

Drag races are often won or lost by a few hundredths of a second. One or two pounds excess tire pressure, a small error in engine timing or a few extra teeth on a rear wheel sprocket make the difference between victory and coming in second. Therefore, drag racing places a special premium on meticulous attention to tuning details as well as rider skill. The briefest delay at the starting line or while shifting will generally cost a rider the race. Quick, controlled reflexes are a prerequisite for drag racing. To win, a rider must waste no human or mechanical motion whatsoever.

Street Racing This specially American form of racing requires two or more willing participants and a section of roadway ordinarily used for public transportation. The race may follow a straight or a winding circuit and it may be as short as a city block or as far away as the state line. The rules of street racing are entirely at the discretion of the participating racers, who also determine what, if any, prize is due the winner. The advocates of street racing emphasize that it is an uncomplicated, democratic and spontaneous form of competition. No special equipment or certification is required; anyone possessing a running motorcycle and elementary driving skills is free to participate on a moment's notice.

The opponents of street racing include many motorcyclists, most citizens and all law enforcement officers, judges and legislators. Street racing, they claim, endangers the safety of racers and anybody else who accidently stumbles into their path. Opponents point out that street racing frequently results in the revocation of licenses, the destruction of motorcycle components and the injury of human beings. Moreover, its practice invariably prejudices the public image of motorcycling and leads inevitably to stricter laws governing the use of motorcycles and less courteous treatment of motorcyclists by both law enforcement officers and the motoring public. Street racers respond that these consequences are a small price to pay for the pleasures of their sport. In fact, it is probably the illegality and danger of street racing that lend the sport much of its appeal.

Whether you, as a motorcyclist, indulge in street racing is ultimately a personal decision. Before you decide in favor of doing so, remember that it is far and away the most deadly form of non-professional motorcycle racing and it is always injurious to the reputation of other motorcyclists.

Flat Track Racing Flat track racing is a primarily American sport, practiced on circular, hard-packed dirt courses by professional and serious amateur racers. Tracks are usually $1/4$ mile to $1/2$ mile in length and the contestants circulate in a counterclockwise direction for a half dozen or more laps. Flat track racers use specially adapted production motorcycles and on some of the longer, smooth tracks, top speeds in excess of 100 MPH are common. Most riders use their inside or left foot, which is equipped with a smooth surfaced metal plate, as a "third wheel" for extra balance in the corners.

The high speeds and congested traffic of a flat track course make it a dangerous form of racing. The majority of spills result in only a few bruises, but

The action on a flat track is fast and rough.

serious injuries are not unknown. Flat track racing is primarily a spectator sport, the motorcycle equivalent of stock car racing. Many spectators claim it is the most exciting form of motorcycle competition. To find out for yourself, watch a few races. But do not try the sport unless you are already an experienced dirt rider and reconciled to the prospect of high-speed spills.

Scrambles Scrambling is the American version of European motocross racing. It is the most popular and widely practiced form of motorcycle racing in this country and it is an almost entirely amateur racing event. A scrambles course can be laid out on most any dirt surface. The course is usually about $1/3$ mile long, with a series of left and right-hand turns of varying radius and usually one small jump for added excitement. Envision a small road racing course carved in the dirt and you will have an accurate picture of a scrambles track.

Local motorcycle associations usually sponsor scrambles racing in a variety of classes with riders grouped both in accordance with the engine size of their motorcycles and their level of ability. Therefore, competitors are evenly matched and the races closely fought. Riders wear an approved helmet, leather riding suit, goggles or a face mask, gloves and sturdy boots. The motorcycles used are either production racers, which can be purchased in nearly ready to race form from a dealer or specially modified street or trail riding motorcycles. Modifications include the addition of high performance engine components, lower gearing, sturdy handlebars, special dirt tires and the removal of lights, heavy fenders, mufflers, horn and any other accessories that do not contribute to the racing performance of the motorcycle. Scrambles motorcycles are light, powerful and agile versions of ordinary trail or "street scrambler" bikes. Long-term mechanical reliability and street legal equipment are sacrificed for greater power throughout a wide range of engine speeds and low overall weight. The short straightaways and sharp curves of a scrambles course place a premium on maneuverability and quick acceleration rather than high top speed.

Nearly all scrambles racing takes place at speeds below 50 MPH. The rough surface of a scrambles track and the congested traffic conditions result in numerous spills and minor accidents. Due to the low speeds and ample protective equipment, scrambles riders rarely suffer significant injury. Most riders who fall quickly remount their motorcycles and continue the race only slightly the worse for wear.

Although the racing is hard, it is almost always clean and friendly. The competitors usually know each other well and bring their family and friends to help with the mechanical and household chores. Family picnics and laughter are an integral part of scrambles racing. The racers strive hard to win, but they are equally concerned that they and their friends enjoy themselves, too. The good cheer and hard racing makes scrambles competition a near ideal sport for the spectator and competitor alike.

TT Racing This hybrid form of competition employs a course combining elements of the scrambles circuit and the flat track. Riders negotiate gentle, high-speed sections, sharply cut corners and, usually, a jump. TT racing requires that a rider master the techniques of flat track and scrambles racing. The ideal TT motorcycle should have the sheer power of a flat track racer and the agility of a scrambler.

Motocross Motocross is the European equivalent of scrambles racing. But a motocross track is rougher and steeper than a scrambles course and the competition includes professional athletes for whom motocross racing is a way of life. The major European motocross racers are internationally known stars. The quality of racing is very high and the competition is correspondingly fierce. Professional motocross racers neither give nor ask for mercy. They race to win, since that is their principal means of earning a livelihood.

Motocross racers compete on motorcycles that are similar in looks and performance to scrambling motorcycles. Factory sponsored racers ride exotic one of a kind bikes loaned to them by their sponsor for the express purpose of winning. Riders without the good fortune of factory sponsorship, use production model European or Japanese dirt racing motorcycles, modified to meet the special conditions of motocross. Recently, American scrambles racers have begun to construct their own motocross circuits and master the art of riding them.

Enduro Racing The object of enduro racing is not to cross the finish line first, but to cross it at the specified time or to reach it in the first place. Enduro riders must negotiate a variety of difficult countryside—hills, swamps, thickly wooded forests, rivers and sand washes—at a specified average speed. Announced and unannounced checkpoints are set up to monitor the progress of contestants and score them on the basis of their punctuality. Enduro races are similar to sports car rallying except they are conducted on motorcycles across rough terrain.

Sheer horsepower is not an important attribute for an enduro motorcycle. Enduro racing requires a motorcycle with high ground clearance, light weight, low-speed engine power, maneuverability and a high level of mechanical reliability. Most contestants modify trial riding motorcycles to suit their personal definition of the ideal enduro motorcycle. Since much of the action in an enduro race happens far out in the woods, this form of competition does not rank high as a spectator sport. The low cost of competing and the high level of safety make it an attractive form of competition for riders. Enduro racing is hard work and requires considerable skill to do well, but it is nearly as safe and much more fun than watching Sunday afternoon television.

COMPETITION CYCLING 143

A factory prepared enduro motorcycle. Note the knobby tires, enclosed rear drive chain and tank mounted carrying pack. The wire between the brake pedal and frame prevents the accumulation of brush in that space.

Hare and Hound Racing The origin of the term hare and hound racing is uncertain, but some racers claim it is a polite way of referring to a wild goose chase. Hare and hound racing requires a vast amount of open space; it is a speed contest to reach a distant objective—known as the finish line—either by the shortest possible route or along a vaguely defined course. The desert country of Southern California and Nevada is the home of hare and hound racing. A hundred or more motorcycles often start out together and race across the sand washes and juniper-studded hills in a wild effort to reach the finish line first in their class. After the race is over, contestants and sponsors begin the search for riders whose motorcycles suffered mechanical ailments or collided with immovable objects before completing the race.

In recent years, the concept of hare and hound racing has grown to include annual endurance races across a variety of inhospitable terrain. The Elsinore Grand Prix is one example; another is the famed Baja course, which begins near the Mexico/California border and continues to La Paz, at the southern tip of Baja California.

The various forms of hare and hound racing require a motorcycle with the sheer speed of a flat track racer and the reliability of an enduro bike. Since brute horsepower and reliability rarely occur together, riders usually opt for a compromise between these two virtues.

Hill Climbing Hill climbs follow the shortest possible path from the bottom of a steep hill to its summit. Hill climb courses fall into two categories: "climbable" hills, where the victory goes to the riders who reach the summit in the shortest elapsed time; and "unclimbable" hills, where the winner travels the greatest distance toward the summit. Most of the "unclimbable" hills have been conquered in the past few years. But only expert class racers can reasonably hope to reach the top of these imposing hills. Most riders must remain content to fail partway up the slope.

144 CHILTON'S COMPLETE GUIDE TO MOTORCYCLES

A hill climb competitor starts on his way toward the top.

This sturdy "knuckle head" Harley-Davidson was still competing at local hill climb events after nearly a quarter century of use. Note the shortened fuel tank that concentrates weight on the front wheel of the vehicle.

Spectators lend a helping hand to a rider who almost made it to the summit of a Missouri hill climb course.

Nearly any trial riding or dirt racing motorcycle can be adapted for the purpose of hill climbing. Sheer horsepower is not important. Instead, a hill climber needs a broad, smooth range of usable power and a low overall gear ratio. Cleated dirt tires and low weight are important to successful hill climbing in the amateur classes. Expert class hill climbers use a variety of specially modified motorcycles, usually equipped with low, long frames, small front wheels, chained rear tires and massive engines of 1,000 cc's or more. These ungainly motorcycles are useful for no purpose other than climbing hills. In the hands of a skilled rider, however, they accomplish their mission with awesome efficiency. Watching an expert hill climber assault a formidable course is among the most dramatic sights in any form of racing.

Hill climbing requires a certain measure of raw courage combined with the ability to unload safely from a motorcycle partway up a steep hill. Riders who lack one or both these attributes should content themselves with a spectator role.

Observed Trials This form of motorcycle competition emphasizes rider style, precision and control above all else. An observed trials course consists of various "sections" which a rider must negotiate without stopping or placing his foot on the ground for balance. Slippery, off-camber paths, rock strewn creek beds, wet grassy hills and steep gulches are excellent trials sections. A trials rider must thread his way over fallen logs, up slippery rocks and through deep bogs. In England and Europe trials riding is an important international motorcycle event with factory sponsorship and professional riders. In this country trials riding remains almost exclusively an amateur form of motorcycle competition, like enduro riding.

Proper trials riding requires a specialized motorcycle with little steering rake, high ground clearance, very low overall weight and a broad power band that supplies tractor-like amounts of low speed torque. Trials machines have large diameter, narrow-section front tires and the controls are positioned, so that the rider can operate them comfortably while standing up on the foot pegs. Trials riders rarely use a motorcycle seat; by standing, a rider can readily shift his body weight and the weight of the entire motorcycle in response to the varying obstacles he must negotiate.

Trail riding experience is a useful training ground for observed trials competition. If your experience and interest lie in slowly negotiating rough terrain, then it is likely you will find observed trials an ideal form of competition. Be prepared, however, for your share of frustration. Trials riding looks to be a simple enough sport, but it requires years of practice to do well.

Ice Racing Northern and Eastern Europe are the center of ice racing, but the sport is also practiced in Canada and some of the colder parts of this country. Ice racing is like flat track with the exception that the riders race on a forzen lake or river. It is a cold and difficult sport. Despite the fact that ice racing motorcycles are equipped with steel spikes in their front and rear tires, traction is less than perfect and riders must take care to avoid the churning spikes of their own and competitors' tires. Most motorcyclists consider ice racing to be somewhere on the far side of the lunatic fringe. But advocates of the sport, though few in number, claim it is a perfectly reasonable and enjoyable form of competition.

Sidecar Racing Sidecar racing is rare in this country, but common in En-

Trials riding demands intense concentration and precision control at all times.

gland and the rest of Europe, where road racing and certain forms of enduro competition include sidecar classes. A sidecar passenger does not merely go along for the ride. He must move about with the agility of an acrobat in order to balance his three-wheeled vehicle. When a sidecar rig turns in the direction opposite the chair, the passenger must hang out on the far side of the sidecar to counterbalance the tendency of the third wheel to lift off the ground. When the rig turns in the direction of the chair, the passenger shifts

The grand old man of trials riding, Sammy Miller, demonstrates his flawless style before a group of spectators.

his weight off the third wheel and onto the rear wheel of the motorcycle. The driver and passenger must work together in perfect coordination to keep their vehicle on course and traveling at the maximum possible speed.

Sidecar racing outfits look not at all like the three-wheeled utility vehicles used by police agencies and delivery services in this country. The rider kneels down inside a streamlined fairing, while his passenger occupies a narrow platform resting a few inches off the ground. Low slung frame designs and short legged front suspension systems radically reduce the overall height of a sidecar rig to the point where the handlebars rest only a few feet off the ground. Watching a sidecar driver and passenger drift their exotic rig through a corner at somewhere near 100 MPH is among the most dramatic sights in motorcycle racing.

Bench Racing Bench racing is the simplest and safest form of racing. It requires only two or more participants and any area suitable for animated conversation. The length of bench racing sessions can vary from a few minutes to an entire afternoon or evening, depending on the endurance of the

Sidecar road racers are among the most exotic and beautiful—but also most dangerous—of all competition motorcycles.

competitors and their ability to spin convincing yarns. Bench racers generally try to achieve one or both of the following objectives: to obtain or exchange information about various motorcycle designs or kinds of motorcycle racing and to demonstrate to the competition their superior courage or experience in one or another area of racing.

Although prior racing experience and the ownership of a racing motorcycle are important assets for participation in a bench racing session, they are by no means necessary. A participant need only speak knowledgeably on the subject of racing, regardless of whether or not he has accumulated any previous racing experience. From the viewpoint of a prospective competitor, bench racing sessions can prove a highly valuable training ground. Bench racing participants are generally eager to share their experience and their mistakes. Therefore, a novice can harvest a vast fund of information on most any aspect of motorcycle racing once he learns to distinguish the wheat from the chaff of bench racing.

A Final Word on Racing

Millions of motorcycle owners throughout the world have little interest in racing. For them, motorcycles are simply an efficient and convenient means of transportation. Riders who regard a motorcycle from a purely practical standpoint, as an economical and expedient way of getting from one place to another, are unlikely to participate in any form of motorcycle competition. Nevertheless, these riders are indebted to the sport of motorcycle racing for the rich dividends it has paid them. The reason is quite simple. Due to the demand for smooth, reliable, fast motorcycles, manufacturers must con-

Amateur racing is a way of life each Sunday afternoon for many thousands of Americans.

stantly improve their products. One important way they do this is to adopt innovations and improvements born on the race course to production touring and trail bikes. Many of the design features of the modern motorcycle—such as telescopic front forks, swing arm rear suspensions, rotary valves, alloy cylinder heads, overhead camshafts and hydraulic disc brakes—are a direct application of innovations that proved their worth on racing motorcycles. Since motorcycle manufacturers quickly apply the lessons learned from competition, the production touring and trail riding motorcycles of today offer a level of performance and reliability superior to the pure racing machines of twenty years ago. The high pitch of racing related research and development in this country, in Europe and in Japan promises to yield an equally healthy dividend of production motorcycle improvements during the years to come.

In the United States, most motorcycles are used as sporting and recreational vehicles in addition to whatever practical value they have for getting their owners to school, to work or out to the park on Sundays. Manufacturers throughout the world provide the American motorcycle market with the kind of high performance motorcycles Americans demand. The spirited machines we purchase are often little more than comfortable, detuned racing motorcycles equipped with the accessories required for use on public roadways. If

Spectator participation (seen here at the Spanish Gran Prix) is an integral part of motorcycle racing.

you enjoy operating a motorcycle like most Americans own, then you will probably also enjoy watching the experts demonstrate the full riding potential of a machine that often differs only superficially from your own motorcycle.

Perhaps watching competition riders may convince you to go racing yourself. Competition experience will make you a more skillful and confident motorcyclist, if you apply the safety lessons learned on the track to riding on public roads. But even if you have no desire to race, try watching a few competition events. The experience can help you become a more knowledgeable and competent motorcyclist, in addition to whatever pleasure it brings you.

Chapter 9

The Accessory Market

In the United States, in Europe and elsewhere around the world, motorcycles serve as more than two-wheeled platforms to transport a rider from the proverbial point A to point B. They become, in addition, an extension of their owner's ego and an expression of his identity. Motorcyclists have a near universal propensity—though not always the budget—to modify their two-wheeled vehicles in response to the dictates of individual need and personal preference. For reasons of economy or ideology, the underdeveloped and socialist nations encourage only minor utilitarian modification of their domestic products. Most everywhere else, however, motorcyclists can pick and choose from among a dazzling array of accessories. Cycle manufacturers and specialty parts producers compete fiercely for their share of the vast accessory market. A motorcyclist intent on proving the point could readily spend more money for accessories and modifications than he paid to purchase his basic vehicle.

The practice of tailoring motorcycles to suit individual taste has from time to time been carried to extreme limits. A few years back English motorcyclists seeking the ultimate vehicle were in the habit of switching entire engine and frame units. Thus was born the Triton, a Triumph powered Norton, and the Vinton, a hybrid Norton equipped with a 1,000 cc Vincent powerplant in its frame. American motorcyclists, not to be outdone, have created a variety of equally radical motorcycle designs ranging from Peter Fonda style choppers and behemoth full-dress Harley-Davidsons to Porsche powered touring cycles, 5,000 cc drag racing bikes, and a few even more bizarre designs.

The creation of a fully custom motorcycle demands, of course, near fanatical dedication coupled with an ample bank account and considerable mechanical ingenuity. When the accessory market fails to accommodate his specialized needs, the custom bike builder must produce his own parts. Custom motorcycle building, as it is practiced in the United States, England and on the Continent, is less a hobby than a way of life requiring the skills of an engineer and the temperament of an artist. The result, however, often justifies the effort required to produce it. Quality custom builders create one of a kind motorcycles that are at once mechanical masterpieces and works of art that have earned a place in respected art galleries as models of outstanding modern design.

Although most motorcyclists can admire the result of a custom builder's effort, they lack the inclination or resources to own a completely rebuilt motorcycle. Instead, the average motorcycle rider is content simply to modify his present motorcycle with various bits and pieces of equipment.

But which bits and pieces does a rider select? The contemporary motorcyclist is faced with the task of choosing from among many thousand accessory products, each one of which promises to enhance in one way or another his motorcycling pleasure. The marketplace is so vast that an unwitting victim could easily find all his spare moments consumed by the act of thumbing through the hundred or more catalogs of accessory equipment and trying to decide what items are best for him. Not only would our victim need to familiarize himself with those general products of use to most every motorcyclist, but he would also be obliged to check out the suppliers that offer their goods exclusively for one particular kind of motorcycling. Entire booklet length catalogs are available in every area from motorcycle clothing to motocross riding and long distance touring. Motorcyclists in need of even the most specialized parts can often find a producer or distributor devoted exclusively to his interests. Thus a motorcyclist in search of road racing parts for a Norton would discover that even his needs are served by a specialty distributor—in this case the Paul Dunstall Organization, Ltd., which has built an international reputation as a producer and supplier of parts and even entire motorcycles for the competition oriented Norton enthusiast.

Each rider must of course decide for himself what his own needs are. As the wise Romans declared: *"de gustibus non est disputandum."* Put into simple English, this means that in matters of choice there is no disputing. It is not the objective of this chapter to specify which or what accessories a motorcyclist should buy, but rather to indicate the choices he has available and how he can best fit these choices to his particular needs.

The single most important consideration in selecting accessories is the use to which they will be put. The enduro or desert rider has no more need for a set of fiberglass saddlebags than the long distance touring enthusiast requires a spark arrestor or upswept exhaust pipes. In fact, accessories that enhance a rider's comfort or safety under one set of circumstances can prove downright dangerous when used in circumstances other than those for which they were intended. Safety bars (or crash bars as they used to be known), for example, can protect a rider and his machine in the event of a mishap on the highway. But those same bars installed on an enduro or trail bike would serve to detract from a motorcyclist's riding pleasure and increase the likelihood of an accident.

Regardless of the uses to which a rider puts his motorcycle, whether it is

THE ACCESSORY MARKET

on the highway, on trails or around a race track, nearly every accessory he might want can be grouped into one of five broad categories. Motorcycle accessories serve basically to increase a rider's *safety* and *comfort* or to enhance the *appearance*, *performance* or *serviceability* of his motorcycle. Some accessories serve a dual or even a triple purpose—aiding, for example, a rider's comfort and the appearance or reliability of his motorcycle. Other accessories may prove valuable for one purpose only at the cost of compromising equally important virtues. The radically elevated handlebars fashionable among outlaw motorcycle gangs may enhance a motorcycle's appearance (beauty, of course, being in the eye of the beholder). These handlebars are, however, clearly detrimental to rider safety and comfort. Such considerations are important to the selection of accessories and later in this chapter they will be discussed in more detail. For the present, however, we shall consider only the principal purpose for which motorcycle accessories are intended.

Safety Accessories

Various accessories related to motorcycling safety have already received mention in Chapter 5, on motorcycling safety. But the subject of motorcycle safety is so important to the development and perhaps even the survival of motorcycling, that several of the issues raised earlier deserve more extensive discussion.

The accessories that enhance motorcycling fall into two categories: those that a rider wears and those that he attaches to his motorcycle. We will examine each of these categories in turn.

Helmets It is a well known fact that the contents of the human head heal only slowly and imperfectly if at all after suffering substantial injury. Moreover, medical science has conclusively established that the brain is both necessary for the continuation of life and not readily subject to transplant from one owner to another. Many parts of the human body can, when necessary, be replaced. But nobody has yet discovered a suitable substitute for the original equipment head with which each of us is born.

Given these irreducible facts, it behooves every motorcyclist to protect his skull and the contents thereof with a specially designed motorcycle helmet. For a long time it was thought that any old helmet would do, so long as it included a hard shell and protective foam rubber or suspended straps to keep the wearer's skull out of direct contact with the shell. Then, following the death of a young sports car driver from massive head injuries, research was begun in earnest to determine why existing helmets so often failed to save lives. The Snell Memorial Foundation (named after Peter Snell—the above driver) and other research organizations quickly discovered the answer. Existing helmets did not dissipate the energy of impact. Instead, they merely absorbed the impact and then transmitted most of it to their contents—namely, the human skull. Further research soon led to the development of true energy absorbing liners, which are now used in the construction of all quality safety helmets. Football helmets, surplus German Army helmets and related headgear may provide a user with protection against abrasion or the impact caused by falling off a door step. For any other use, however, such as absorbing the impact of a vehicle accident, they are of little more use than the cardboard shipping boxes in which they arrive. Even the British, who long favored "porridge pot" style helmets (so named for their shape and their level of effectiveness), have adopted a compulsory helmet law requiring motorcycle riders and passengers to wear safety helmets that meet modern impact standards.

In the United States, the industry sponsored Z90.1 standard, and the stiffer Snell Memorial Foundation 70 Standard, insure that a conforming helmet will provide a user with protection from impact. Helmets that meet these or other protection standards will so state on the helmet and in the manufacturer's advertising information. No motorcyclist should consider wearing or allowing a passenger to wear a helmet that fails to meet the Z90.1 standard. Motorcyclists should bear in mind, however, that Z90.1 is a minimal protection standard; higher quality helmets can meet much more demanding performance tests than those required for Z90.1 certification.

It is a trite but valid observation that in safety helmets as in most other consumer product areas, the customer usually gets what he pays for. Certainly there may be a few bargains available on the helmet market. As was noted previously, only an engineer equipped with a testing laboratory can tell for sure whether that helmet with the foxy bronze metallic paint job is a good buy for the money or a nicely painted invitation to the world beyond. Unless a prospective buyer knows for sure, he should select a helmet somewhere near the top of the line offered by a well recognized manufacturer of safety helmets.

Furthermore, it stands to reason that the more helmet a rider buys, the more protection he will receive. The "shorty" style helmets favored by police departments may have much to offer in the way of style and comfort. Unfortunately, they tend to slip out of place at highway speeds, which is inconvenient and dangerous. They also provide no impact protection for the area about the ears and the back of the skull, which can prove painful and perhaps fatal.

Full coverage helmets are available in two styles: the traditional open-face type, long favored by motorcycle riders and the enclosed competition style helmets that extend around the jaws and the lower portion of the user's face. Enclosed helmets are hotter, heavier and more expensive than the open-faced models, but they offer greater structural rigidity and invaluable protection to a rider's jaws and lower face area. For everyday riding, the open-faced style is considered adequate by most motorcyclists. The greater strength and protection afforded by an enclosed helmet makes it a sensible choice, however, for the rider who favors safety above all else and for most every kind of racing and high speed use.

Patches of reflectorized material are an important and in some states a mandatory accessory to the safety helmet. Helmets should be visible both during the day and at night. A bright color, such as international orange or traffic safety yellow, aids visibility during the daytime. Reflectorized material is necessary, however, to enhance night time visibility. How much material to use and where to place it is a matter of rider preference in states that do not require the use of such material. Motorcyclists who are in doubt might consider the statutes of one Western state, which declare that each motorcycle helmet "shall be coated with a reflectorized substance, or have attached thereto a reflectorized material, on both sides and the back thereof, with a minimum of four square inches of such coated substance or attached material in each of such locations."

THE ACCESSORY MARKET 155

A full coverage helmet and face shield offer maximum rider protection on the road and off.

In other words, use twelve square inches of reflectorized material divided in equal proportion (but cut in whatever shape you desire) between the two sides and the back of the helmet.

As a final word of caution, remember that a safety helmet only has a safe life of a few years, presuming that the helmet simply rests on the wearer's head waiting to serve its ordained purpose. After a helmet is called upon to serve that purpose, namely, protecting a user's head from impact with hard objects, the helmet should be replaced or returned to the manufacturer for relining even if the outer shell is not cracked or otherwise damaged. The reason, which deserves repetition here, is simple enough: helmet liners are designed to absorb a single massive impact, which compresses the lining material and makes it unfit for additional use. If a helmet has once saved your life or prevented a crippling head injury, then it has surely earned a vacation to the factory or full retirement.

Face Protection Facial protection equipment includes a variety of accessories designed to protect a rider's mouth and lower facial area, his eyes, or his entire face. Mouth protectors, or moulded synthetic mouth guards, are used primarily by motocross riders and other off-road riders plagued by stones and other hard objects hurled at them from the wheels of competing motorcycles.

Face protectors, in turn, serve to protect a rider's eyes or his entire face. Full face protectors include a wide variety of plastic shields that either snap onto a helmet or flip up and out of the way when not in use. Unlike goggles, face shields offer the advantage of comprehensive wrap-around protection for the entire face. Bugs, stones, road tar and related objects are kept at a safe

A helmet with goggles and a visor, a mouth protector, protective gloves, well padded riding pants and knee-high boots—the working dress of a motocross racer.

distance from the user's face. For a number of years following their introduction, bubble style face shields were prone to a variety of drawbacks: they fogged up unexpectedly, scratched easily, flipped up at the wrong moment, burned readily and caught the windstream when a rider turned his head while traveling at high speed.

Improved designs have, however, overcome most of these liabilities. New surface coatings reduce the chances of fogging or scratching while improvements in shape and chemical composition have enhanced the aerodynamic characteristics and flame resistant properties of most shields. So strong are the modern shields that at least one brand has withstood the blast of a 12 gauge magnum shotgun shell fired from a distance of 25 feet. About the only problem to which even the better designs remain prone is flying mud. Competition riders overcome this problem by taping several face shields on top of each other. As soon as the front shield becomes dirty they tear it off, exposing a clean shield beneath. Road riders, who cannot afford the luxury of discarding dirty shields every few miles when the weather turns rotten, must be prepared to stop quickly in the event that a passing vehicle deposits a facefull of mud or dirty water on them.

Undeniably, face shields afford a rider the maximum available protection. Unfortunately, the shields are hot in summer and confining all year round. For city riding, low speed competition events (as in trials events or enduro races) or short distance highway use, the full face shield offers more protection than most riders feel is necessary. The alternative, of course, is a pair of goggles or quality glasses. Goggles have the advantage of providing near total eye protection: the lenses are shatterproof plastic or (hopefully) impact resistant glass and only the smallest particles of foreign matter can enter through the ventilation slits. Eyeglass wearers traditionally have been faced with the problem that only oversize goggles would fit around their glasses, and even the largest goggles are not a comfortable fit. Presently, however, a workable though expensive alternative (about $50) is available in the form of closefitting motorcycle goggles with the user's prescription bonded to the viewing surface.

Last and certainly least in the field of eye protection are ordinary glasses, either in the form of a rider's own eyeglasses or an accessory pair of (usually tinted) riding glasses. Unlike a face shield or motorcycling goggles, glasses have the important disadvantage that they allow foreign matter to enter the eye from around the sides. In addition, they can also slip off the user's face at highly unfortunate moments.

In most states, glasses are legally adequate eye protection. Motor vehicle statutes commonly include statements to the effect that "the operator and any passengers thereon shall have in place on his helmet a face shield or shall wear, covering his eyes, goggles or eyeglasses made of safety glass or plastic lenses." Although glasses may be perfectly legal, to use them in place of additional eye protection is highly imprudent in nearly any form of competition riding or for highway and expressway use. Ordinary glasses may be the most comfortable form of eye protection. Alas, they are also the least effective protection available. Riders who either must wear prescription glasses or who insist on wearing glasses in place of other eye protection, should insure that their lenses are safety treated for hardness or, better yet, constructed from plastic and that the frame bows are securely fastened behind their ears or secured by a connecting elastic band.

Body Protection   Since human skin is no match for pavement or for cold and wet weather, motorcyclists should dress appropriately. Shorts and a tee shirt may be comfortable hot weather motorcycle apparel, but they are a standing invitation to a painful case of pavement rash in the event of a mishap. Abrasions, in fact, are only one danger to which a thinly clad motorcyclist exposes himself. Hot exhaust pipes and cylinder fins, protruding bits of sharp metal, flying hunks of gravel and a sudden rainshower are unavoidable facts of motorcycling. Proper dress will go a long way toward mitigating their unhappy consequences.

Leather jackets and pants provide the best available body protection from abrasion, impact and the elements. Unfortunately, leather is also expensive, hot in the summertime and evocative of the black leather jacket look that has done so much harm to the public image of motorcycling.

As for the question of expense, the issue is simply one of how much money a rider has to spend and how highly he values his own skin as opposed to cowhide. In regard to the public image of leather in general and black leather jackets in particular, there is no rule that requires a motorcyclist to wear black as opposed to brown or some other color leather garment. Nor, of course, are all leather pants skin tight nor all leather jackets equipped with metal studs, rabbit tails or eagles on the back. A customer in the market for leather motorcycling attire has available a wide range of attractive styles and colors from which to choose.

Foot Wear Like other parts of the human body, feet require protection from abrasion, heat and impact. Sandals are no more appropriate gear for a motorcyclist than are penny loafers useful to a mountain climber. Sturdy shoes are the minimum footgear for motorcycling and any riding in the dirt requires high boots preferably equipped with low heels and a steel arch support.

Although motorcycle boots should be sturdy, sheer size and strength are not useful features. Massive reinforced toes and wide, soles will in fact prove a liability as they detract from a rider's ability to work the gear shift level and rear brake pedal. So select a boot that is comfortable and sturdy though not oversize for the task at hand.

Hand Wear Gloves serve to protect hands from abrasion, the elements and the sweat, grime and consequent blisters produced by gripping the handlebars for hours at a time. In warm weather, thin, perforated, open-backed driving gloves work best. To reduce the likelihood of blisters, insist on a pair with seamless palms. Cold weather driving, for those riders willing to endure the tribulations of winter cycling, requires well padded gloves. One wintertime expedient long favored by European riders is handlebar muffs. These heavily insulated accessories fit over the handlebar grips and controls. A rider places his bare or lightly gloved hands inside the muffs. The result? Warm fingers and positive contact with the handlebar control levers.

Kidney Belts In days gone by motorcycles had rigid frames and their riders suffered from various forms of kidney trouble. In response to the constant pounding, riders began to strap across their lower backs a wide leather belt often decorated with metal studs and various mottos or insignias. Modern motorcycle suspension systems and the widespread use of asphalt paving have eliminated the need for kidney belts on the highway. But rough country riding and especially off-road competition subject kidneys to dangerous pounding; consequently, many dirt riders continue to use body supporting belts. These modern belts are not, however, adorned with studs nor even made of leather. Instead, they are orthopedically designed from elastic and various other synthetic fibers to hold a rider's kidneys gently yet securely in place.

Auxiliary Lights Most full size touring motorcycles come equipped from the factory with a bright headlight and a readily visible tail lamp. Some smaller motorcycles and machines intended largely for off-road use, roll away from the assembly line with only minimal lighting—a headlight that rivals the effectiveness of a flashlight strapped to the handlebars and a taillight/brakelight visible only on moonless nights. If a motorcyclist finds himself in possession of a vehicle equipped with inadequate lighting, he must

Handlebar mittens are a warm and safe solution to one problem of cold weather cycling.

decide whether to risk his neck riding at night, to venture out only between the hours of dawn and dusk or to install substitute lights.

Fortunately for riders who elect the last alternative, the accessory market is loaded with bright taillights and powerful driving lamps able to bring the brightness of day into an otherwise gloomy night. But before installing additional lights, a rider should insure that the power output of his alternator or generator can supply the additional wattage. If not, the electrical system must be reworked to the point where it can produce the extra current.

Horns The same that was said of lighting holds true of horns also. Highway motorcycles equipped with a shortlived or weak voiced horn deserve an effective replacement. Here again, a motorcyclist can choose from among a wide range of accessory horns including air-driven trumpet systems powerful enough to wake the dead.

Mirrors Most state laws require that a motorcycle be equipped with at least one rearview mirror. A mirror, or better yet two mirrors, may not be a substitute for direct visual inspection of what lies behind. Nevertheless, rearview mirrors allow a quick and accurate check of following traffic. Most manufacturers distribute their own mirrors, which attach to a threaded mounting post on the handlebar. Original equipment mirrors, because they are produced for a particular motorcycle or series of motorcycles in mind, generally afford a clear, vibration-free view to the rear.

Alternately, a rider may buy a universal style accessory mirror designed to fit a wide variety of motorcycles. Such mirrors vary considerably in quality, so the buyer must beware. A cheap mirror is no bargain if it rusts, vibrates, or reflects imperfectly. Beware also the convex mirror favored by a few riders. These nasty items afford a wide field of view but at the cost of making all objects seem more distant than is actually the case. Consequently, a forgetful rider, which includes most of us at one time or another, can readily suppose that an overtaking vehicle is much farther away than it actually is. The result of this supposition could prove most unhappy.

Safety Bars Safety or crash bars are tubular bars attached to the front and sometimes also the rear of a motorcycle to protect the machine and its rider in the event of a spill. In theory, the motorcycle slides along the ground on its safety bars rather than the operator's leg or chest. Sometimes the bars work and occasionally they do not. On large touring motorcycles used for highway travel, safety bars make sense. They are of less value, however, on smaller motorcycles and a dangerous liability in any situation where they might snag on a tree branch or curb, thereby causing an accident.

Comfort and Convenience Accessories

The number of comfort and convenience oriented accessories presently on the market is countless. Plush seats, padded passenger backrests, accessory handlebars, custom handlebar grips, ride-off centerstands, cigarette lighters and running boards are but a few of the convenience items available to a motorcyclist. Any attempt to catalog and evaluate each and every one of these accessories would require a separate book, and a lengthy one at that. Yet the number of major comfort oriented accessories is relatively small. Consequently, the following section will be limited to a brief examination of only the more common accessories in this category.

Windshields Until a decade ago, windshields were the sole form of protection a motorcyclist had against the wind, rain and flying objects. At that time, most touring motorcycles were massively heavy and powerful machines that cruised at speeds which seem relatively modest in light of our modern standards. Given these circumstances, a windscreen was an entirely practical and nearly necessary touring accessory. True, the windshield was aerodynamically unstable in crosswinds and it consumed considerable horsepower. But it was the only choice available.

Even today a few traditional touring motorcycles, such as the Harley-Davidson Electra Glide, still look right and travel reasonably well with a windshield. For short distance touring, however, a faceshield is a cheaper, safer and more attractive alternative, while for long distance travel, a full fairing offers undeniable advantages over the plastic windshield. Moreover, the lighter weight touring motorcycles lack the sheer power to pull a windshield at high speed and in adverse wind conditions.

The Fairing Motorcycle fairings came into existence as streamlined shells bolted onto the forward portion of road racing motorcycles. The shells served to increase top speed, reduce fuel consumption and protect a racer from windblast. The road racing fairing, however, requires that a rider crouch low behind a narrow and confining shell.

A properly designed fairing will enhance the pleasure of long distance riding. Note the adjustable air vents on the windscreen of this model.

Road fairings, on the other hand, combine the virtues of a traditional windshield and the road racing shell. A swept back windshield is attached to a fiberglass housing that surrounds the front of the motorcycle. The headlight, turn signals, and often the instruments are attached directly to the fairing.

Fairings used for road touring often reduce wind resistance and increase gas mileage slightly, depending on their size and efficiency. But fairings have come into widespread use on touring motorcycles because they afford an increased level of rider comfort. Wind, rain, bugs and the other tribulations of long distance touring are kept at arms length from a rider, thereby allowing him to better enjoy the pleasures of motorcycling. Quality fairings do not come cheaply and their installation is usually accompanied by an increase in mechinical noise, which is reflected upward toward the rider. In addition, fairings reduce the air circulation available to an engine at low speed and they preclude any off-road excursions. Nevertheless, the creature comforts available from a fairing are sufficiently compelling that they are coming into increasingly widespread use among long distance riders.

Well styled fiberglass saddlebags, safety bars and a handlebar fairing/windscreen need not detract from the appearance of a heavyweight touring machine.

Luggage Carriers Luggage carriers are available in a variety of shapes and sizes ranging from simple parcel carriers to massive luggage racks and elaborate contoured fiberglass saddlebags. A motorcyclist can spend anywhere from half a dozen dollars to upward of one hundred dollars for the privilege of carrying his personal possessions about in style.

The kind of luggage carrier a motorcyclist will require depends largely on the kind of motorcycling he intends to do. The long distance touring enthusiast who plans to take it all with him will need oversize saddlebags and, if there is room, a metal rack on which to tie additional luggage. Day riders, boulevard cruisers and the dirt rider require only a limited carrying capacity. For them, the traditional answer is a bolt-on luggage carrier attached to the rear fender. A rider can either lash his books, extra clothing or what-not to the rack, or he can place his possessions in a pack for protection from the elements and strap the pack to his luggage carrier.

Exposed luggage carriers, however, are not without their dangers. The straps that hold the luggage in place can work loose and wend their way into the spokes or the luggage itself can work loose and end up in the same place or out on the highway. Improbable as this chain of events may seem, more than one rider has come to grief as a result of it happening.

A neater, safer and highly economical solution for carrying less than a full load of luggage is available in the form of a baja pack or strap-on cycle pack. This roughly cylindrical or rectangular pack is strapped onto the rear fender, seat or gas tank of a motorcycle. A zipper closure and waterproofed material provide a neat, protected environment in which to store extra clothing, tools, lunch, or even a female companion's purse.

Sissy Bar The sissy bar is a tubular back rest extending upward and backward from the rear of a motorcycle seat. Sissy bars range from a short loop of tubing to towering monuments decorated with ornamental spikes, iron crosses and like configurations. Moreover, all sissy bars serve as supporting back rests for a passenger and provide an inexpensive (usually) and convenient attachment point for items of luggage ranging from a spare helmet to an entire backpack.

Despite the usefulness of a sissy bar, they are not without their drawbacks. Beauty, of course, is in the eye of the beholder. Yet many motorcyclists would argue that except on a specially customized motorcycle, the sissy bar is visually unattractive. More practically, the bar invites a passenger to lean backward into a semi-reclining position. The resulting passenger comfort is obtained, however, at the cost of distributing a passenger's weight rearward. Since motorcycles carry the majority of their weight on the rear wheel, the addition of a passenger simply aggravates this condition. As a passenger leans back onto the sissy bar, the balance point moves even further toward the rear, thereby tending to create an unstable and dangerous distribution of weight. The practice of attaching luggage to a sissy bar also places additional weight precisely where it is least needed: behind the rear axle and well above a motorcycle's center of gravity. Every additional pound of weight placed above the existing center of gravity detracts from the handling and responsiveness of a motorcycle. Side-mounted saddlebags can also place an excess burden of weight on the rear wheel, but they offer the advantage of carrying that weight as near the ground as possible.

Footrests The chopper fad and a revived interest in long distance touring have brought in their wake a renewed search for enhanced rider comfort. Chopper riders, who enjoy a semi-reclined seating position, hit upon the expedient of mounting a metal bar perpendicular to the front downtubes of a motorcycle frame. The bar is equipped with rubber footpegs on which a rider can rest his feet while cruising along the highway. The result is a relaxed riding position that provides a restful respite from the normal footpeg location.

So long as a motorcyclist encounters no impediments to his smooth progress down the highway, high-mounted footrests are perfectly functional, except that elevated feet raise a motorcycle's center of gravity. In the event that a rider is suddenly required to apply the rear brake or change gears, however, he must shift his weight distribution abruptly and reach down blindly for the foot controls. A slight shift in weight and an equally minor delay in reaching the foot controls may not seem consequential. Yet under the wrong circumstances they can make the difference between rounding a corner safely or shooting off the road; between maneuvering out of danger or striking a vehicle head-on.

In other words, elevated footrests should be used cautiously or not at all.

Appearance Accessories

The temptation to dress up, redecorate or otherwise modify the appearance of a motorcycle is an irresistible urge for many owners. Whether the consequences of this urge are worth the effort is largely a matter of individual judgement. Since standards of beauty are, as we said before, formed in the eye of the beholder, there exist no universal criteria with which to judge the product of a customizer's labor.

Nevertheless, a customizer should decide which route he wishes to take before wandering through the marketplace of bobbed fenders, pleated vinyl seats, trumpet-shaped mufflers, fluted gas tanks, translucent red ignition wiring, elongated fork tubes, decorative license plate holders, chrome plated chain guards and rearview mirrors shaped in the form of an iron cross. By careful selection of his accessories within the framework of an overall plan, an owner can transform the appearance of his motorcycle into an attractive expression of his individual taste. On the other hand, the haphazard attachment of appearance accessories will usually compromise the aesthetic appeal and often degrade the mechanical integrity of an otherwise perfectly attractive and functional motorcycle. Factory designers know their business well; an integrated and thoughtful approach to redesign is usually necessary to improve upon their effort.

The original equipment accessories provided by the manufacturer are most always of high quality and carefully engineered to function properly on that motorcycle. If a motorcyclist is going to modify the appearance of his machine, then he should first determine to his satisfaction that the accessories he plans to install are of at least as high a quality as those the manufacturer saw fit to install at the factory. He should also satisfy himself that the intended improvements will in no way compromise the performance, safety or reliability of his motorcycle. Modifications to a motorcycle's suspension or exhaust systems deserve especially careful consideration. Both these systems receive special attention from factory engineers. Any attempt to replace them with more attractive components nearly always detracts from the reliability and all around performance of a motorcycle.

Performance Accessories

Ever since the first primitive motorcycles began roaring down dusty roads, their owners have sought ways of going just a little bit faster than the manufacturer intended. Over the years, motorcycle producers have developed an increasingly sophisticated technology of speed in order to satisfy their customers. But many of these customers continue to search out ways of extracting still more performance from the factory product.

There are only three basic methods of enhancing the performance of a motorcycle: its overall weight can be reduced, its coefficient of friction can be reduced or its power output to the rear wheel can be increased. The reduction in weight by lightening or removing parts usually requires sacrificing comfort or legality since the horn, lights, battery, fenders and centerstand are usually the first parts to go. To decrease the drag or air resistance requires the addition of a bulky competition fairing. Moreover, the effect of decreased resistance is significant only at high speeds. So most motorcyclists intent on obtaining improved performance resort to modifications of the engine itself.

More power can be extracted from an engine by drawing a greater volume of air-fuel mixture into the combustion chamber(s) of the engine, by burning that mixture more thoroughly or by extracting the burned mixture more effectively. Oversize carburetors, larger valves, highlift long duration camshafts, high compression pistons, lightened flywheels, modified ports, long stroke crankshafts and tuned exhaust systems all serve to accomplish one or more of these aims. The addition of any one or two engine modifications will usually yield a marked increase in peak horsepower. When a number of modifications are undertaken in concert, however, the results can prove startling. A docile 40 horsepower day cruiser becomes a screaming 50 or even 60 horsepower roadburner. When the same performance enhancing accessories are attached to a large displacement superbike tuned by the factory to produce 60 or more horsepower, the result is awesome to behold. Zero to 60 MPH acceleration times dip into the five second bracket or below while top speed climbs into the range of 120 MPH and beyond. The rider of a fully modified, large displacement motorcycle has at his disposal more horsepower than most grand prix road racers had on tap only 15 years ago.

But motorcyclists intent on converting their vehicle into something other than the factory intended, should carefully examine the costs and risks before marching down to the nearest parts counter. In the first place, quality performance accessories do not come cheaply. A rider can easily sink many hundreds of dollars into the performance hardware needed to fully rework an engine. Second, there is the problem of skilled labor. If the owner is not himself a qualified mechanic, he will need the services of one who is. The time and knowledge required to properly build up a reworked engine will run a rider's total bill for parts and labor to half a thousand dollars or more. Third, there is the question of what our intrepid performance enthusiast ends up with. He may have the fastest motorcycle in West Eggville—when the motorcycle is running right. Performance modified engines are no joy to live with. They usually start hard and require frequent, even constant, tuning and they break down with alarming frequency. Worst of all, modified engines usually develop their increased horsepower only at high engine speeds. They often produce substantially less low and mid-speed torque than before modification. In other words, the low speed performance and all around flexibility of an engine generally suffer for the sake of increased top-end power.

Finally, the novice speed enthusiast should realize that only half the battle of building a high performance engine is installing the parts right. The other half of the battle involves the fine tuning needed to get the engine running right. Simply hanging some performance parts on an engine can be an invitation to disaster. For example, if a long duration, high lift camshaft or a more efficient exhaust system is installed, the carburetors must usually be rejetted, colder spark plugs installed and the ignition timing must often be modified. Failure to undertake one or more of these steps can result in the near total destruction of a modified engine. The cost of buying and installing performance accessories is often only the first in a series of expenditures that confront the owner of a modified engine.

So what is a performance oriented motorcyclist to do? Probably his best bet is to purchase a larger, more powerful motorcycle equipped from the factory with the power and performance he desires. Alternately, he can undertake either those modifications that enhance performance while in no way compromising the smooth, flexible running of a motorcycle. Or he can embark on a gradual program of modifications, intended to accomplish a specific objective.

The modifications that improve performance while extracting no liabilities will not produce a radical increase in power. Instead, they consist of the fine tuning work and the minor handling modifications that pick up where the factory left off. Precise ignition timing, spot-on carburetion, correct tire pressure and the appropriate weight fork oil will not convert a day cruiser into a road racer. But such attention to detail *will* yield a smoother, more responsive and more enjoyable two-wheeled motorcycling experience.

Motorcyclists intent on modifying an engine to obtain substantially increased power do so, of course, at their own risk. Nearly every motorcycle manufacturer voids his warranty in the event performance goodies have been substituted for the factory engine parts. The risks of modifying an engine can be reduced by experimenting cautiously, however. Does a dirt bike rider wish to obtain a bit more mid-range power with only a small sacrifice in reliability? Then perhaps he should try a slightly larger carburetor or a higher compression cylinder head. Before buying these accessories, however, he is advised to check around. Who else has attempted these modifications to the same make and model motorcycle? Who manufactures the parts he used? What size carburetor jets and what ignition setting worked best? For what kind of riding was the bike used? Who else has tried the same or similar modifications? What were his results?

It costs nothing to ask these and a dozen related questions. But the time so spent can prove highly valuable. Perhaps you noticed an advertisement in a motorcycle magazine for a camshaft guaranteed to wring an additional 7.4 horsepower from a Guzzlefire V-3 cycle. And your local motorcycle dealer just happens to have such a camshaft on sale. But before you buy it, ask around. What happens to the low speed performance? Is an entire kit needed, or just the cam? How much faster will the valve lifters wear? What kind of guarantee is offered? The answer to these questions might prove discouraging, but the expense and nuisance of rebuilding a blown engine is far more discouraging.

Service and Protection Accessories

This catch-all category includes the thousand and one products available to protect a motorcycle from mechanical failure, the elements and human mischief. These accessories will not enhance the appearance of a motorcycle or increase its performance. They serve instead to preserve and protect an important investment. The single most important item in this category is probably the collection of tools a rider needs to keep his motorcycle properly adjusted. The subject of tools has been discussed, however, in previous chapters (see Chapter 6, on preventive maintenance and Chapter 7, on bike tripping). Consequently, this section will skip over the subject of tools and examine instead some of the other servicing accessories a motorcyclist might consider purchasing.

Theft Protection Ever since motorcycles came into being, there have existed motorcycle thieves. Although such thieves are held in properly low esteem, their numbers have increased rapidly in the past few years and their methods of operation are becoming increasingly sophisticated. The recovery rate of stolen motorcycles is not a source of encouragement to motorcycle owners or law enforcement officers. In many metropolitan areas, the police concede that when a motorcycle is missing for 72 hours, the chances are very high that it is gone forever.

Most motorcycle manufacturers equip their products with the traditional steering head lock as a token gesture of defiance to thieves. Unfortunately, no self-respecting cycle thief is much bothered by the sight of an engaged steering head lock. Even if the lock cannot be jimmied, which is rarely the case, the motorcycle can be rolled, dragged or lifted away.

Consequently, many motorcyclists invest in a lock and chain, preferably the strongest lock and heaviest chain they can find. Even the best lock or chain is not immune to the effects of a large bolt cutter or a cutting torch. A sturdy, hardened chain will, however, deter a casual thief and slow down even the professional. So, by all means, consider buying some heavy chain and a strong lock if you park a motorcycle where it might be stolen. To protect the finish of a motorcycle and yourself too, either purchase plastic coated chain or encase the chain in a discarded bicycle innertube and wrap the lock with a few layers of plastic tape.

In addition, a motorcycle owner should give thoughtful consideration to the best method of attaching a chain to his motorcycle. Whenever possible, the chain should secure the frame of the motorcycle to a stationary object such as a telephone pole, parking meter or fence post. More than one motorcyclist has attached a chain not around the frame, but around a wheel, only to discover that an obliging thief has taken his entire motorcycle except for the wheel. If no immovable object is available, the next best alternative is to secure the chain around the frame and rear tire of the motorcycle.

In addition to the traditional lock and chain, there are also available electronic theft alarms that emit a loud, piercing sound when an unwitting victim tampers with the motorcycle. So long as the alarm functions when the need arises and so long as someone in the vicinity hears the alarm and decides to respond, then the device will prove a worthwhile investment. Nevertheless, every motorcyclist should bear in mind that there exists no commercially available anti-theft device, mechanical or electronic, that cannot be circumvented by a professional thief equipped with a few minutes time and the right tools. The best protection remains the human eye backed by a good insurance policy. So park your motorcycle in a conspicuous, well-lighted place and obtain motorcycle theft insurance coverage from a reliable underwriting firm.

Motorcycle Covers Motorcycle owners who lack a garage or covered storage area should consider the purchase of a motorcycle cover. A little bit of rain, snow or summer sun will do no damage to a cycle. But constant exposure to the elements diminishes the appearance of any motorcycle. Inevitably, the paint fades, the rubber rots and the brightwork begins to dull. An owner wishing to preserve his investment can retard these processes by keeping his motorcycle covered whenever it is sitting idle.

A Skid Plate Bashing through the woods and jumping over rocky terrain are respectable enough activities, so long as they are done safely and with an eye toward preserving the environment. However, motorcycles used for off-road riding should themselves be preserved by the use of a sturdy metal skid plate. Engine cases are not only among the most expensive components of a motorcycle, but they are also among the most difficult to replace. The best method of preventing a broken case or a ripped out drain plug is to bolt a skid plate beneath the frame. Skid plates are light in weight, inexpensive and sensible insurance against the costly problems that can pop up unexpectedly when riding off-road.

Accessory Gauges Many of the problems that befall any kind of machinery happen without warning: a fuse fails, a cable snaps, a piston ring breaks. Many mechanical failures are preceded, however, by warning signals such as the whining of a wheel bearing or a fluttering ammeter gauge. For whatever reason, few motorcycles come equipped with extensive warning indicators. Nor in fact would some motorcyclists have much use for an extensive array of monitoring devices. The trail or enduro rider, for example, needs a light, simple machine unencumbered with instruments or warning lights. Long distance touring riders, on the other hand, can benefit from an ammeter or voltmeter to monitor the electrical system and an oil temperature or head temperature gauge with, perhaps, an oil pressure warning indicator.

Since total failure of a motorcycle's lubrication system happens only rarely, an oil pressure indicating light is not of high importance. But an ammeter will often warn of impending electrical problems while an oil temperature gauge is an important accessory to any air-cooled, four-cycle engine. When oil temperatures climb dangerously high, it could be the result of an oil leak or simply because the lubricant cannot handle the heat load generated by a particular set of riding circumstances such as riding double on a scorching summer day along an uphill grade. An oil temperature gauge allows a motorcyclist to spot impending problems before they become critical.

Oil Coolers An increasing number of touring motorcycles are either factory delivered or owner-equipped with an oil cooler. High speed driving on a hot summer day can cause oil temperatures to soar. An oil cooler will effectively bring these temperatures down to within safe limits. Oil coolers are neither cheap to buy nor simple to install, but they can give a motorcycle owner increased peace of mind and permit his engine to enjoy an extended lease on life.

Fuel Filters Most motorcycle manufactures—and many car producers too—equip their vehicles with only minimal protection against the ravages of impure gasoline. Motorcycle carburetors are becoming increasingly complex, yet the majority of manufacturers continue to equip their fuel systems with no more protection than metal or plastic mesh filters. Mesh filters suffice to keep pebbles, large flakes of rust and safety pins out of the carburetor. They are of little help, however, in trapping the small bits of dirt and grime that can clog carburetor orifices.

Motorcyclists who want to keep their fuel supply clean and pure can overcome this problem by installing an accessory in-line fuel filter. These filters are inexpensive (usually only a dollar or so), simple to install and they effectively block the passage of water and even microscopic impurities. Like a number of other accessories already mentioned, the auxiliary fuel filter is cheap insurance against the possibility of bothersome problems. In fact, the price is so low that it is wise to buy two filters: one for installation now and a second one as an emergency spare in the event you forgot to change the first one before the accumulation of gunk and crud blocks the flow of gasoline.

No review of the accessory market can pretend to offer a definitive examination of each and every item a motorcyclist might see fit to purchase. The preceding review is no exception. The principle objective has been less to survey the entire market than to offer some reasonable shopping advice for motorcyclists intent on wandering through that marketplace of competing wares.

Despite the profusion of local, state and federal consumer protection laws, the rule of *caveat emptor* still holds true. The buyer must beware. More specifically, a potential customer should play it safe, avoid the temptation of impulse buying and keep his purchases to a minimum.

Playing It Safe When a rider's own safety is at stake, money should be no object, or at least of somewhat less importance than would otherwise be the case. The additional fifteen dollar cost of a better grade safety helmet is well worth the difference—unless you value your cerebral matter at only thirty-five rather than fifty or more dollars.

A rider should also give careful consideration to accessories that enhance his own comfort or protect his motorcycle. The most useful accessories, however, are those that serve more than one function. Motorcyclists who purchase a foul weather riding suit do so largely for reasons of comfort. But a warmer, drier cyclist is a safer cyclist, too.

Impulse Buying Like every other group of consumers, motorcyclists often make purchases not in response to rationally perceived needs, but to satisfy spur of the moment wants. The temptation of impulse buying is unhealthy to the extent that many such purchases serve a given purpose only at the expense of compromising other goals. If a motorcyclist is willing to accept the risks and liabilities resulting from his decision, that should be his choice. But it is important for him to realize the tradeoffs that often result from impulse buying. Thus, the radically extended front forks favored by some riders may enhance the appearance of a motorcycle, although such claims are open to question. Nevertheless, these forks are not conducive to a rider's safety or to the structural integrity of his motorcycle. At least a few riders will continue to use extended front forks so long as the fad persists and the law permits. They should, however, first give all due consideration to what the consequences may be.

Keeping It Simple The danger of burdening a motorcycle with accessories that hinder as much as they enhance is self-evident to most observers of the sport. There exists a related temptation for motorcyclists to burden themselves with an excess of gadgets and so-called convenience accessories. Just as the best photographers do not travel about with the surplus of gadgets many amateur photographers consider essential, most experienced motorcyclists rely more on their skill and experience than on an array of supporting accessories. In the eyes of many an old time motorcyclist, and some recent converts too, simplicity is central to the motorcycling experience. To abandon that simplicity, they would argue, is simply one more step down the road toward motorcycles that are merely two-wheeled automobiles, with all the comforts and drawbacks thereof.

Chapter 10

Motorcycling and the Environment

More than three million motorcycles are presently registered in the United States. Worldwide motorcycle production totals in excess of three million vehicles anually. So vast a number of motorcycles is bound to have an effect, and a significant one at that, on the environment. Each individual motorcycle contributes very little to this total impact. Yet the overall impact is no more than the sum of the impacts created by each individual motorcycle. Consequently, every motorcyclist owes it to himself, to his fellow riders and to the environment to act in a fashion that will conserve the environment and preserve the sport of motorcycling as we know it today.

To be sure, the ecological consequences of motorcycling may count for little in comparison with the impact of cars, trucks and buses. The total number of motor vehicles operating on our roads is nearly forty times greater than the number of registered motorcycles. Cars, trucks and buses account for more than sixty times the mileage racked up annually by motorcycles. Since these four (and more) wheeled vehicles travel so many more miles, weigh so much more and require engines that are so much larger, they contribute vastly more damage to the environment than do two-wheeled vehicles.

Even though four-wheeled vehicles must bear a far greater burden of responsibility for deteriorating the environment and depleting our stock of fossil fuel, motorcyclists have little cause to rejoice. The number of two-wheeled vehicles increased drastically in the past decade: from 1960 to 1970 motorcycle registration grew fivefold.

Not only has the number of cycles mushroomed, but the wide availability of sophisticated all terrain motorcycles has enabled the motorcycling community to take their vehicles into environments that were previously inaccessible. Then too, motorcyclists are conspicuously obvious on our highways and about town. The noise, smoke emission and highly visible riding style so commonly associated with motorcycles has created a singularly unfortunate impact on the public. Although the majority of citizens are willing to tolerate motorcycles in their midst, there is no broadly based layer of public sentiment in favor of motorcycling as a sport or as a method of basic transportation. Finally, the motorcycle, because it shares with other motor vehicles a gasoline powered internal combustion engine, is automatically open to suspicion on the part of those who object to any and all sources of environmental damage.

For all of the above reasons, motorcycles and the sport of motorcycling are under attack from a number of quarters. The best available evidence suggests that this trend will continue for a number of years to come. Regrettably, many motorcyclists still believe that public opinion counts for very little. Let me do my thing, they say, and you are free to do as you please. But this attitude no longer prevails among the general public. A variety of activities that were once thought to be within the private domain are now considered by public opinion and by statute to be public acts. Simply stating the magic phrase, "It's a free country" no longer gives anyone license to run roughshod over issues of public concern. Today the question of just what constitutes the public interest is open to increasingly broad interpretation. Not so long ago the issues of clean air, noise and the allocation of petroleum resources were matters of limited concern. Consequently, manufacturers and users of motor vehicles were free to do as they pleased. Recently, however, these three areas have felt the impact of public opinion. Manufacturers and owners of motorcycles alike are discovering that they can no longer do as they please.

When people are under attack and especially when they believe that attack to be without justification, there is a natural tendency to counterattack blindly and without forethought. The recent history of environmental debate in this country has followed just this course. Attack and counterattack have followed in quick succession without either side giving pause to consider the needs and concerns of the opposition. This state of affairs, though not surprising, has proven highly unproductive.

If a consensus of thought and opinion is to emerge, all parties—for actually the debates has been more than two-sided—must concede that there is room for give and take and for compromise. The owner of a motor vehicle, whether it has two wheels or four, must understand the consequence of his actions and assume responsibility for those actions. His motor vehicle does not exist in a legal, moral or environmental vacuum. The rights of other people and other interests, both public and private, deserve all due respect. Not only must motorcyclists obey the law—though they are of course welcome to fight it in the courts or through channels of political action. They are also accountable for breeches of judgement, courtesy and fair play in matters beyond the reach of the law. Using a motorcycle to chase domestic animals or to pursue wildlife is a violation of the responsibility each motorcyclist must bear. So too is littering a violation of this responsibility even when it is not a violation of law. Pedestrians no more want to see the sight of discarded oil cans or spark plug wrappers laying by a curb than do backpackers wish to hear the sound of unmuffled motorcycle engines in an area reserved for their use and enjoyment. Even though it may be a free country, we are not free to trespass upon the rights of other persons or groups.

Just as pedestrians, backpackers and other interest groups have rights that must be respected, so too do motorcyclists deserve special rights and privileges that we call freedoms. The freedom to operate a motorcycle wherever and however a rider so wishes simply is no longer a reasonable freedom. Motorcyclists *can* reasonably expect, however, that the law and public opinion will guarantee them the right to other less broadly defined freedoms such as the right to operate a properly equipped (for example, with a spark arrestor) motorcycle in designated off-road areas of ample size and with the appropriate terrain. In the event that motorcyclists are not accorded reasonable freedoms or find that reasonable freedoms previously accorded them are being eroded, it is their right and responsibility to themselves, to other motorcyclists and perhaps even to the public at large to fight—legally—such infringements upon their freedom.

How best to resist these infringements is a complex issue that deserves thoughtful consideration by every motorcyclist. A portion of this chapter is devoted solely to the issue of protecting motorcyclists from encroachment on their activities and on the sport of motorcycling. Yet every motorcyclist owes it to himself and his fellow riders to expand his knowledge of this subject beyond the information that can be offered within the pages of an introductory volume. In a society where many interest groups are clamoring for their fair share of scarce resources, it is important that every group make its voice heard.

Before examining the issue of rights and responsibilities, it is necessary, however, to consider first the obligations and responsibilities of every motorcyclist. The reason for proceeding in this fashion is simple enough. To the extent that motorcyclists understand and accept the responsibilities that go hand in hand with motorcycle ownership, they can more effectively lay claim to the rights and freedoms due them. For it is an axiom of American political life that freedom is accorded only those who are thought to act responsibly.

The Ecology Problem

Motorcycling is no more harmful to the environment than any other form of gasoline powered transportation. Motorcycles, in fact, wreak less environmental havoc than nearly any other motor driven vehicle. What Thomas Firth Jones said of off-road motorcycling is true of the entire sport: "Motorcyclists are not the most dangerous or destructive users of the woods, by any means, but we are certainly the most conspicuous." In the public mind motorcycling ranks high on the list of environmentally unsound activities. Why is this so? The roots of the problem are many and intertwined. Yet one fact emerges clearly. The public image of motorcycling is heavily one-sided. The sins of a few have overshadowed the good deeds of the majority. A number of motorcyclists, and a few manufacturers too, have failed to respect accepted standards of environmentally sound behavior. Whether their actions were willfull or simply the consequence of ignorance matters little. The fact remains that motorcycling's track record in the field of ecology and environmental protection traditionally has left much to be desired.

Where have these failings occurred and what needs to be done? Motorcycling's problem areas include sound pollution, air pollution and ground pollution. We will look at each of these subjects in turn.

Sound Pollution During the early days of the automobile, every motor driven vehicle emitted considerable noise. Valves clattered, pistons slapped against their walls, carburetors gasped, gears whined and, most of all, exhaust pipes emitted a wheezing rasping sound remindful of a patient in the terminal stages of a respiratory disease. As automotive technology and consumer expectations grew more sophisticated, the motorcar became increasingly silent. With the advent of hydraulic valve lifters the engine racket subsided while carefully baffled mufflers coupled with the addition of tailpipe resonators reduced exhaust noise to a mere whisper. Modern automobiles are as nearly silent in operation as current technology permits.

The history of motorcycling, however, followed a rather different course. The asthmatic sound of early day motorcycles gave way to the barely muffled roar of highly tuned four-stroke engines and the high pitched buzz of the modern two-stroke engine. While automotive engineers were perfecting the internally baffled muffler, most motorcycle designers stuck fast to older and less efficient designs that use a perforated tube surrounded by fiberglass packing. Motorcycles were judged not by how quiet they were, but by how pleasing was the exhaust sound to the ear of the listener. Since the listener often placed volume of sound above all else, LOUD noises invariably issued forth from two wheeled exhaust pipes.

Not only did motorcycle manufacturers show a singular disregard for the ear drums of riders, passengers and pedestrians, but many motorcyclists took it upon themselves to modify original equipment exhaust systems. Off came the factory installed mufflers and in their place went an accessory exhaust system consisting of a straight pipe or a trumpet shaped muffler equipped with only the most primitive and easily removable baffling system. The result was a rumbling thunder-like blast of sound loud enough to shake acorns off an oak tree. In consequence, motorcycles acquired—and some do still deserve—a reputation as the loudest motor vehicles this side of a steam driven locomotive.

In all fairness to motorcycle manufacturers, it is important to remember that the motorcycle is a more difficult vehicle to soundproof than the automobile. Air-cooled engines, because they lack the noise deadening waterjacket and double iron walled cylinder block of a water-cooled engine, are inherently noisy. Witness to this fact is the Volkswagen, which emits more engine noise than automobiles equipped with a water-cooled engine of similar displacement. Two-cycle engines, because they produce twice as many power strokes as the four-cycle engine, present especially formidable obstacles to sound silencing. In addition, the relatively small size of a motorcycle relative to an automobile offers little space for a bulky exhaust muffling system. Finally, the practice of employing one exhaust pipe for each cylinder does not readily lend itself to silent operation. Multiple exhaust silencing systems emit more sound than does a single muffler shared by two, three or four cylinders.

For these and related reasons, the task of effectively silencing a motorcycle is not without some complexity. Yet the technology to do so does already exist and it is by no means prohibitively expensive. Hydraulic valve

Watercooling is the key to the low noise level of this Suzuki 750 cc touring cycle.

lifters and closely fitted pistons (both of which Harley-Davidson has used for over two decades) will go a long way toward quieting the noise of a reciprocating engine. The use of water-cooling silences even the racket of a two-stroke engine, as Suzuki and other manufacturers have demonstrated. Where water-cooling is combined with the rotary or Wankel engine, an almost totally noise-free powerplant results.

Perhaps the day will never come when a motorcycle glides by emitting the eerie sound of silence. Yet relatively quiet motorcycle exhaust systems require neither especially sophisticated technology nor an inflated price tag. For years now, The Bavarian Motor Works (known around the world as BMW) has produced remarkably quiet motorcycles ranging in size from 250 cc up to 900 cc touring goliaths. BMW's secret weapon in the battle against noise is simply an effective set of mufflers engineered to absorb as much sound as possible. These mufflers are neither substantially larger nor that much more expensive to build than the mufflers attached to a number of other road going motorcycles. They merely do a more efficient job than the competition.

Recently, other manufacturers have begun to do their part in the war on noise pollution. The Honda Motor Company has pioneered such features as double walled exhaust tubing, internally baffled muffler designs and single piece exhaust systems that do not lend themselves readily to the substitution of customer installed mufflers. An increasing number of manufacturers are voiding their warranties in the event that an owner tampers with the factory installed exhaust silencing system. Motorcycle manufacturers are taking these steps with full knowledge that unless the industry polices itself, restrictive state or federal sound control legislation that is waiting in the wings will do the job for them. Even the world of motorcycle racing has responded to the need for sound reduction. An increasing number of off-road competition events require that motorcycles be equipped with a working muffler. ISDT races include a sound level test, failure of which results in the loss of

MOTORCYCLING AND THE ENVIRONMENT

Sound muffling equipment has a place even on pure racing cycles. Note the muffler attached to the exhaust system of this Honda CR-250 Elsinor.

valuable bonus points. AMA sanctioned short track motorcycles and Novice class dirt track cycles must be muffled to 92 decibels (A scale) at 50 feet.

How can individual motorcyclists participate in the war against noise pollution? First and foremost, motorcycle owners should resist the temptation to modify factory installed exhaust systems. The sounds of silence should take precedence over any attempt to dress up an exhaust system with accessory mufflers or to modify the exhaust system in an effort to extract more horsepower. In addition, motorcyclists should support and encourage manufacturer efforts to develop more effective exhaust silencing systems. Motorcycles will remain a source of objectionable noise only so long as owners and buyers permit that situation to exist. As soon as motorcycle consumers demand quiet machines, motorcycle producers will supply appropriately silenced vehicles.

The advent of quiet motorcycles may cost a few dollars more and will surely sadden the heart of many an old time rider who enjoys the sound of an unmuffled engine at full song. But in the long run all motorcyclists will profit from quieter machines. In the first place, there are the advantages that result from a more favorable public image. Second, motorcyclists and nonriders alike will benefit physically, and perhaps psychologically too, from the reduced sound level. Research studies have conclusively shown that high noise levels, even though they may be pleasant to some ears, produce unwelcome physical and psychic side effects including altered endocrine, cardiovascular and neurological functions. Continued exposure to excessive noise can contribute to irritability, reduced resistance to infection, heartburn, indigestion, ulcers, high blood pressure and heart disease. Third, more effective sound control will especially benefit off-road riders. It is an axiom among environmentally minded cycle enthusiasts that less sound will produce more ground. In other words, quiet motorcycles will yield increased access to privately and publicly owned back country riding areas. Few motorcyclists would argue the point that a well muffled exhaust system is a cheap price to pay for preserving access to trail riding terrain. Noise is a readily overcome form of pollution, yet it has proven the single most important reason cited for the closure of land to off-road riding.

As a final point in favor of quiet motorcycling, every rider should bear in mind that if motorcyclists do not clean up their act, the government will do so legislatively. Under the Noise Control Act of 1972, the Environmental Protection Agency (EPA) is required to set noise emission standards for products that have been identified as major noise sources—among which the EPA most assuredly presumes to include motorcycles in general and trail bikes in particular. Given these circumstances, most motorcyclists would agree that self-policing is preferable to statutory regulation.

Air Pollution The effect of motor vehicle emissions on the atmosphere has received widespread publicity. The internal combustion of fossil fuel releases into the environment large quantities of carbon monoxide, nitrogen oxides, hydrocarbons and particulate matter. Man is not, of course, the only producer of these contaminants. Natural processes also generate these substances and in a quantity greater than does man. In fact, it has been established that nature is the source of nine times the carbon monoxide emission and five times as much airborne hydrocarbons as man produces. The Great Smoky Mountains of North Carolina and Tennessee were so named for their characteristic haze, generated by the effect of sunlight on hydrocarbon substances released by pine trees.

Nevertheless, vehicular sources of atmospheric contamination are a legitimate source of concern. Vehicle emissions occur not randomly but in pockets of concentration about urban areas. Mother nature's self-cleaning action is often sufficient to dispel these concentrations with only mildly harmful consequences for man and the environment. But when the concentrations become too great for the self-cleaning action to work or when this self-cleaning action breaks down temporarily (as happens during an atmospheric inversion), the consequences can prove disastrous.

Just what role do motorcycles play in the production of atmospheric pollutants? Simply because motorcycles depend on gasoline fired engines, they contribute to the pollution problem. How much pollution they contribute is an altogether different and much more complex question. According to a 1970 study conducted by the Environmental Protection Agency in the Los Angeles Basin, motorcycles were responsible for the generation of 27 tons of reactive hydrocarbons daily. The total daily hydrocarbon production for all internal combustion engines was reported to be 1,601 tons. In other words, motorcycles contributed about 1.7 percent of the total motor vehicle related hydrocarbon contamination in the basin. Motorcycles constituted in 1970 about 2.6 percent of all registered motor vehicles in the country and a somewhat larger percentage of motor vehicles in the Los Angeles Basin. Consequently, these figures suggest that motorcycles may contribute less than their per-vehicle share of contamination.

Nevertheless, many questions remain as yet unanswered. Whether or not motorcycles contribute less pollution per mile traveled and whether or not they generate about the same volume of pollutants relative to their engine size simply is not known for certain. A preliminary study conducted for EPA reportedly concluded that the "air pollution impact of motorcycles on individual metropolitan areas is not known at this time." The gaps in existing research data are so great that it is not even known for certain whether it is easier or more difficult to clean up the emissions produced by a two-stroke engine. Since a two-stroke engine, like the diesel, emits a high level of visible particulate matter (and also because the two-stroke produces twice as many exhaust strokes per revolution), many persons have assumed that the two-stroke engine is inherently dirtier than the four-stroke. Yet particulate matter is only one small chapter in the pollution story. Thus diesel engines, though they often produce a high level of particulates, generate far less of the highly dangerous nitrogen oxides than does the four-stroke gasoline engine.

Much of the technical debate concerning relative emission levels and the question of who has the dirtiest engine is entirely beside the point, however. Some of the most important facts are established beyond doubt. We know, for example, that motorcycle engines do release contaminants into the atmosphere. Furthermore, EPA has so far exempted motorcycle manufacturers from the increasingly stringent emission control standards that apply to automobile engines. Motorcycle manufacturers fully expect, however, that they too will be required to clean up their act. In anticipation of this event, most large motorcycle manufacturers have quietly been preparing for the day when they must substantially reduce exhaust emissions.

Automobile manufacturers have already pioneered the development of emission reduction technology. It was a motorcycle manufacturer (Honda) who led the way in meeting the stringent 1975 emission control standards. There is every reason, therefore, to suppose that motorcycle producers will experience little difficulty in reducing exhaust emissions to far below their untreated levels. It is important, however, for individual motorcyclists to support and cooperate fully with emission reduction efforts. As motorcyclists we might regret the small loss of horsepower that could at least temporarily accompany the introduction of pollution control technology to two-wheeled vehicles. But there are nearly four million motorcycles registered in the United States and the number continues to grow rapidly. Moreover, every motorcyclist must fulfill his obligations as a citizen and as a human being. One of these obligations is to be part of the air contamination solution rather than part of the pollution problem.

Ground Pollution During the 1960s, that segment of motorcycling which attracted the most public notice was motorcycle gangs and the outlaw rider. An outpouring of books, film and newspaper exposés focused public attention on the exploits (some real and some probably imagined) of a motorcycling minority whose sole purpose in life seemed to be the offending of public sensibilities.

The decade of the 1970s has brought in its wake a diminished concern for the activities of the outlaw motorcycle rider. Gangs do still exist. Yet they create less havoc and attract far less interest than was the case a decade ago. Public concern has instead turned toward a wholly new motorcycling group: the off-road rider. Where once motorcyclists were thought a threat to public safety and an affront to morality, they are now accused of defacing the landscape. A sudden rise in the popularity of trail riding has prompted many environmentalists to envision wilderness areas wholly overrun by untold millions of trail bikes. Off-road riders in turn have found an increasing amount of back country terrain closed off at just the time that their numbers were expanding dramatically. The resulting confrontation between motorized and non-motorized users of the land has generated more heat than light.

Professional land managers classify dirt going motorcycles in the overall category of ORVs or ORRVs—off-road (recreational) vehicles. The list of grievances presented by opponents of the ORV include an array of environmental misdeeds ranging from the destruction of flora to the pollution of surface waters, littering, disturbing the nesting and feeding patterns of wildlife, noise pollution, soil compaction, the harassment of hikers, trail and stream bank erosion, the creation of forest fires, air pollution, sedimentation of surface waters and the creation of ORV junkpiles in wilderness areas.

ORV operators have at one time or another committed all of these sins and then some. For ORVs are motor powered machines and their owners are all too human beings. It is a simple but sad fact that every increase in the number of ORV owners will bring a corresponding increase in environmental problems. The Bureau of Land Management (BLM), which administers vast tracts in our Western States, annually removes some 25,000 tons of litter from its lands. If the number of ORVs were to double in size next year, it is altogether likely that the volume of litter strewn about BLM land would increase in nearly equal proportion.

Moreover, the ecological sins laid at the feet of ORV operators are entirely real. Motorcycle tires, for example, do compact the soil and cause soil erosion. The consequences of compaction and erosion are many and unfortunate. Compaction kills soil nutrients, increases the rate of surface runoff and destroys the ability of soil to support plant life. Erosion alters the shape of the land, washes away topsoil and causes silting at the point of deposition. The environmental consequences of ORV pressures on the land can show up miles from the site of impact.

Clearly, ORV related problems exist. How best can we conserve the environment yet satisfy the various interest groups competing for the use of backcountry terrain? The solution lies neither in accepting the demands of those who insist on total banishment of ORVs nor in allowing ORV operators free access to all publicly owned lands. Instead, both sides must work together toward developing policies with which everyone can live. ORV owners will have to concede that motorized vehicles simply do not belong in certain wilderness areas while their opponents must forsake the notion that every acre of publicly owned land should be preserved intact forevermore.

The solution to the problem of competing land uses must rest on an under-

MOTORCYCLING AND THE ENVIRONMENT

Intensive motorcycle use—seen here at the start of the Spanish Gran Prix—can have a substantial impact on the local environment.

standing that with proper management there is more than enough land to go around. The Bureau of Land Management alone administers nearly one half *billion* acres of federally owned land. Although BLM is the largest public manager of land, it is not the only government landlord. The U.S. Forest Service, the U.S. Parks Department, the military services and each of the individual states and counties own sizable amounts of raw land. Although this publicly owned land is concentrated in the more sparsely populated parts of the United States, it represents a vast and largely untapped land bank of more than 250 acres per off-road vehicle in the country.

Not all of this terrain could or should be opened up to ORVs. Ranching interests, the mining industry, lumber companies and various departments of the military have already leased much of the available land for their own use. The point remains, nevertheless, that this vast reservoir of land is sufficiently large to accommodate a variety of interest groups so long as each group is willing to share its usage rights with other groups. Certain combinations of usage are, of course, simply not compatible. For example, jeeping enthusiasts and bird watchers can no more harmoniously share an area than can hunters and hikers happily coexist at the same time on a given tract of land. Allowing such combinations of people to occupy the same area inevitably causes more problems than it solves. The concept of multiple land use requires the joining together of environmentally and socially compatible interest groups, such as motorcyclists and snowmobiles, or four wheel drive vehicles and a lumbering operation.

Just how best to divide up our land resources among competing interest groups is a subject that legislators, public officials and sportsmen will grapple with for years to come. Clearly, however, certain lands must be reserved for a single purpose while other terrain can reasonably sustain multiple usage. Recreational and scenic areas must be categorized by the kinds of usage to which they are best suited. What are these categories? There exists no one universally accepted or patently superior method of categorizing land usage. Presented below, however, is one system that makes sense for motorcyclists and non-motorized users of the land, too.

Protected Lands Certain environmentally fragile areas simply cannot withstand the onslaught of mechanized man without suffering rapid deterioration. When such terrain is also of high scenic value it must be rigidly protected from the introduction of any intensive use except along officially designated roadways.

What kind of land falls into this category? A well known example is high altitude tundra. This landscape is so delicate that in certain areas even unregulated pedestrian use will wreak environmental havoc. Access by motorized vehicles must be prohibited and even pedestrian use must be subject to careful regulation. Less drastic examples of land reasonably deserving a protected status include wetlands, much coastal shoreline and high altitude meadows. Our National Park system and formally designated "Wilderness and Primitive Areas" are properly closed to off-road recreational vehicular use. By definition, Wilderness Areas must evidence virtually no signs of human intrusion. The use of motor vehicles in such an area would rapidly compromise its wilderness status.

Restricted Use Lands Many recreational areas already bear the more or less permanent evidence of man's presence. Moreover, these areas include a somewhat less fragile environment and lack the majestic scenery of a National Park. The unrestricted use of off-road vehicles would certainly prove detrimental to the existing ecology. Yet such areas can sustain limited off-road vehicular traffic without causing significant environmental damage. Vast portions of our national forest lands fall into this category. In these areas, motorcycles and other ORVs deserve the opportunity to use designated trails. Colorado's Pike National Forest uses just this system. Motorized vehicles are permitted to travel off-road at various strategically located trailheads that have been developed from existing trails for their use. Hikers are free to use these trails or to follow the many footpaths that are barred to vehicular use. The TVA Land Between the Lakes recreational area employs a similar system featuring a specially designated trail riding area reserved for motorcycle use.

What happens if the vehicular paths suffer environmental damage? The answer is simple enough. Environmental damage of the sort under discussion here rarely proves irreversible. In extreme cases the trail must be closed permanently to prevent further damage and to permit nature to heal its wounds. More often than not the solution lies in rebuilding the trails to eliminate an environmental hazard or closing the trail until such time as nature has repaired the damage—at which point the trail can be reopened for vehicular use. The principle of crop rotation is a proven method of conserving agricultural land; similar techniques are being employed with increasing frequency to conserve recreational land while allowing that land to support the maximum feasible range of recreational activities.

Use of this dry, rock filled stream bed (at the site of the Scottish Six Day Trials) protects the neighboring vegetation from vehicular damage.

The question of when and where to open or close national forest and other limited access lands to ORV use presently rests with local land managers. Consequently, there exists no uniform policy even from one forest area to the next within the same state. A rider must check with the appropriate land manager (generally a U.S. Forest Service or State Department of Natural Resources employee) to determine what is the prevailing policy that governs the use of ORVs in a given area.

A spark arrestor—such as the one built into the muffler of this Honda Motosport 125—is a necessary piece of trail riding equipment.

Managers of public land are required to balance the goals of environmental protection and recreational use by a variety of interest groups. A motorcyclist who arrives at a recreational area previously open to ORVs only to find it closed may be sorely tempted to ride where he is not now welcome. He should resist that temptation. His favorite area may be closed for the time being to restore accumulated environmental damage. Or it may be closed because temporary conditions, as spring snowmelt, heavy rains or extreme dryness, have rendered the area too fragile for vehicular use. Whatever the reasons for the closure, they should be respected both for the sake of the environment and for the sake of future riders who may wish to use the area.

Free Access Land The majority of publicly owned land is environmentally sturdy and lacking in special scenic value. Though this land should be conserved as a valuable natural resource, it can sustain considerable vehicular use without losing its economic value, its scenic beauty or its environmental integrity. Whether such terrain should be made available to ORVs on a lease basis, according to a pay as you go plan, through special user excise taxes or free of charge, is not at stake here. What matters is that land in this category represents a largely untapped source of recreational space where motorcycles can move freely.

What if such land becomes stripped of its vegetation or begins to suffer the consequences of erosion? Again, the answer is simple enough. In that case, vehicular use must be limited or prohibited until such time as conservation practices or nature unaided can restore the land to its original condition. Over-intensive use of such lands is an ever present danger. But just as professional conservationists have learned to predict and control the effects of over-intensive cattle grazing or timber cutting, so too can they estimate the level of unrestricted vehicular activity a parcel of land can support before sustaining environmental degradation of one kind or another.

Intensive Use Land All the previous use categories presuppose that the land will be preserved intact. Vegetation, wildlife and drainage patterns would suffer no significant impact. To the extent that vehicular use threatens to upset any of these patterns, it must be curtailed. Yet there exist throughout the country tracts of land largely devoid of vegetation, wildlife and special scenic value. Such land often exists at the fringe of development areas, in and about areas of surface mining activity, along utility line easements and interspaced about areas of more substantial scenic or recreational value.

Land in this category is a likely candidate for intensive ORV use or conversion into an area devoted exclusively to motorcycling. The notion of organized cycling in an area given over solely to motorcycles is hardly new. California's Saddleback Park is simply the best known example of a growing movement. Why are motorcycle parks gaining in popularity? Because if properly designed, they have much to offer motorcyclists and non-motorcyclists alike. First, recreational areas devoted to motorcycling provide a safe playground area with a variety of inviting two-wheel terrain. Second, so long as motorcycle parks are properly situated, they allow riders to play all day long without offending those who do not enjoy the sight or sound of motorcycles. Third, motorcycle parks contain the environmental impact of intensive motorcycling activity within a manageable area where the proper conservation measures can be used to prevent, retard or repair the wear and tear that would otherwise result.

What is the best way to organize and manage a motorcycle park? Actually, no single method is best in every situation. The park can be privately owned, like Saddleback Park, or it can be publicly owned, either by a special district or a unit of government such as a municipality, a state or the federal government. The notion of a city owned motorcycle park may seem curious indeed. But it is entirely within the legal authority of a government unit to construct such a facility and many cities have undertaken far more ambitious projects. Consider, for example, the City of Denver, Colorado. More than a generation ago, Denver obtained a vast tract of land located 60 miles from the city and on the other side of the Continental Divide in order to create a municipal ski resort. That resort, which is known to skiers throughout the country as Winter Park, has proven over the years an extraordinary success. The excess revenues generated by the park are annually plowed back into it for better trail grooming and for the expansion and upgrading of facilities.

The example of Winter Park illustrates what is possible. The development of a motorcycle park is nowhere as difficult an undertaking as Winter Park. In fact, a motorcycle park is no different in nature than a municipally owned golf course or shooting range. If skiers can enjoy publicly owned ski slopes and golfers can benefit from public golf courses, then there is no reason why motorcyclists should not have at their disposal public motorcycling parks.

Any mention of public facilities and services raises the issue of financing: how will the money be raised and who will pay? A recreational amenity can be financed in a number of ways. In the case of privately owned parks, commercial loan financing is often available to underwrite the capital costs. A unit of government wishing to establish a motorcycle park can budget a portion of its general revenues or issue bonds to finance its capital costs. User fees assessed at the gate or on an annual basis can also pay the operating expenses and pay off capital expenditures. Local units of government are even eligible for federal grants-in-aid, as from the Bureau of Outdoor Recreation, to finance recreational projects such as a motorcycle park.

An alternate source of financing rests with an excise tax collected on the sale of motorcycles and motorcycle accessories or assessed in the form of a registration surcharge. In the years before World War II, Congress enacted legislation establishing user excise taxes on the sale of sport fishing and hunting equipment. This tax money is channeled into special accounts known as the Dingle-Johnson Fund (for sport fishermen) and the Pittman-Roberson Fund (for hunters). Money from these funds is disbursed on a formula grant basis to undertake a wide variety of activities that benefit fish and game sportsmen. The individual states receive a proportionate share of the funds to use for restocking lakes, acquiring open space for hunting and for enhancing the population of game and wildlife. This method of financing projects of benefit to special interest sportsman groups has proven highly successful. Motorcyclists and industry spokesmen would do well to explore carefully excise tax methods of underwriting two-wheel recreational projects.

The development of new and more sensible land allocation policies will require an intensive group effort by the motorcycling industry, individual owners and their appointed spokesmen. Motorcyclists and industry spokesmen must think and act not so much on the basis of their own self-interest but in terms of what is good for the sport itself. In addition, motorcyclists must learn to consider the environment as more than a commodity to be bought, sold and consumed. Rather, we must view it as a finite resource to be conserved. The environment can survive and survive well the intrusion of ORVs, but only if each one of us acts positively to protect and conserve rather than to consume and exploit it.

Motorcycling, in other words, is not inherently and inevitably at odds with the interests of a quality environment. The concept of ecological motorcycling is no contradiction in terms. What we do to and with the environment is largely our own choice as motorcyclists and as citizens. Since we have that choice, at least for the time being, it is our obligation to use it wisely.

The injunction to act wisely requires merely that motorcyclists make proper use of the grey matter contained within their helmets. The application of common sense and a measure of consideration for the environment and for its users will go a long way toward solving the ORV ecology problem. For the benefit of readers who may wish to know just what is involved in acting wisely, the following list of do's and don'ts is presented. This list, which has been adopted from a similar list prepared by the AMA for trail riders, offers a series of guidelines for responsible motorcycling.

Ten Essentials for Responsible Motorcycling

Do	Don't
Ride in appropriate places	Don't ride on private roads or private land without first seeking permission of the owner or manager
Ride where others have preceded you	Don't ride on fragile or virgin environments that wound easily or heal slowly

MOTORCYCLING AND THE ENVIRONMENT 185

Off-road riding is a source of entertainment for over a million Americans. But it must be done with an eye toward protecting the environment.

Stay on trails	Don't create your own trails
Keep your motorcycle properly tuned	Don't allow an untuned engine to pollute the environment
Buy a quiet motorcycle and keep it that way	Don't modify mufflers or substitute loud accessory equipment
Ride with an eye to minimizing environmental damage	Don't spin the rear wheel needlessly and don't cause ruts and consequent soil damage to loose or damp soils
Obey the law on and off the road	Don't try to make your own rules
Consider the needs of other users of the road and the land	Don't spoil the recreational pleasure of other users
Belong to an organized group of fellow sportsmen	Don't assume your voice will be heard alone
Communicate with land managers and users	Don't act aggressively Don't act defensively Don't ignore the concern of others

Some Environmental Virtues of Cycling

So far in the course of this chapter, motorcycles have emerged largely in the role of environmental villains. As a subcategory of the motor vehicle, cycles are heir to the environmental failings of that larger category of vehicles. The case against motorcycles is not the least bit one-sided, however. Off-road motorcycling does generate harmful side effects. Yet hikers can also cause damage to the back-country environment. If the number of hikers is sufficiently large or if a small number of hikers act in a sufficiently careless fashion, substantial environmental damage will soon result. In many respects, the difference between hikers and off-road motorcyclists is largely a matter of degree rather than a difference in kind.

The environmental problems that we face today are largely the result of mechanization. Motor vehicles, however, are only one part—and a small one at that—of the overall problem. Let's consider just one particular form of pollution: namely, waste heat or thermal pollution. A study of the 4,000 square mile Los Angeles Basin indicates that the motor vehicle contributed only one third of the total waste heat generated in the basin and will contribute barely one fifth of the waste heat generated throughout the basin in the year 2000. When we further assume, on the basis of the EPA sponsored Los Angeles Basin study cited earlier in this chapter, that motorcycles contribute less than two percent of all motor vehicle pollution, then we can reasonably suppose that motorcycling accounts for approximately one half of one percent of the waste heat generated in the basin. If present projections prove accurate, this figure would decline to about one third of one percent by the year 2000. In other words, motorcycles are a miniscule contributor to the overall pollution problem.

Nor do motorcycles contribute substantially to the total output of vehicular pollution. The less than two percent share attributable to motorcycles may not be utterly inconsequential. Yet it is hardly a subject worthy of excess concern in comparison to the overall problem of motor vehicle pollution. Simply because cars, trucks and buses travel so many more miles and consume so many more gallons of gasoline than motorcycles, they are a much more significant part of the problem. A mere two percent reduction in car, truck and bus emissions would prove more beneficial to the environment than reducing motorcycle emissions to zero.

In fact, under certain circumstances motorcycles are a more environmentally sound method of transportation than the passenger car. The typical passenger car used in this country has an engine capacity on the order of 200 cubic inches and carries an average of less than two occupants. In other words, an automobile requires roughly 100 cubic inches of engine displacement—and pollution potential—per occupant. Let's look at the motorcycle in comparison. The average motorcycle has an engine capacity in the vicinity of 300 cc (21 cubic inches) or less and carries always one rider and occasionally a passenger. The typical automobile employs an engine *ten times* larger than the average motorcycle and ordinarily carries less than twice as many occupants. Autos therefore typically require between six and eight times the engine capacity per occupant.

Because of differences in engine speed at any given velocity (motorcycles are geared "lower" than automobiles) and for a number of other technical reasons, the typical motorcycle may not be six or eight times as pollution free a method of transporting occupants down the road. Yet motorcycles could well generate three, four or even five times less emissions per occupant than the normal passenger car. Considerable research is needed to demonstrate precisely how much less pollution per occupant is emitted by a motorcycle. For the time being, it seems safe to conclude that a switchover from automobiles to motorcycles could realize a substantial reduction in environmental damage.

Since motorcycles are smaller and lighter than even the most compact automobiles, they go much further on a gallon of gas. How much further depends. Automobiles normally consume 10 to 25 miles per gallon while motorcycles can travel about three to four times as far on a gallon of gasoline. Motorcycles therefore make sense as a method of conserving scarce petroleum resources. A motorcycle rider and passenger together consume approximately the same amount of gas per person as the occupants of a fully loaded full size American passenger car. As we know, however, automobiles rarely carry anywhere near their full load of passengers. So under normal driving circumstances the motorcycle emerges as a practical and effective method of reducing gasoline consumption.

The advantages of the motorcycle relative to a passenger car become especially obvious in an urban environment. Consider the example of a housewife—or a student or a businessman—who drives to the corner grocery store to pick up a copy of the Sunday newspaper or to get a pack of cigarettes or to have a prescription filled. Does there exist any earthly reason to take a two ton vehicle equipped with a 250 horsepower engine on a six block trip to the drug store? Of course not. Does it make much sense to use a one ton car powered by a 100 horsepower engine? The one ton car makes more sense than a larger car. But neither vehicle is appropriately sized to the task. Both are wasteful of energy and needlessly burden the atmosphere with contaminants. For short urban trips the motorcycle is an appropriately large personal transportation vehicle. An engine displacing 100 cc is more than powerful enough to transport a rider down residential streets and along many major transportation arteries within a city. Yet a motorcycle of this size—which is only 6 cubic inches—produces vastly less pollution than even the smallest automobile and consumes far less gasoline, too. As an added bonus, a lightweight motorcycle in the 100 cc class weighs about 200 pounds or less. Six or more such vehicles can conveniently fit in the parking space reserved for a single large passenger car.

Especially in the milder parts of the country where motorcycles can be used nearly all year round, the two-wheeler makes sense as a basic method of personal transportation in the city, in suburbs and in small towns. European nations, where gasoline has always been a precious commodity, long ago recognized the virtues of two and three-wheeled methods of motorized transportation. The motorcycle sidecar combination, which is an especially efficient method of transporting from one to as many as four persons, enjoys great popularity throughout Europe. In England, the government has favored three-wheelers with preferential tax advantages that free their owners from the otherwise steep tax rates assessed on the owner of a four-wheeled vehicle. A similar taxing structure to induce the emergence of more economical methods of personal transportation could prove beneficial in this country, too.

The Freedom of Motorcycling

So far this chapter has emphasized the responsibilities of a motorcyclist to his fellow riders, to the public at large and to the cause of safe, ecological motorcycling. What can motorcyclists expect in return for responsible conduct on their part? Basically, they can expect fair and impartial treatment from the public and from both appointed and elected officials. Like every other citizen, motorcyclists deserve the right to participate in the making of those decisions that either directly or indirectly affect them as owners and operators of two-wheeled motor vehicles. To participate in decision making does not guarantee each individual motorcyclist, or even all motorcyclists acting in concert, that they will get what they want. Motorcyclists deserve to be heard, however, and to be given a full and honest explanation of the rationale for any adverse decisions.

Before motorcyclists are heard, they must learn to speak up in a clear, unified and reasonable voice. Shrill words and mixed views will accomplish nothing of value. Instead, the motorcycling community must marshal its facts carefully and work hand in hand with lobbyists and public relations specialists to present its concerns to state and federal legislators and to the public at large. Individual motorcyclists will need to follow impending legislation closely and establish channels of communication through which they can alert and mobilize other motorcyclists. Industry representatives and the staff of motorcycling associations must listen carefully, as the AMA has begun to do, at the local level of motorcycling and intensify their lobbying efforts. Too often in the past lobbying has simply taken the form of last minute attempts to kill harmful legislation. Lobbying, however, is a dual edged effort directed both at blocking the passage of unwanted bills and at encouraging the passage of helpful legislation.

The series of successful dialogues that the AMA arranged in response to Executive Order 11644 is a case in point. On February 8, 1972, the President of the United States released Executive Order 11644, which recognized that recreational vehicles have a right to the use of public lands and required various federal agencies with a responsibility for the administration of public lands to develop guidelines that would promote the recreational use of those lands while minimizing conflict among the various users and protecting the nation's resource potential. The Legislative Department of the AMA launched a massive publicity campaign with its individual members, among motorcycling clubs and at more than 6,000 dealerships. As petitions began to flow in, the staff of the AMA met with regional and Washington based public land administrators. Special presentations were made at fact-finding sessions the U.S. Department of the Interior conducted in nine major studies. The result of this extensive lobbying effort was public acknowledgement by the President, by the Director of the U.S. Bureau of Outdoor Recreation, by Congressmen and by federal and state land managers that ORV users in general and motorcyclists in particular can speak with a unified and reasoned voice of their right to share the use of public lands.

The notion of an extensive lobbying and public relations effort does not sit comfortably with many motorcyclists, however. Motorcycle riders traditionally have valued their personal freedom above all else. They ride a motorcycle not out of a concern for public affairs or the desire to present a favorable public image but in order to escape physically and psychologically from such concerns. Collective group action seems contrary to the spirit of individual freedom that pervades motorcycling. In addition, many motorcyclists who recall the era of the 1950s and the early 1960s simply assume that any attempt to overhaul the public image of motorcycling is hopeless. Too many politicians and citizens are dead set against us, they say.

Nevertheless, motorcycling's public image is changing, and for the better. Largely as the result of an intensive advertising campaign by manufacturers and the AMA's public relations effort, a new public image of motorcycling is beginning to emerge. No longer does the typical citizen associate motorcycles exclusively with deviant behavior and offensively loud noises. He has heard repeatedly that one meets the nicest people on at least one brand of motorcycle and he probably knows from experience that there is some truth in the expression—for in all likelihood a relative or a friend or a neighbor of his owns a motorcycle. The day of the motorcycle gangs is gone at least for the time being and in its place is an enhanced (the trail bike problem excluded) public image. To be sure, this image could well stand further improvement. Yet the prospect of improvement is good indeed.

Anyone who doubts that motorcyclists could organize themselves into an effective lobbying group should consider the success other sportsmen groups have enjoyed. Whether or not an individual is favorably or unfavorably disposed toward the National Rifle Association (NRA) is entirely a matter of personal preference. Both friends and enemies of the association concede, however, that it is an effective lobbying organization. Over the years the NRA has achieved an enviable track record in its effort to defend the interests of its membership. Industry representatives and sportsmen groups work effectively with the NRA toward achieving their goals. Over the past few years individual segments of the motorcycling community have learned to lobby with increased sophistication and effectiveness. Nevertheless, motorcycle owners, distributors and their organizational representatives could profit from the lessons learned long ago by the NRA.

Active participation in the NRA has not cost hunters and gun enthusiasts their freedom or their independence. As individual sportsmen they continue to hold their own convictions and to practice their sporting activities as they see fit. Motorcyclists who elect to participate in organizations such as the AMA that enhance the image of motorcycling or that are lobbying for two-wheeled interests need fear no loss of freedom. Collective group action will not compromise the spirit of motorcycling or the freedom of individual motorcyclists. The cost of participation in this collective action amounts to no more than nominal membership dues in a motorcycling organization and perhaps a bit of spare time to help out.

What does a rider receive in turn for his money or time? Principally he is buying a share in the mutual effort to preserve and expand the freedom of all motorcyclists. More specifically, he helps to support several vital activities. First, his time and money provide for an effective public forum in which his views and the views of his fellow motorcyclists can be heard. Second, he is demonstrating that he, like other motorcyclists, does not intend to sit passively on the sideline while decisions are made that affect one or more segments of the motorcycling community. Third, he helps to plan for a future that will be consistent with the needs and expectations of as many motorcyclists as possible.

Too often in the past motorcyclists have fallen victim to the attitude that "whatever will be will be." Every man defended his own self-interest on the assumption that nothing more was possible. Efforts at planning for the future occurred only rarely and only on a small scale.

What is needed instead is a large scale effort to shape the future itself. Simply planning for the future is only a matter of preparing to roll with the punches. By striving to plan the future itself motorcyclists can take the initiative rather than respond to the initiative of others. Freedom rarely befalls those who wait patiently on the sidelines for it to happen. Instead, it is bestowed upon or retained by those individuals or groups who actively pursue it. If motorcyclists wish to preserve and expand their traditional freedoms, then they too must actively and collectively seek that goal.

A Glossary of Motorcycle Terms

AMA   American Motorcycle Association
ape hangers   High and narrow handlebars so named because their users must assume an ape-like appearance
ATV   All Terrain Vehicle
bank   To turn a motorcycle into a curve or corner
bike   Slang for a motorcycle
bore   The inside diameter of an engine's cylinder. See also *stroke*
cafe racer   A road-going motorcycle fitted out to resemble a pure road racing motorcycle
camshaft   A cylindrical steel rod that employs eccentric lobes to open the valves on a four-cycle engine. See also *overhead camshaft*
carburetor   A device that mixes fuel and air in the proper proportion and feeds the resultant mixture into the cylinders of an engine
centerstand   A spring loaded platform attached to the lower frame rails of a motorcycle. When engaged it provides two additional points of balance, thereby allowing a motorcycle to stand upright at rest
chair   Slang expression for a motorcycle sidecar
choke   A mechanical device that reduces the air flow to an engine in order to speed cold weather starting and warm-up
chopper   A custom built motorcycle characterized by extended front forks and a low, semi-reclining seating position
clip-ons   Short low mounted handlebars that are attached to the fork tubes of a motorcycle
compression ratio   The ratio between the maximum volume of an engine cylinder/combustion chamber area and the volume of its contents when the piston is fully extended. A cylinder with a displacement of 250 cc and a combustion chamber capacity of 50 cc would have a compression ratio of 6:1 (300:50)

compression release A valve that allows a rider to manually release engine compression, thereby helping to start large capacity four-cycle engines or increasing the compression braking capacity of two-cycle engines

cylinder A hollow metal sleeve inside which the piston travels back and forth. Numerous rows of finning cover the outside of an air-cooled cylinder to enhance its ability to dissipate heat

cycle Slang for a motorcycle

disc brake A braking system that employs a front or rear wheel mounted steel disc. Application of the brake lever presses a heat resistant pad against the side of the disc in order to generate friction and thereby reduce the forward motion of a vehicle

displacement A measure of the size of an engine. Displacement refers to the volume of gas (usually expressed in cubic centimeters) each piston can draw into its cylinder. All other things being equal, the larger the displacement of an engine, the more power it will produce

drive chain A series of links and rollers that transmit power from a transmission to the rear wheel of a motorcycle. See also *primary chain*

enduro A type of dirt going motorcycle designed to travel comfortably over and through a wide variety of rough terrain and soft surfaces. Also a type of motorcycle competition over rough terrain and soft surfaces

EPA The Environmental Protection Agency. The folks who make the rules regarding vehicle exhaust emissions

expansion chamber A specialized exhaust system for two-cycle engines that uses exhaust pressure waves to extract more efficiently gases from the combustion chamber

factory racer A competition motorcycle prepared on a one at a time basis by the manufacturer of that motorcycle. Factory racers are rarely offered for sale to the public; instead, they are intended for use by factory hired racers

fairing A moulded fiberglass shield attached to the front of a motorcycle for the purpose of streamlining the vehicle and/or protecting its rider from the elements

forks The front suspension legs of a motorcycle

fouling The accumulation of deposits on the tip of a spark plug. Fouling retards the proper flow of electricity across the electrodes of a spark plug, which can cause hard starting or prevent an engine from operating at all until the spark plug is cleaned or replaced. Improperly tuned two-cycle engines are especially prone to spark plug fouling

four-stroke A type of engine that produces one power impulse every four revolutions of its crankshaft. Four-cycle or four-stroke engines employ camshaft activated valves to control the flow of gas into and out of the cylinder(s). See also *two-stroke*

groove The path taken by the majority of competitors around a race course. Also the most efficient path around a corner

hog Slang for a Harley-Davidson V-twin motorcycle

horsepower What makes the wheels of a motor vehicle go around. Horsepower is a measure of the mechanical force produced by an engine. By and large, the faster an engine is rotating, the more horsepower it produces

ISDT International Six Days Trial. The annually held king of international trails competition events

kickstand (also jiffystand) A spring loaded lever attached to the frame of a motorcycle. When engaged the kickstand serves as a third point of balance, thereby allowing a motorcycle to stand upright at rest. See also *centerstand*

knobbie A tire equipped with wide-spaced, deep lugs designed to provide maximum traction in a variety of off-road surfaces

minibike (also minicycle) A two-wheeled motor powered vehicle equipped with small wheels (less than 15 inches in diameter) and a low seat

A GLOSSARY OF MOTORCYCLE TERMS

motorcross   The European version of scrambling, but employing a rougher and more challenging course. Refers also to the type of motorcycle used in motorcross competition

NHTSA   The National Highway Traffic Safety Administration (a part of the Department of Transportation). The folks who make the rules regarding motorcycle safety

OR(R)V   Off-Road (Recreational) Vehicle. A vehicle, including but not limited to motorcycles, designed to travel across off-road environments. This group of vehicles includes dirt going motorcycles, four wheel drive trucks, jeeps, snowmobiles and ATVs

overhead cam   (abbreviated OHC) A method of activating the valves of a four-cycle engine whereby a camshaft mounted on top of the engine directly opens the valves without need for push-rods, rocker arms or other indirect linkage. See also *camshaft*

points   Ignition points control the delivery of the spark to an engine's cylinders

primary chain   A series of links and rollers that transmit power from the engine crankshaft to the transmission. See also *drive chain*

road racer   A high performance competition motorcycle intended exclusively for use on paved road racing circuits

rotary valve   A thin metal disc attached to the crankshaft of some two-cycle engines. As the disc rotates, a cutaway portion allows the fuel-air mixture to pass from the carburetor into the cylinder(s)

RPM   Revolutions Per Minute. A measure of the rotational speed of an engine

scooter   A two-wheeled motor powered vehicle with small wheels (less than 15 inches in diameter), an enclosed engine, leg shields and floorboards. Also slang for a motorcycle in certain parts of the country

scrambling   (also scrambles) A form of off-road motorcycle competition along a winding dirt track about 1/3 mile long

security bolt   A bolt and plate assembly that locks the bead of a tire to the rim, thereby preventing rotation of the tire on its rim. Tire rotation, which readily occurs at the low inflation pressures used for off-road riding, rips out the valve stem from a tube

sissy bar   An unswept bracket attached behind the rear seat of a motorcycle

skid lid   Slang expression for a safety helmet

skid plate   A metal plate attached beneath a motorcycle engine to protect it from damage while riding off-road

spark arrestor   A device that captures and extinguishes sparks before they can escape from the tip of an exhaust pipe

sprocket   A toothed wheel that meshes with a chain to transmit rotational force from one point to another

steering damper   A device built into the steering head of a motorcycle or attached between a fork leg and the frame of a motorcycle and designed to absorb the shock of deflecting side forces, thereby enabling a rider more readily to keep his motorcycle moving in its intended direction

street racing   What you should not do

street scrambler   A road going motorcycle fitted with various off-road motorcycling accessories

stroke   The length of travel of a piston inside an engine cylinder. See also *bore*

superbike   An expensive large displacement motorcycle offering high performance levels

swing arm   The rear suspension arms of a motorcycle, which connect the frame to the rear wheel

tachometer   A measuring instrument that shows the speed, measured in RPMs, at which an engine crankshaft is rotating

touring   Long distance travel by motorcycle

trail bike An all purpose dirt going motorcycle

trials A form of off-road motorcycle competition (and a type of motorcycle) that stresses precise control at low speed over short sections of challenging terrain

twistgrip The tubular device attached to the end of the right handlebar. The twistgrip controls the flow of fuel-air mixture to the carburetor(s), thereby acting in the same capacity as an automobile's gas pedal

two-stroke A type of engine that produces one power impulse every two revolutions of its crankshaft. Two-cycle or two-stroke engines employ their pistons or a crankshaft mounted rotary valve to control the flow of gas into and out of the cylinder(s). See also *four-stroke*

universal tire A motorcycle tire equipped with a tread pattern and other construction features intended to provide satisfactory traction on both paved and hard packed off-road surfaces

waterpumper Slang for a liquid cooled motorcycle engine

wheelie The operation of a motorcycle solely on its rear tire with the front wheel raised off the ground

Z90.1 The industry imposed standard for the performance of safety helmets

Index

accidents, 58, 83-97, 130
air cooling, 66
Allstate, 61
American Automobile Association, 128
American Motorcycle Association, 184, 188-189
aquaplaning, 81

baja pack, 162
Barrington, James T., 77
battery, 30, 112
BMW, 12, 19, 21, 174
Bonneville, 17
boots, 158
brake, 36, 67, 68, 104-105
    cable, 103-104, 105
    lever, 71-72
    light, 72, 104, 108
    linings, 104
    pedal, 72-73
Brakebender, Henry, 63-64
bridges, 81
British, 12, 18
Buick, 99
Bultaco, 9
Bureau of Land Management (BLM), 178-179
Bureau of Outdoor Recreation (BOR), 184, 188
button,
    kill, 72
    starter, 72

cable,
    brake, 103-104
    choke, 103
    clutch, 64, 103-104
    instrument, 103
    throttle, 103-104
California, 30, 79, 80, 88, 143
camshaft, 33

Canada, 145
carburetor, 66, 111-112
    tickler, 73
centrifugal force, 69
chain,
    adjuster, 75
    drive, 68, 106-108
    flying, 107
    primary, 108
Charlottesville, 79
Chicago, 60
chrome molybdenum, 31
clutch, 66
    cable, 64, 103-104
    lever, 70
compression release, 70-71
Connecticut, 62
consignment, 24, 56
cornering, 69
credit card, 130
cylinder, 66
    four, 11, 13, 17
    single, 11, 33
    triple, 11, 13, 17
    twin, 11, 33

day cruiser, cruising, 116-119, 129
dealer(ship), 24, 25, 47, 53, 61
debris, 80
Denver, 118, 183
Department of Transportation (DOT), *See* "U.S. Dept. of Trans."
Dingle-Johnson Fund, 184
dogs, 82
drainage trough, 80
Dunlop, 105
Dunstall, Paul, 152

easy rider, 19-21
Ellison, Ralph, 86
Elsinore, 143
engine characteristics,
   road-going, 7
   off-road, 33-34
England, 9, 14, 138, 145, 152, 187
Environmental Protection Agency (EPA), 176-177
equilibrium, 68-70
Euripedes, 24
Europe, 138, 145, 146, 149
Executive Order, 188
exhaust system, 8, 18, 34, 173-176
   pipe, 8, 34, 66
exposure, 83-84

fairing, 160-161
Federal Highway Administration, 94
fender, 8, 34
Ferrari, 13, 99
fiberglass, 34, 91, 95
file, 100
financing, 53-55, 183
finder's fee, 55
foot controls, 95
   rest, 163
footpeg, 34, 36, 96
Ford, 99
Fourteenth Amendment, 88
four-cycle, 17, 33, 34, 66, 70, 177
frame, 7, 18, 31, 65

gas,
   economy, 186-187
   filter, 111, 168
   line, 111, 112
   tank, 8, 34, 95, 111
   tap, 73
gauge,
   accessory, 167-168
   feeler, 100
   spark plug gap, 100
Germany, 9
gloves, 158
goggles, 157
Grand Prix, 138
gusset, 31
Guzzlefire, 5, 48, 52, 124, 166
gyroscopic precession, 63, 68

hammer, soft headed, 100
handlebar controls, 70-72
handlebars, 36-37, 70-72, 96, 153
Harley-Davidson, 125, 151, 160
headlight, 50, 62, 86-87, 158-159
helmet, 50, 62, 87-92, 153-155
hill climb, 33, 143
Holland and Holland, 22
Honda, 9, 17, 21, 174, 177
horn, 30, 159
hot rod, 18-19, 20, 21, 22
Hummingbird, 10
hydrocarbons, 176-177

IBM, 44
ignition,
   coil, 96
   switch, 73
Illinois, 88
inspection cap, 75
institutions, lending, 54-55
insurance, 58-62
   collision, 60-61
   comprehensive, 60-61
   liability, 60-61
invisible rider, 86-87

Iowa, 88
Italy, 9

jacket, 157-158
Japan, 9, 138, 149
Jawa, 18
Jones, Thomas Firth, 172

Kawasaki, 17
kerosene, 108, 110, 111
kidney belt, 158
King of the Road, 65

lever,
   brake, 71-72
   choke, 72
   clutch, 70
   kickstarter, 73-74
   shift, 74
license, operator's, 56, 130
litter, 80
loan, 54-55
Los Angeles Basin, 176-177, 186
lube gun, 100
lubricant, 103, 110
luggage carrier, 162

management by objectives (MBO), 6
map, 117-118, 128-129
margin of safety, 85-86
masterlink, 107, 108
minibike, 8, 14
Minnesota, 79
mirror, 94, 159-160
Mississippi, 88
motocross, 39, 41, 42, 141, 142
Moto Guzzi, 21
motorcycle,
   dual purpose, 6, 9, 12, 22, 68
   full size, 38-40, 44, 45
   heavyweight, 9, 12-14, 15, 22, 52
   lightweight, 9-11, 22, 25, 37-38, 44, 45, 52
   middleweight, 9, 11-12, 22, 23
   off-road, 8, 28-49, 178
   road-going, 6-27, 37
muffler, 34, 66, 173-176
Murphy's Law, 98

National Highway Traffic Safety Administration (NHTSA), 88, 90, 91, 95
National Rifle Association (NRA), 189
National Safety Council, 79, 87, 93
Nebraska, 62
Nevada, 143
New Jersey, 62
New York, 56, 60
North Carolina, 176
Norton, 151

objective hazards, 80-83
objectives, 26
off-road (recreational) vehicle, (ORV or ORRV), 178-185
oil,
   cooler, 168
   engine, 110-111
   filter, 110
   fork, 111
   lubrication, 100, 110-111
   penetrating, 100
   transmission, 110
Oklahoma, 56

Panther, 18
Park, National, 180
park, motorcycle, 183-184
Peerless, 25, 55
Pike National Forest, 180

INDEX

Pirelli, 105
Pittman-Roberson Fund, 184
plain jane, 18, 21, 22, 52
plates, license, 51, 107
pliers, 100
points, 66
pothole, 78, 80
pollution,
    air, 176-177, 186-187
    ground, 177-185
    sound, 173-176
    thermal, 186
polycarbonate, 91
Porsche, 151
protector,
    face, 87, 155-157
    mouth, 155

racer,
    dirt, 42-43, 44, 48
    flat track, 42
    desert, 42
racing, 11
    bench, 147-148
    drag, 139-140
    enduro, 142
    flat track, 37, 140-141
    hare and hound, 143
    hill climbing, 143-145
    ice, 145
    road, 138-139
    scrambles, 141-142
    sidecar, 145-147
    street, 140
    TT, 142
railroad crossing, 80
rake, 67, 145
roughrider, 43-44, 45

saddlebag, 113, 121, 152, 162
Saddleback Park, 183
safety bars, 152, 160
San Francisco, 60
sealer,
    non-hardening, 100
    silicone, 101
seat, 8, 34
serial number, 57-58
shock absorber, 7, 68, 74-75
shuffle, bureaucratic, 50
sidecar, 14-17, 145-147
sissy bar, 162-163
skid plate, 167
Snell, Peter, 153
Snell Memorial Foundation, 153, 154
spare parts kit, basic, 125
spark arrestor, 34, 152
    plug, 112
    gap, 100
spoke, 108-110
sprocket, 66, 107-108
State Department of Natural Resources, 181
State Farm, 61
state of tune, 17, 18
steering, 7, 8, 66-67
    damper, 67, 73
    geometry, 13, 28
    lock, 73, 166-167
stolen motorcycle, 48, 57-58
street scrambler, 6, 22, 25
Supreme Court, 88
suspension, 7, 32-33
    front, 7, 32, 66-67, 111
    off-road, 32-33
    rear, 7, 32
    road-going, 7

Suzuki, 22, 42
swing arm, 68, 103

tail light, 159
Tennessee, 176
tire, 8, 35
    iron, 100
    knobby, 35, 105
    pressure, 106
    gauge, 100, 106
    ribbed, 8, 105
    sidewall, 35
    tread, 8, 81, 105-106
    trials, 35, 105
tools,
    emergency, 125
    essential, 99-100
    useful, 100-101
touring, 9, 12, 18, 113, 119-131
track,
    multi, 14
    single, 15, 17, 65
traction, 7, 8, 36
traffic, 10, 11, 13, 14, 37, 82
    marking, 82-83
trail, 67
    bike, 41-42, 44, 45
    maintenance, 179-185
    riding, 9, 29
transmission, 64, 66, 74, 107, 110
traveler's check, 130
trials,
    bike, 145
    competition, 145
tricycle, 14
Triumph, 17, 21, 151
twistgrip, 71
two-cycle (stroke), 11, 17, 33, 34, 66, 71, 173, 177

used motorcycle, 24, 47-49, 57-58
U.S. Department of the Interior, 188
U.S. Department of Transportation, 86, 94
U.S. Forest Service, 179, 181
U.S. Geological Society, 117-118
U.S. Geological Survey, 117-118
U.S. Parks Department, 178

valve, 33, 66
    stem puller, 100
Vermont, 45, 79
Vincent, 17, 151
Volkswagen, 99, 173

Warmshoe, Jack, 64
weight, unsprung, 34, 36
    distribution, 7, 32
    transference, 71
wheel, 14
    balancing, 108-110
    rim, 8, 35-36, 109
Wilderness Area, 180
windshield, 87-88, 160
Winter Park, 183
Woods, Robert, 26
worst case thinking, 84
wrench,
    allen head, 100, 125
    crescent, 99
    open-end, 99, 100
    socket, 99, 100
    spark plug, 100
    torque, 100

Yamadakta, 5

Z90.1, 88-91, 154